West Haven

West Haven

Classroom Culture
and Society in
a Rural Elementary
School

Norris
Brock
Johnson

The University of North Carolina Press
Chapel Hill and London

To all the children
who have passed
and will pass through
the portals of
West Haven
Elementary School

Library of Congress Cataloging in Publication Data

Johnson, Norris Brock, 1942–
West Haven, classroom culture and society in a
rural elementary school.

Bibliography: p.
Includes index.
1. Education, Rural—United States—Case studies.
2. Education, Elementary—United States—Case
studies.
3. School environment—Case studies. I. Title.
LC5146.J64   1985   370.19'346'0973   84-17371
ISBN 0-8078-1630-2

Contents

Figures

Appendixes

Acknowledgments

An empty classroom is a motionless assemblage of paraphernalia and a quiet kaleidoscope of color until brought to life by the energy and passion of children. This book is about public school classrooms, and it could not have been written if I had not been so warmly welcomed as a momentary part of the life children bring to the classrooms of West Haven Elementary School. The principal, teachers, personnel, and more than a few of the children saw the value of this project and provided appreciated insight into the intricate issues surrounding classroom life.

My stay in West Haven was supported by grant #MH5894-01 from the National Institute of Mental Health. Partial support for interpreting the research information was provided by grant #1-0-101-3284-VC851 from the University Research Council, University of North Carolina at Chapel Hill. The writing and rewriting of manuscript drafts were aided by two generous grants from the Spencer Foundation. This book is adapted from a doctoral dissertation submitted to the University of Michigan Department of Anthropology, and some material appeared in previous publications of mine:

"Classroom Spatial Environments: Their Impact on Differential Grouping and Interaction." Reprinted from *School Desegregation and the School Principal*, edited by George W. Noblit and William J. Johnson (1982), pp. 222–50. Copyright by Charles Thomas Press.

"Education as Environmental Socialization: Classroom Spatial Patterns and the Transmission of Sociocultural Norms." Reprinted from the *Anthropological Quarterly* (1982), Volume 55, pp. 31–43. Copyright by the Catholic University of America Press.

"The Material Culture of Public School Classrooms: The Symbolic Integration of Local Schools and National Society." Reprinted from the *Anthropology and Education Quarterly* (1980), Volume 11, pp. 173–90. Copyright by the Council on Anthropology and Education, American Anthropological Association.

"School Spaces and Architecture: The Social and Cultural Landscape of Educational Environments." Reprinted from the *Journal of*

American Culture (1983), Volume 5, pp. 77–86. Copyright by the Popular Culture Association.

"Schools and Schooling: Anthropological Approaches." Reprinted from *Psychosocial Influences in Retarded Performance, Volume 1: Issues and Theories in Development*, edited by Michael J. Begab, H. Carl Heywood, and Howard L. Garber (1981), pp. 287–307. Copyright by University Park Press.

I am most thankful to Dr. T. Elaine Prewitt.

PART I

On the Education of Children

1
In Elementary School

In elementary school your child learns many things. All his experiences at school are designed to produce in him a desire to learn, to help his neighbor, to like his school, to honor his home, and to love America.

West Haven Public Schools, *Elementary School Report Card*

With few exceptions, all of us spent a good portion of our lives in public school classrooms. We may recall faces, sounds, or places—some pleasant, some not so pleasant. In our society elementary schooling is one of the most profound experiences of childhood, and its effects always remain with us. Apart from our families and mass media such as television and films, public schooling, mass education, remains our most powerful vehicle for the social and cultural conditioning of children.

This book is an account of preschool through sixth grade day-to-day classroom life in the rural, midwestern elementary school I term West Haven. Public schools and school classrooms are a small society and culture—a way of life into which children are initiated and conditioned to adhere. The West Haven Elementary School report card tells us that in addition to reading, writing, and arithmetic classroom life presses children to adopt particular norms for behavior ("to help his neighbor"), important cultural values ("desire to learn"; "to honor his home"), and core social goals ("to love America"). My purpose is to describe the social and cultural reality of everyday classroom life and to note the conditioning effect of the process of elementary schooling on children.

3

4 West Haven

I lived in West Haven for nine months investigating the manner in which seemingly isolated rural villages in the United States subtly are linked to the wider national society and culture. Schools, as described in Part II, are critical to the history and development of West Haven, and I wanted to understand how the public school system helps tie the village to the outside world. So, like the journalist Martin Mayer (1961:xiii), "I decided to see for myself what was going on in the schools." One must begin in classrooms, the workplace of the educational system. It is there that the important sociocultural conditioning of students takes place, relevant to their eventual participation in American culture and society.

I studied classroom life at West Haven as both a participant and an observer. I sat in one of the small children's chairs throughout the classroom day, squatted on the floor with the children while stories were read, and squeezed between them when invited to eat lunch with the classroom group. This strategy brought me close to the reality of classroom life. Sitting at a table with the children during mealtime, for example, gave me a good idea of what they eat as well as the manner in which they are taught to eat it. Sitting in their hard and cold chairs helped me understand that learning the way of life of the classroom is physically demanding. Sitting on the floor looking up at a teacher who was reading a story told me about the importance of height, space, and social distance to the nonverbal conditioning of children to the status/role structure of the classroom society. My participation in the life of the classrooms enhanced the children's involvement with me as I was not just another official visitor silently sitting in the back of the room, watching them. I occasionally ate with them, helped them tie their shoelaces, played with them, and helped them read and study their lessons.

The children and teachers, though, could not help reacting to my presence as an observer, and their reactions provided information about the classroom culture and society. Many of the boys, for example, "showed off" for me by bullying other males, and their behavior revealed how males rank each other in the status hierarchy of the classroom social system. Girls practiced sometimes not so subtle flirtation rituals on me, and their behavior provided information about the sex-role norms common to classroom life at West Haven. Teachers tried to reinforce "good" behavior in their students while I was present, and teachers often quickly glanced at me to see if I had noticed student

behaviors they label as "bad." Teachers' choices about what student behaviors to negate and reinforce, and what behaviors to label good and
bad, further made evident the norm and value system at work in the
classrooms. Most teachers were concerned that I view only what they
term "regular classes." When I asked to observe a class session, teachers tried to get me to visit on "regular" days because they might not
be "doing anything" on the day I requested—only "reviewing," doing
"group work," or "taking a test." Teachers, I learned, define a "class"
depending on whether information is transmitted from teacher to student in particular ways; anything else is not considered a "class." I
stressed that my interest was in viewing the routine of ordinary classroom days and not what goes on in any particular "regular" classroom
session.

Recording and Narrating Classroom Observations

At West Haven I observed classroom sessions, in sequence, from
preschool through the twelfth grade. Individual classroom sessions were
observed all day for at least three days each, and I concentrated on
intensive observation during the middle of the school year when the
routine of classroom life had been established. Study of the grade-to-
grade process of schooling revealed patterns of student initiation into
classroom society and culture as well as the nature of education as a rite
of passage. I spent five months studying public schooling at West Haven. The most detailed of the sets of elementary school classroom observations are presented here.

All-day observations, over several days, reveal subtle patterns in
the routine of ordinary classroom life. Classroom days, for example,
are composed of specific, recurring events and activities (Burnett 1970,
1976). *Events* are the major incidents occurring during the classroom
day: the entry of students into the classroom, work routines, play periods, mealtimes, and the like. *Activities* are the smaller clusters of behaviors (Barker and Barker 1961) making up the major event segments of
the classroom day. For example, classroom entry and exit event patterns
are composed of predictable and regularly recurring subpatterns: the
way teachers address students, the ritualized greetings and exchanges
between teachers and students, the ordered movements between classrooms and play areas. The routine events and activities of classroom life,
recorded by observers, rarely are presented to readers as the basis around
which interpretations of schools and the process of schooling might be

built. Despite a vast store of information on schools and schooling most of this material does not describe for us the day-to-day reality of classroom life. Presenting descriptions of actual classroom events and activities more clearly communicates the reality of schooling than does the customary presentation of generalizations about classroom life. Readers must be "taken into the classroom," as Harry Wolcott (1974:1) suggests, "to see what really goes on, as opposed to what we would like to go on." Ideally, the narrative presentation of descriptions and interpretations of classroom life is the most desirable reporting format. For every classroom session observed, I wrote descriptions of events and activities on the left side of my notebooks; on the right side, I noted my impressions of what I had seen. Those descriptions of elementary school classroom life are presented here along with my interpretations of them—descriptions on the outer side of the page, commentary on the inner margin of the page. The narrative descriptions follow the preschool through sixth grade day-to-day event and activity stream of selected classroom sessions as they occurred. The inner margin commentary highlights important social and cultural features of classroom life. Classroom events and activities themselves take center stage in this account of contemporary public schooling in our society. The narrative descriptions, and accompanying interpretation, communicate the reality of the social and cultural conditioning that is the life blood of public schooling.

Classroom Life and Sociocultural Conditioning
Classroom life, as well as the grade-to-grade process of schooling, is a vehicle for the social and cultural conditioning of children. By *social conditioning*, I mean that when they go to school children are pressed to become part of an ongoing group of people occupying a specific geographic territory; that is, to become part of a society. As a society, school people share a common language and set of customs to which children are expected to adhere. As territorial groups, schools possess a collective identity (Park School, West Haven School, Washington School, and so forth). The statuses and roles important to the organization and functioning of school society are defined sharply ("teacher"; "student"; "administrator"). Subgroup identity is expressed through named subdivisions in the society ("primary school"; "secondary school"). The narrative descriptions in Part II show that going to school conditions children to adhere to specific patterns of social relationship characteristic of classroom life. Becoming a student is a process of incorporation into an

existing social group. By *cultural conditioning* I mean that when they go to school, children are pressed to adopt the way of life of the classroom, the classroom culture, as their own. A culture is a fairly persistent patterned interaction of distinctive behaviors, ideas, and physical objects. The component features of cultural systems tend to be mutually reinforcing and coalesce into distinctive themes. A pervasive theme in contemporary American culture illustrated in the classroom observations, for example, is our belief that human beings are perfectable and the masters of a rational, mechanistic universe (DuBois 1955; Shimahara 1975). This generalized theme in American culture is expressed at West Haven Elementary School through recurrent behaviors (the prevalent emphasis on work), ideas (such as the emphasis on regular student progress through school), and objects (the classroom emphasis on the student manipulation of machinery and tool technology).

To what cultural way of life, to what values and habits of mind are the children at West Haven initiated and conditioned to adhere? What forms of social relationship do public school classrooms consistently emphasize? What behaviors, ideas, and objects routinely make up classroom life?

Classroom culture and society are apprehended by identifying the meaning of seemingly mundane events and activities. A cross-cultural outline of educational events and activities by Jules Henry (1960) (see Appendix A) provides a means for translating classroom events and activities into social and cultural terms. The outline is a classification scheme intended to standardize descriptions of educational processes, for the purpose of efficient cross-cultural comparisons, in widely differing types of societies. The categories in Henry's outline were used to identify and then label the social and cultural features of the event and activity stream of the classroom days at West Haven. I wove this interpretation into the commentary begun during initial classroom observations. Major social and cultural themes emerge through the classroom-to-classroom comparison of standardized interpretative categories. Grade level to grade level changes in the frequency of occurrence of these features, as sampled, are presented in the series of figures in Appendix C. Part III reflects on the preschool through sixth grade social and cultural themes on which elementary schooling at West Haven places emphasis and comments on the manner in which these themes echo the mission of schooling in contemporary American life.

EDUCATION: THE REPRODUCTION OF CULTURE AND SOCIETY

Education is the systematic transmission and inculcation of social and cultural information. Cultures and societies are fragile, and the perpetuation of custom and tradition depends on the unfailing education of young people. Education is a conserving process. The passing on of core social and cultural information ideally leaves little to chance, and all human groups exhibit similar vehicles for social and cultural conditioning. Two common features of every system of education, as vehicles for social and cultural conditioning, are initiation and rite of passage.

Initiation and Rite of Passage
The initiation aspect of education exposes young people to core features of the social and cultural system into which they are to be incorporated. In premodern societies, initiation customarily takes the form of ritually preparing prepubescent children for the display and transfer of sacred knowledge (Brown 1963; Eliade 1958, 1959:162–63; Whiting, Kluckhohn, and Anthony 1958). The pattern of experiences surrounding baptism as preliminary induction into religious life or the pattern of experiences characteristic of adolescent induction into fraternal or military life are familiar examples of initiation in modern societies. In each instance initiation experiences signal the beginning stages of a long process of conditioning and mark the point in a person's life at which a child or adult is ushered into new levels of expected participation in a culture or society.

After initiation, young people are provided clearly defined sets of conditioning experiences as they are incorporated further into their sociocultural system. These sets of age-related experiences are termed rites of passage; they refer to the process people undergo in being conditioned to adopt, by stages, a way of life. Arnold Van Gennep (1960), in *The Rites of Passage*, argues that the life of any individual ought to be viewed as a series of interrelated biological and sociocultural transitions. Birth, education/schooling, social puberty, occupational specialization, marriage, father/motherhood, and death are age-related life stages defined and given meaning by various sociocultural systems. Passage through a sociocultural system, just like passage through life, is marked by different sets of conditioning experiences as people move deeper into various levels of participation in their sociocultural system.

Initiation and rite of passage are primary vehicles for the reproduction and regeneration of culture and society. These concepts customarily are applied to the study of sociocultural conditioning in premodern societies, but they also can help us better understand the educational life of our society. It is said that modern life has reduced the significance of initiation and rite of passage (Siegel 1965), and both are thought incompatible with the structure of contemporary societies (Gluckman 1962:36–37). Initiation and rite of passage, however, are universal phenomena of enduring human importance organizing educational experiences in every human group in a variety of ways; they receive less emphasis in societies like ours, to be certain, but they do occur (Burnett 1969; Lancy 1975; Young 1965).

Public schooling is mass initiation and rite of passage adapted to the educational requirements of stratified, multicultural, nation-state societies. In particular, the process of preschool through twelfth grade public schooling initiates young people into aspects of American culture and society. Like any other prepubescent initiation and rite of passage situation, elementary schooling efficiently separates children from their families, transmits core social and cultural information, shapes appropriate feelings, behaviors, and habits of mind, and ceremonially confers status identities to those successfully completing the passage. "There is no evidence," says Van Gennep (1960:xvii), "that a secularized urban world has lessened the need for a ritualized expression of an individual's transition from one status to another." Passage through the social and cultural way of life of school classrooms changes young people. Children enter school behaving, thinking, and feeling one way, and most of them exit behaving, thinking, and feeling in other ways. Classrooms turn young people into students, then provide sets of conditioning experiences preparing them for various levels of participation in the wider society and culture.

Schools, Stratification, and National Integration

Forms of education as institutionalized techniques for sociocultural conditioning vary with the kind of society in which they occur. The "school" is a comparatively recent phenomenon, about six thousand years old at most, and occurs only in certain types of state societies (Cohen 1970, 1971, 1975; Watkins 1943). Schools developed as an educational adaptation to pressures accompanying a state's participation in civilizational networks with other states, such as occurred in early Mesopotamia (Kramer 1959:2–5), the Greek Peloponnesus (Marrou 1964:56–57), or dynastic China (Wilkinson 1964:15; Wittfogel 1963:320). Schools invariably were connected to the temple or to the palace, were attended only by the children of elite subgroups, and trained people responsible for maintaining the political and economic relationships between and within states. Schools exhibit physical and sociocultural characteristics that can be supported only by large-scale societies: full-time specialized personnel, permanent buildings for instruction, codified texts, and so forth (Cohen 1970:56). The development of states out of heterogeneous subgroups and regions requires maintenance of a minimal level of social and cultural integration. States must foster and then perpetuate unifying ideologies reinforcing local-level identification with political units encompassing various geographic regions; they must generate and promote a sociocultural orientation universal to the state as a whole rather than particular to specific subgroups or regional locales. Schools are state-level institutions cutting across geographic regions to promote interdependence among diverse populations.

The structure of the state societies in which they occur mandates that schools simultaneously stratify and homogenize the children of client populations. Stratification is the organization of a society on the basis of fixed inequality of subgroup access to strategic life resources such as adequate food, shelter, work, and information (Fried 1960). Stratified state societies such as our own are a form of political organization for the maintenance of social and cultural inequality. All state societies are composed of subgroups the members of which have differentially ascribed life chances in the society as a whole, and schooling is a major institutional arena for sorting out children for various levels of participation in the social system of stratification. The structure of schooling reproduces the structure of society such that the children who are required to attend invariably are conditioned to stratified social and cultural relationships (Bourdieu 1973b; Bourdieu and Passeron 1977; Bowles 1971, 1972; Bowles and Gintis 1976). Public schooling is implicated intimately in the reproduction and regeneration of unequal divisions in the wider society and culture.

Schooling in stratified state societies occurs both in a localistic and in a nationalistic sociocultural context. Mass education links and tends to homogenize diverse regional, ethnic, and linguistic populations for various levels of participation in national social and cultural networks. Mass education is a vehicle for the transmission of national values, habits of mind, and ways of life to local settings (Carnoy and Werthein 1977; Warren 1967; Wylie 1976). "Education," as John Singleton (1967:2) notes in his study of a contemporary Japanese school system, "in every modern society is in some degree an instrument of national policy." The school is the only national-level contemporary public institution in which all new members of the society are required to participate (Safa 1971:211), and public schooling is crucial to the ongoing process of social and cultural integration at the national level (Paulson 1971:401–15; Steward 1972:43–52; Wax and Wax 1971). National integration is so important that authorities often force schooling on colonial populations; in many cases, the schoolteacher closely follows on the heels of the soldier and the missionary (Carnoy 1974; Collier, Jr., 1973; Dumont, Jr., and Wax 1969; Wax 1967).

Schooling is a powerful national institution that standardizes social norms and cultural values among diverse subgroups and regional populations. Schools have the difficult task of simultaneously stratifying and homogenizing children, and schools cannot properly be understood without considering the type of society in which they occur.

2
West Haven
The Village and the School System

All the world's a stage
And all the men and women
Merely players.

William Shakespeare,
As You Like It

West Haven, with a population of 2,793, is a rural village in the midwestern United States. Now almost evenly divided between black and white residents, the village first was settled by Yankee farmers migrating inland from the eastern seaboard and presently is home to German, Swedish, Polish, Scandinavian, and Jewish ethnic and religious groups.

The few service institutions in the village are branch offices of "outside" agencies, as they are termed. The village bank, for example, has a home office located in a major regional town twenty kilometers to the north. Across the street from the bank is a small post office. The electric power company is located in a new office building at the other end of the village. The telephone company is directly across the street. West Haven built a single-story brick building to house its new fire and ambulance service several years ago. A four-person police department is housed in the township hall, a converted frame house next to a small barbershop. The village previously had to depend on a town six kilometers away for police, fire, and ambulance service. Across the street, a small waiting area inside an automobile service station houses the Greyhound bus station. Health care and service agencies used by West Haven residents are located outside the village; hospitals, doctors, and dentists are at least six kilometers away. There are no local newspapers, movie theaters, or radio or television transmitting facilities in West Haven.

The village retains a veneer of autonomy but strategically is placed

12

within major urban and industrial networks. No industries are based in West Haven, and the economic life of the village is dominated by extensive labor migration. A three-hour drive on nearby expressways will take one to several major furniture, textile, automobile, and steel manufacturing cities. During the 1950s, emigrating families moved into West Haven but continued to work in these cities. Many parents live in West Haven but commute daily to places of employment, often making one-way trips of more than one hundred miles. The Greyhound bus, the automobile, and the superhighway are crucial to the development and continuing growth of West Haven. During my observations at the school, children told me of living with grandmothers, aunts, and even older brothers and sisters while their parents are away at work. During home visits, I talked to parents about labor migration and schooling. The sacrifices they make, they say, are hard but are the only way to provide "a decent living" and "a decent education" for their children. The school invariably is mentioned in conversations about West Haven. Most parents expect the school to provide *in loco parentis* care for their children and to prepare them for employment opportunities parents feel they themselves did not have. Most parents expect the school to teach their children not so much how to survive in West Haven, but how to survive in the world outside West Haven. Parents expect the school to be more oriented toward the wider society than toward the local community. Upon graduation from high school, most young people move away from West Haven to live in cities their parents previously fled.

The school is the major public institution in West Haven. The school complex is located a quarter of a kilometer south of the village (see Figure 1). This complex is the result of the consolidation of seven regional schools established in various parts of the surrounding township, the earliest in 1865. These early private schools were supported by residents. The Smith-Hughes Act of 1917 provided West Haven with federal funds that aided construction of a central school facility, now the high school building. West Haven in return promised to institute instructional programs in agricultural science, home economics, and manual training. As an agricultural community (see Hatch 1979:138–164; Fuller 1983) West Haven skillfully used federally sponsored instructional programs to help develop the township, the village, and the school system. In 1920, West Haven became the first district in the state to consolidate its private regional schools under a central administration.

The single-story elementary school building (A), built in 1951, cur-

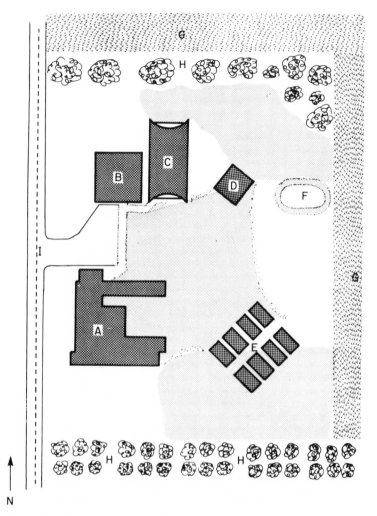

Figure 1. The West Haven School Complex

Legend

A. Elementary building

B. Secondary building

C. Gymnasium

D. Bus garage

E. Middle grade converted
    mobile homes

F. Track

G. Open fields

H. Orchards

I. State highway

rently houses 350 students. West Haven had not completed construction of the middle school building at the time of my research, and eight aluminum-sided converted mobile homes temporarily house third and fourth grade students. The secondary school building (B), built in 1923, currently houses 480 students. The bus garage (D) is corrugated aluminum painted green with white trim. The gymnasium (C) is the newest building in the school complex. The playground is worn clean of grass and topsoil, and contains swings, slides, ten large earthmover tires half sunk into the sand, a teeter-totter, and a netless basketball hoop atop a pole.

SCHOOLING AND ENVIRONMENTAL CONDITIONING

The school buildings children are required to frequent and the spatial areas with which and in which they interact are much more than passive wrappings for classroom life. The buildings, spaces, and associated artifacts that make up public school environments of traditional design (Gump and Good 1976) physically manifest and replicate core themes in American society and culture. Sociocultural information is presented to children in public schools both consciously and unconsciously through physical and spatial school environments as well as through teachers in classrooms.

The relationship between people and the environments we construct for ourselves is reciprocal. Buildings and architectural spaces, on the one hand, are products of human social and cultural activity. The components of sociocultural systems are mutually reinforcing; thus, people tend to build physical environments and define physical spaces congruent with other aspects of culture and society (Bourdieu 1973a; Paul 1976; Williams 1972:206–38). The physical environment, says Amos Rapoport (1976:7–35), is a set of "symbols representing ideas and practices in the social realm." Physical and spatial environments are nonverbal stores of social and cultural information; they concretize dominant sociocultural themes, make visible the conceptual order of sociocultural systems, and serve as "material manifestations of metaphysical ideas" (Leach 1976:39). Through our continual interactions with them, physical and spatial environments help make us, especially children, social and cultural (Bourdieu 1973a; Moore 1981; Richardson 1974). As well as interacting with and receiving information from other human beings, we always are interacting with and presented information from the socioculturally charged forms and spaces we inhabit.

The school complex at West Haven possesses important sociocultural characteristics physically and spatially enduring apart from the people who temporarily inhabit them. Public school spaces and architecture, like other physical environments, are a nonverbal curriculum, what Basil Bernstein (1977) would term a "visible pedagogy," some aspects of which literally are more interpretable than others. Even before children enter any particular classroom, the physical and spatial information in the school complex nonverbally orients them toward and cues their adherence to behaviors and habits of mind that will be imparted through their classroom experiences.

School Spaces and Artifacts

The spatial separation of the school complex from the village, for example, is significant socioculturally. Children at West Haven go to school either by walking up the sidewalk from the village or by being bused there from outlying rural areas in the township. Spatial isolation is an important physical characteristic of formal education in state societies (Cohen 1970; Watkins 1943) and is a nonverbal expression of the intent to remove schooling from the sphere of kinship and the family, the merging of which is characteristic of small-scale preindustrial societies. A special place created at West Haven for the express purpose of educating children is called a *school*, and schooling at West Haven is distinguished spatially from kinship and family-based childrearing that also occurs in the village. Schooling is a distinct enterprise spatially segmented out from other aspects of village life, and most public school complexes are isolated physically from other activities. Physical separation often is marked by fences, high walls, or other artificial barriers (Eddy 1965:64), or, as at West Haven, by more natural and subtle means. The West Haven school complex is isolated from the village by orchards and plowed fields to the north, plowed fields and stands of wild grass to the east, fruit orchards to the south, and the state highway to the west. People at West Haven, putting forth their own explanation of this physical separation, invariably say that the school is isolated so children can be more easily watched and protected.

The school complex at West Haven, in any case, is a special set-apart place where special events and activities occur. The trees and fields surrounding the school complex, natural boundaries planted at the time of site construction, serve as unintended though functional rite of passage boundary markers. Boundary signs, ceremonially placed, mark the presence of groups inhabiting specific territories for specific purposes. A minister and high-ranking village elders were present at the ground-breaking ceremonies dedicating the school complex at West Haven. This rite of consecration, as Van Gennep (1960:15) would term it, was accompanied by the installation of a small bronze plaque noting the date the earth was broken to begin construction of the complex. The bronze plaque is a physical symbol of the resultant collective identity of the families who, before consolidation, sent their children to separate regional schools in the township. The physical space of the complex was demarcated, isolated from the village, and claimed for special purposes by a specific group of people. A boundary marker signals this special purpose, especially to approaching strangers. Celebrations in the village accompanied the dedication of the school complex. Christening libations purified the earth, and this special place was purged and prepared primarily for occupation by children.

Other physical features mark the school complex as a distinct space with a distinct purpose. Approaching the complex from either end of the highway, the first thing one sees is the flagpole in front of the elementary building. The flagpole is the tallest structure in the village. Boundary markers are intended to be seen at a distance, and the flagpole visually marks off school from nonschool space. Next to the flagpole and facing the highway is another boundary marker, a large kiosk. The kiosk is made of red brick, and the message area is enclosed in safety-tempered glass. The glass case displays the name of the school complex, the mascot (a grimacing bulldog) with which the complex symbolically is associated, and the leaders (principal and superintendent) of the group found there. Underneath is a blank space on which school-related events and activities such as sports events, homecoming, or parent-teacher day are advertised to outsiders passing by. The kiosk physically defines territory and nonverbally offers social, cultural, and political information about the school complex.

Access to the isolated school complex is monitored and highly controlled; access from the state highway is the only permitted point of entry. Passing from the highway into the school complex one crosses a narrow, portal-like threshold. The flagpole and kiosk are placed prominently near this threshold. These artifacts are "guardians of the threshold," as Van Gennep (1960:24) would term them, and threshold markers control access to special spaces by signaling a taboo against unauthorized entry. School people at West Haven are aware of this threshold taboo and recognize that special rites of passage are required to enter and leave the complex. Similar to crossing into a foreign territory, unauthorized personnel entering the school complex at West Haven are required to obtain passes to proceed; the passes are distributed by male administrators in both the elementary and secondary buildings. Persons permitted unmonitored entry customarily include students, staff, and administrators; except for students, school people permitted unmonitored entry to the complex are required to be certified by the state. Unsanctioned entry or exit are met with retribution and sometimes with legal action. It is important, I was told, to keep "strangers" away from the children. Passions are strong about this matter. Teachers and administrators spend considerable time and energy controlling movement in and around the school complex. Administrators say that parents storming through the school complex, or "barging" into classrooms, are subject to suits for illegal entry. Though students are not required to possess passes to enter or leave the school complex, they nonetheless must adhere to the rules and prescribed routines for sanctioned passage. Required deference to prescribed rite of passage rules is important nonverbal information about what people and agencies (administrators, the state) control the school complex, a fact of which most students and parents are aware. The social and cultural information concretized in the physical and spatial school environment contextually cues for appropriate behaviors. Some students intentionally violate these nonverbal cues, thereby indicating that the rules are consciously understood. Indeed, the nonverbal rules are made more conscious through their overt violation.

There are physical and spatial signs and symbols that the group claiming primary possession of this school complex represents the nation-state rather than the specific local village of West Haven. Federal funds from the Smith-Hughes Act in large part were responsible for the construction of the school complex. People in West Haven are aware of state and national influence with respect to the lack of control they have over school matters such as classroom curricula and the certification of teachers. There are, however, more subtle levels of influence. Again, consider the flagpole. Flags are important physical symbols of identity and are pervasive group markers. Normally, there are two flags on the pole at West Haven: a state flag and a national flag. The political information symbolized in these flags is that the school complex is associated with both these supralocal (outside West Haven) units. West Haven does not have a village flag, but the school flagpole always has the national flag displayed on top and the state flag displayed below. Ranking and hierarchical placement convey, literally, the comparative importance of each political unit. The information displayed symbolically is that the nation-state has sovereignty over the school complex and that the school complex is primarily a nationally rather than primarily a locally controlled space. Much of the sociocultural orientation expressed in the elementary school classrooms, as we will see, is toward the national level rather than toward the local level of West Haven.

The presence of state as well as local political units is represented symbolically through the display of hierarchically presented anthropomorphic animals. On the state flag is the picture of a wolverine bearing qualities of human facial expression—the animal has human teeth and a humanlike smile. The presence of the state is conveyed through a symbolic association with this specific animal. In the classroom, students are taught to associate specific animals with specific political units: the eagle with the national unit, the wolverine with the state unit, and so forth. On days of special school events such as basketball games, the school flag is attached to the pole below the state flag. The hierarchical placement of these flags is nonverbal information about the political principle of ranking. Ranking, among other things, defines the relationship of the West Haven local school complex to the state and to the federal government. There is a picture of the school mascot, the bulldog, on the school flag as well as on the kiosk. Students are familiar with this particular symbolic association and often speak of the school as the *Bulldogs* rather than as *West Haven*. Each school complex in the region, indeed, throughout the state, symbolically is associated with a different animal. Sporting events such as basketball games often are conducted as a competition between different animals inhabiting neighboring territories. West Haven has had several state basketball champions, and people are aware and proud of their identity with these culturally defined school spaces and artifacts.

Schooling as a Spatial Rite of Passage
Rites of passage refer to ceremonies dramatizing a person's spatial separation from one place, transition to another place, and incorporation into a new space. Rites of passage always involve a spatial context for ceremonial changes in status (Eliade 1958:4–13; Van Gennep 1960:15–25). With respect to this spatial frame of reference, children

in West Haven are first separated from their home and village context, then transported to the isolated school complex where they experience a twelve-year sequence of transforming events and activities. These experiences, in part, prepare children for incorporation into a new place and state of being—as young adults ready to participate, on various levels, in the wider American culture and society outside the school. Schooling at West Haven is a rite of passage the initial separation phase of which physically is manifested in the spatial isolation of the school complex from the village.

People at West Haven make a distinction between *elementary, middle*, and *secondary* schooling. These terms provide information about the different rank, status, and prestige accorded each phase of schooling. Physical space often concretizes and replicates nonphysical ideas otherwise expressed through verbal language (Austin 1976; Griaule and Deterlen 1954; Vogt 1965). A student's progress through the named stages (elementary, middle, secondary) that constitute the process of schooling is passage through physical space. Schooling at West Haven occurs neither in one place nor at one time. Although this spatiotemporal state of affairs is so common as to be taken for granted, it is not a cross-cultural norm. Childhood rites of passage among the Hopi, for example, traditionally are held in a round, semisubterranean, communal *kiva* (Eggan 1956; Tuan 1977:120–21). The *kiva* is isolated from other village activity and is used only for educational purposes. The *kiva*'s nondivided, communal, internal structure is quite different from the succession of spaces through which children at West Haven are required to pass. Indeed, by schooling we mean the progressive passage of children *through* successive spaces. A student's rank, status, and prestige in school are symbolized in the classroom and grade level spaces they occupy. People at West Haven use the phrase "having gone to school" to mean children having experienced each component phase of schooling in its fixed sequence. Just as the *kiva* physically manifests and reinforces the communalism in Pueblo society, navigating the school complex at West Haven is contextual conditioning for participation in ranked societies, such as our own, emphasizing differences in status and prestige.

Just as buildings can be interpreted as concretized social norms and cultural values, so too can the form of the spaces between buildings (Van Gennep 1960:18) be interpreted. The twelve-year passage through the elementary building to the middle school mobile trailers to the high school building involves crossing several socioculturally important spaces. These architecturally defined spaces, for example, symbolically give emphasis to the age grouping of children that occurs at West Haven. Each school building houses children grouped on the basis of age, and school authorities maintain strict spatial separation between age groups. Students going from one building to another, carrying messages back and forth, for example, are required to possess special passes and badges of authorization to do so. Teachers and administrators react with anger upon discovering a high school student without a pass in the elementary building or vice versa. The yearly, formal crossing of these architecturally defined spaces by a group of children always is accompanied by elaborate ceremonies making public their transition to a new rank, status, and school space. With respect to the symbolic significance of public school spaces, Figure 1 also illustrates an important distinction we make between work and play in that playgrounds and athletic spaces are separated physically from school spaces. In the early grades play activities occur inside the elementary building and remain confined to specific areas within the classrooms. Over the several years between preschool and the middle grades, however, these inside play areas are deemphasized until they are moved outside the building. Work, not play, spatially becomes associated with the school buildings themselves. Teachers say the purpose of this spatial separation of work and play is to keep the noise of recess away from the classrooms, which it certainly does. The symbolic information, however, is that learning, not play, is supposed to take place in school. As the teachers often remind children, schooling is "work," and they tell children there is a specific time and place for work and a specific time and place for play. This distinction between work and play, manifested spatially, is an important lesson conditioning children for participation in both the local-level and national-level sociocultural system of which the elementary school is an integrated part.

THE ELEMENTARY SCHOOL BUILDING

A red brick exterior makes the elementary school building appear warm and expansive. The interior walls of the building are a dark, natural brick, and recessed fluorescent lighting and skylights punctuate the spotless white acoustic ceiling tiles. The hallway walls are covered with the artwork of the children; the paintings and drawings provide a sensate, stimulating, and personalized school environment. More than in the middle and high school buildings, the elementary school physical environment, by conscious intent, visually entices new students.

Public school environments for the most part are designed extra-locally, and local choices customarily are made from among sets of standardized architectural plans. The design features of traditional public school architecture are fairly standardized. The buildings, spatial features, and physical artifacts found at West Haven are pervasive. Neither West Haven teachers, administrators, nor parents (let alone students themselves) exercised control over the design of the school complex or its buildings.

Building Design Principles and Sociocultural Themes

West Haven's elementary school building physically and spatially manifests several core sociocultural themes (see Figure 2). The architectural design principle of the elementary school building is based on the replication of rectangular forms. There is an "aesthetic of order" (De-Carlo 1969:22) to the building. Mirroring the school's bureaucratic concern with the precise organization of objects (students) in time and space, the mechanical ordering of repeated forms is congruent with our dominant sociocultural orientation toward standardization.

There is a relationship, in addition, between a society's technology base and its childrearing patterns. Hunting/gathering and some agricultural societies share an emphasis on curvilinear architectural forms; Eskimo (*Inuit*) igloos and native North American tepees can easily be constructed and moved, and in part are physical adaptations characteristic of these types of societies. Inhabiting curvilinear dwellings such as these environmentally orients children toward, and conditions them to adhere to, the principles of communalism and egalitarianism predominant among these people (Balikci 1970:128; Carpenter 1973; Marc 1977:29–66; Niehardt 1961:20–47). Rectilinear architectural forms, by contrast, tend to be associated with ranked and stratified sedentary agricultural and industrial societies. Emphasizing lines rather than curves, rectilinear forms are more easily subdivided than are curvilinear forms. Rectilinear buildings are likely to be multiple-roomed, with each room associated with different domestic tasks.

This sociocultural theme of separation and specialization of domestic tasks in the architectural forms associated with ranked and stratified societies physically is expressed at West Haven through the spatial organization of the buildings within the school complex, as well as through

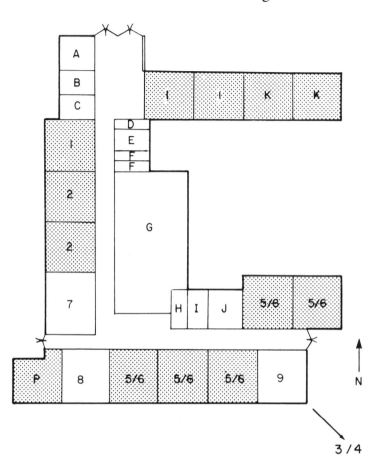

Figure 2. The West Haven Elementary School Building

Legend

1. Administration/Support Areas:

A = principal's office
B = administrative office
C = teachers' lounge
D = supply room
E = maintenance room
F = lavatories
G = lunchroom/multipurpose room
H = kitchen
I = health/nurse's room
J = conference room

2. Academic Areas
(located in converted mobile homes):

P = preschool room
K = kindergarten rooms
1 = first grade rooms
2 = second grade rooms
3 = third grade rooms
4 = fourth grade rooms
5/6 = fifth and sixth grade rooms
7 = music room
8 = art room
9 = mathematics laboratory

the spatial relationship of the school complex to the village. The multi-ple-roomed elementary school building, for example, organizes special-ized task divisions of labor. *Learning* (shaded classrooms) areas are sepa-rated and isolated from *office* and *support* (lunchroom, supply rooms, maintenance, and so on) areas. The administrative sector (A and B) of the elementary school, physically manifesting its "guardian of the thresh-old" (Van Gennep 1960:21) function, strategically is placed at a moni-toring and control position near the main doors. The principal says someone in the office must always "keep an eye" on students and other people around the building. Maintenance areas (D, E, and F) are clus-tered, womblike, toward the protected core of the building, while learn-ing classroom areas fan out to form the edges of the building. Teachers and administrators explain this arrangement simply as a matter of archi-tectural style, which it is. The differentiation of educational functions and tasks, in association with differing school spaces, also can be inter-preted as a physical and spatial manifestation of the separation of func-tions and tasks as an important theme in American culture.

Our culture emphasizes lineality and is oriented toward lines, se-quences, and ideas about life as sequential progress (DuBois 1955; Hsu 1972) through time and space. American culture emphasizes the edges of things (Hall 1959:158–60), and space is considered empty until fleshed out by physical boundaries. The line is basic to our perception of reality. "We see it in visible nature," says Dorothy Lee (1959:110), "be-tween material points, and we see it between metaphorical points such as days or acts." The Euro-American notion of time, space, and reality as particulate and sequential is manifested in public school spaces and ar-chitecture at West Haven. Children at West Haven environmentally are conditioned to lineal orientations toward time, space, and world view through their many years of interaction with the spatial and physical features of the school complex. The learning sector of the elementary building, for example, is expressed as a lineal movement through space (see Figure 2). Students begin the process of schooling in the isolated preschool room, go over to the kindergarten rooms, then counterclock-wise through first and second grades, out of the building into third and fourth grade quonsets, then back into the elementary building for the fifth and sixth grades, isolated in the southeast corners of the building. *Early elementary* (preschool through kindergarten), *lower elementary* (first and second grades), *middle elementary* (third and fourth grades), and *upper elementary* (fifth and sixth grades) are named stages in the sequence of schooling. Each stage of schooling spatially is distinct, and individual classrooms are segmented, isolated by fixed walls, and defined by specialized tasks. Children of specific ages are confined to each isolated classroom segment, and there is little spontaneous interchange between classroom segments. The lineal design principle of the elementary school building tightly organizes and focuses student movement. School spaces and architecture at West Haven physically and spatially manifest a stated educational goal of keeping people separated by age, role, and status (adults invariably are associated with administrative and support areas). Narrow hallway connecting channels enhance the isolation of component school units (classrooms) and funnel students to specific school spaces. The occupation of a particular space by students is symbolic of their status and rank. With a distinct beginning, middle, and end, public schooling is a line along which students are required to move progressively. "We feel we must arrange events chronologically in lineal order," says Dorothy Lee (1959:116), "we arrange events and objects in a sequence which is climactic, in size and intensity, in emotional meaning. In the fulfillment of this course of career—not in the fulfillment of self as point—do we find value."

In a variety of ways, public schools orient and condition children to adhere to particular habits of mind and behaviors instrumental to their eventual participation in the wider society and culture. Public school settings are a quiet though ever present sociocultural reality often overshadowed by the noisy drama of the classrooms they frame.

PART II

Schooling at West Haven

Classroom Experiences

3
The Early Grades
Social and Cultural Transitions

Their zeal for learning the Koran by heart is so great that they put their children in chains if they show any backwardness in memorizing it, and they are not set free until they have it by heart. I visited the *qadi* in his house on the day of the festival. His children were chained up, so I said to him, "Will you not let them loose?" He replied, "I shall not do so until they learn the Koran by heart."

Ibn Battuta,
Travels in Asia and Africa

PRESCHOOL: EDUCATION AS SEDUCTION

Children in West Haven begin their classroom experiences at an early age. Parents view the school as an instrument for social and economic mobility, and the earlier school experiences occur, they feel, the better for their children. West Haven, by state law, makes the preschool program available to all the children in the school district. The only criterion for participation is age; specifically, a child must be four years old by the first day of the year he or she enrolls in preschool. Half-day sessions structure the preschool program.

By an adult's frame of reference, the preschool room is large; by a child's frame of reference, it must appear cavernous. This is the largest classroom in the elementary building. The large size and grand aesthetics of the room reveal the visual effort made to capture the attention of preschool children. Walls are painted pastel blue with pink trim, the floor rug and window curtains are pale blue, and the floor is dark green tile. Recessed fluorescent fixtures in the gray acoustic tile ceiling effuse warm, flowing light. This is the only classroom in the elementary building with windows in three of the walls. The preschool room always appears bright, airy, and spacious. Environmentally, the child's first contact with school is, by conscious design, stimulating and pleasant. The preschool room is visually dense and is decorated lavishly with the children's artwork. Virtually every surface of the room is covered with some

29

sort of visual display. Drawings and paintings hang from a string spanning the length of the front window, and artwork also is taped to the walls and to other surfaces such as the doors. The classroom is personalized; paintings and drawings are made by the children and the teacher, and there are few commercially prepared visual materials. The room is seductive visually; the environment tugs at and captures the eye and stimulates visual and tactile senses. Children tell me they like to come to school because they can play with so many toys. The storage areas in the preschool room are overflowing with toys. The effect on preschoolers of the myriad toys, cavernous classroom space, and lavish teacher attention is demonstrated in the enthusiasm with which children in the early grades come to school.

In every classroom, wall clocks are displayed prominently either above the hallway door or above the front blackboard. All the clocks in the elementary building are synchronized. Classroom life is based on the rigorous time and space coordination of specific events and activities. In every classroom, an American flag is displayed on a pole jutting from an upper corner of the front and side walls. The flag is a continual, nonverbal symbolic reminder that it is the nation-state rather than the local village to which the school is linked and to which the classrooms, and the students in them, primarily owe allegiance.

The furniture in public school classrooms, and its spatial placement, influences the behaviors occurring in that setting. Attention to patterns of furniture arrangement, furniture design features, and the use of physical space reveals subtle, nonverbal aspects of classroom culture and society. The shape and physical arrangement of preschool furniture, for example, reinforce student accessibility to and encourage the exploration of classroom spaces; there is a small amount of furniture in the preschool room defining large amounts of unrestricted classroom space (see Figure 3). Except for the teacher's closet (a private space protected by closed doors), few physical objects in the room inhibit the spontaneous mobility of the children. Compared with more restrictive furniture arrangements in several upper grade classrooms, the large amount of unrestricted preschool classroom space invites movement and mobility. The classroom spatial environment, and its behavioral effect, is intentional. The preschool teacher says that children need room to move about and that the development of muscle coordination is important at this age. Children are introduced to an initial school setting with few environmental restraints. The preschool classroom environment encourages play and is seductive in its accessibility.

The shapes of tables and other pieces of classroom furniture predispose the people using them for specific patterns of social interaction; there is an interactional difference, for example, between round and rectangular tables. Round furniture permits people to remain equidistant from one another, with a common focal point in the center of the table. Round tables, no matter what size, focus the attention of the group inward, thereby stimulating and encouraging mutual interaction. The large round table (A_3) in the preschool classroom is used primarily for group activities; children very rarely work on solitary activities at this table. Adjacent seating reinforces cooperation (Hall 1969), and most of the cooperative and coactive student classroom behaviors over the whole of elementary schooling occur in the early grades. Cooperative and coactive student behaviors are reinforced, environmentally, by the round table shapes common in early grade classrooms. Rectangular tables, on the other hand, encourage interpersonal distance (Hall 1969; Osmund 1957) and discourage every interaction pattern except corner conversation (Sommer 1965). To counter the effect of furniture shape and the placement of classroom furniture on the children's pattern of interaction, the preschool teacher regularly pushes together the six separate rectangular wooden desks (A_4) to form two rows, thereby physically providing a more interactive environment. Sitting at these pushed-together tables, children exchange and share the materials used in various classroom activities and otherwise interact much as they do at the round table. The preschool classroom physically and spatially does not isolate children from one another. The children, though, occupy group tables while the teacher has a personal desk (A_1). Private property and private space are of increasing value to the classroom culture. The teacher's desk is isolated spatially from the children's area, and it is much larger than any child's desk. These physical and spatial features consciously symbolize and designate the high rank and status of the teacher (an adult) in the classroom society.

In the northwest corner of the room, three wooden stoves serve as a toy kitchen, and more girls than boys play in this area. The spatial placement of the classroom's physical features reinforces the separation of male and female activity in the classroom society.

The preschool environment orients children toward behaviors and

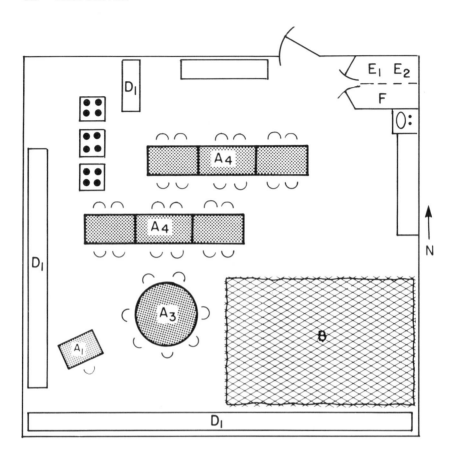

Figure 3. The Preschool Classroom

Legend

A₁ = teacher's desk   B = floor rug
A₂ = teacher aide's desk   C = chair
A₃ = classroom activity desk   D₁ = bookcases/storage areas
A₄ = student desk   E₁ = teacher's closet
                                E₂ = students' closet
                                F = lavatory

                                ▦ = toy stove

types of interaction that reinforce classroom norms and values of cooperation and interdependence. The free play, mobility, and comparatively unstructured activities associated with this grade are congruent with the physical and spatial characteristics of the classroom. Throughout the school year, preschool children are conditioned to adhere to predominant classroom cultural and social themes through their interactions with specific furniture shapes and furniture spatial arrangement.

Cherubic and approachable, the preschool teacher is a white female in her early thirties, who has taught at West Haven for seven years. Her ease and warmth are more the result of her personality than of a professional attitude. Her assigned aides, a black female and a white female, are in their late thirties. Teacher aides are recruited from the school district and are paid with state funds. The children are four and five years of age. There are fifteen children assigned to each half-day session. On the days observed, there are four white females, three black females, five black males, and three white males in the morning session; in the afternoon session there are three white females, three black females, four black males, and five white males. Sex, color, and age are important organizing features of classroom society and are indicated throughout the observations.

Two Preschool Sessions

The monitoring/supervision of classroom experiences by adults.

Spontaneous peer interactions are coactive (groups) rather than autonomous (individual).

This high degree of physical contact/nurturing is confined to the lower grades.

Compare this contact-seeking behavior with the later upper grade stress on autonomy. Emphasis is on literacy training.

9:00 A.M. The teacher arrives to set out books and other materials and to prepare the room for the day's activities. As each bus arrives, the children come in and run down the corridor to the room. The children, especially the girls, tend to hold each other's hands as they whirl into sight. In small clusters, they burst into the room. Most of them smile and say hello to the teacher. They grab her hand or blouse and seem happy to see her. The teacher stops what she is doing to grab and hug them in return, then helps them remove their outer clothing and put it in the closet.

Many of the children run up to the observer to say hello and to talk with him. A few children show the observer the names of various animals in the books the teacher has placed on their desks. Several children open the books without being told.

9:15 A.M. The children engage in free play either among themselves or with the many toys and other materials in the room. They are excited by the toys and play with great enthusiasm. Some go off by themselves while others play in groups.

A black female and male argue, loudly, over the possession of a toy. Both have hold of a toy wheel used in a wooden construction set. The girl is making a car and has only three wheels. The boy has a series of wheels on each side of a long block of wood. Although she is not crying, the boy calls the girl a crybaby. Quickly, the girl snatches the wheel. Before they can continue, the teacher intervenes and gives the wheel back to the girl. She tells the boy he can use it tomorrow. Without any further argument, they both go back to their seats.

9:25 A.M. The children settle down to play with the toys with which they are most comfortable. Though the teacher has laid out materials for them, a multitude of toys remain in the storage areas. Each table and area of the room is a setting for only one activity. Rather than taking a toy or activity to a different area, students tend to go from area to area playing with different toys. Toys are laid out in a certain pattern. For example, modeling (clay) activities are confined to one end of one of the long rectangular tables. This day, most of the children are playing with modeling clay, peg boards, wooden toy trucks, wheel and block

Self-direction. Permitted exploration and mobility.

Event Transition 1

Self-generated activity. No ritual distinction between work and play.

Activities reinforcing the manipulation of materials.

Spontaneous, self-generated social organization.

References to automotive technology and to the manipulation of material items common to industrial society.

Value of emotional restraint; age-related.

Adult decision maker as final arbitrator. Cooperation/sharing are reinforced.

Student emphasis on personal/private property.

Compliance/obedience.

Emphasis on play. Self-generated, spontaneous activity.

Plenitude and consumption. Place/activity coordination. A classroom norm emphasizing order.

Spatial emphasis on the precise organization of material items. Order.

Notice the many material items associated with machine technology.

In loco parentis concern with safety/care of the body.

Physical violence.
This action shows awareness of the classroom norm of sharing.
More instances of physical violence.
Competition. Peer (primarily male) status ranking.

Place/activity coordination.
Value of solicitude for others. *In loco parentis* emphasis on safety.

Spatial emphasis on stereotypic sex-role activities. Notice the mobility/aggressiveness of the males. Recurrent references to industrial, machine technology.
Discipline by cessation of activity. The classroom concern is with safety.
Place/activity coordination.

Sex segregation. Male emphasis on assemblage and construction. Male aggression. Space/activity coordination.

Nurturant, sedentary, nonaggressive (stereotypic) female activities.

assembly kits and are involved in the cutting and gluing of varicolored papier-mâché shapes.

Many of the children, both boys and girls, get into wooden trucks to push them around the room. The teacher intervenes to tell them not to push their trucks too fast.

A black female hits another black female for taking her clay. While so doing, she quickly glances at the observer and the teacher. The teacher did not see her. In a far corner of the room two black males are boasting, loudly, that each can "beat up" the other. They engage in mock combat. One male feigns at karate, playing at kicking the other male in the groin.

A white male scatters toys on the rug area, and the teacher tells him to gather them together because "you might hurt someone." Quite a few of the boys are running around the room pushing the toy trucks. Most of the girls are in the far corner of the room playing with the dolls. The boys rapidly push the trucks around the room and make "engine noises" while yelling and whooping. Children walking back and forth from table to table sometimes are almost run down because the drivers do not slow up or look back. At one point, the teacher goes over to tell them to put all toys with wheels on the shelf. The boys immediately stop and do as she says.

Many of the boys get out decorated paper and cardboard boxes from beneath the shelf area. The cardboard boxes often are stacked one on top of the other. While gaily laughing, several of the larger boys run up and knock down the stacks. This activity is confined to the rug area. Most of the girls are

playing with the dolls or are at one of the tables playing with some of the materials the
teacher provided.

10:00 A.M. The teacher stands up and
tells the children to put away their toys. They
immediately obey. They are told to clean up
their tables. Materials are removed from the
tables and placed in various storage areas
around the room, and the tables are wiped
clean with paper towels.

Event Transition 2

Authority position/
posture = elevated height
(nonverbal signs of status).
Recurring emphasis on
cleanliness and neatness is
common throughout the
period of observation.

10:15 A.M. The teacher's aide arrives and
tells the children to lie down on the rug for a
few minutes. They get blankets from a large
cardboard box in the storage area, and each
child selects a spot and quietly lies down.
They widely space themselves on the rug. No
one touches anyone else. The teacher and aide
exchange greetings and brief conversation.

Event Transition 3

Emphasis on care of
the body is widespread in
its ongoing emphasis.
Self-selected spacing.
Emphasis on au-
tonomy/lack of physical
contact.

10:25 A.M. Today is the birthday of one
of the children. The teacher and aide have
planned a small birthday party. After the
teacher says they have rested enough, the children are told to take their seats. Blankets are
put back in the storage boxes. The teacher
tells a black female to pass out paper napkins
and cups, one to each person. While she does
so, the teacher tells the children to make sure
their hands are clean. Children get up, one at
a time, to wash their hands at the sink, then
quietly return to their seats. The aide, who is
the mother of the birthday child, has brought
ice cream and cupcakes for the party. Some of
the children spontaneously begin singing

Event Transition 4

The uniqueness of the
individual is reinforced.
Rite of passage ceremony.
Ranking/grading by
date of birth. Order as con-
ditional to further activity.
Housekeeping tasks (Goetz
1976:40) = responsibility
training. Regimentation.
Order.

Internalization (learn-
ing) of procedure norms.
Particular foods ceremo-
niously associated with particular events. Spontaneity
and the denial/control of
spontaneity.
Compliance/obedience.

"Happy Birthday." Smiling, the teacher tells them, "Please wait so we might all sing together." The children receive her admonition in good humor, and they all sing together.

The ceremony involves total participation.

The observer has been sitting in one of the tiny chairs in the back of the room. The teacher invites him to join the group. He sits down with the children, and a few occasionally look up and smile but otherwise pay no attention to him. The teacher and aide distribute the food.

Tolerance of interruptions. Task orientation. Food handling by adults.

In the midst of the meal, several children loudly announce that they do not like cupcakes, get up, and toss them in the wastebasket! Neither the teacher nor the aide says anything. These children begin to whine that they want to go outside. The teacher, in a moderate tone of voice, simply says, "No." The children accept this answer, stop whining, and search for something else to do.

An emphasis on accommodation and nurturing that will disappear during the later grades.
The classroom is a limited-access, controlled environment; children are confined for specified periods of time, despite their own wishes.

Immediately after eating, the children get up to put their cups and papers in the wastebasket. They finish eating their food and cleaning their tables. When finished, they sit quietly in their seats.

Food norms are internalized.
Recurring emphasis on neatness and cleanliness.
Militarylike at-attention, waiting position.

Event Transition 5

Authority position (nonverbal sign of status).
Place/activity coordination.
Emphasis on quiet, order, and the passive student reception of information.
Compliance.

10:45 A.M. The teacher goes to sit in a chair on the rug area and calls the children to lie down in a cluster around her. They scurry to do so. When they are quiet, the teacher begins to read them a story. They are told to be "good listeners" and to be quiet while she reads. The children are quiet. The story is about the adventures of three little pigs. As she reads, the teacher pauses occasionally to ask questions about the story—who is doing what to whom, the names of things, and so forth.

Guided recall demands proof/demonstration.

As the story continues, several children become restless and start squirming. Some look away, at the observer, or at something in the room. Because they are not paying attention as she would like, the teacher, in a smiling voice, admonishes them to be good listeners.

Discomfort is tolerated. Control of emotions and self-discipline.

Reprimand so student will please (Henry 1955) the teacher.

As she reads, the teacher holds up the book, sideways, so they can see the pictures. She pauses to ask the names of various animals in the story. They answer and spontaneously make animal sounds while laughing and flopping on the rug. The teacher smiles and laughs. She pauses to ask them to count, out loud, the number of particular animals in the story. The children perk up and strain to see. Wide-eyed, they stare at the picture book, then hold up an index finger to count out the animals.

Categorization/identification.
Little separation of work and play.

Demonstration/proof required.

Play is characterized by much more coactive activity than routine classroom instruction.

A girl asks if she may go to the bathroom. The teacher says, "Yes." Quietly, she gets up to go to the bathroom, closing the door behind her. There is a small red light near the door handle, and she turns it on to mark her presence. The teacher continues the story. Exiting, the girl closes the door behind her and goes quietly to sit back down on the rug. The other children remain enthralled with the story.

Permission requesting (Goetz 1976:40). Deference to adult authority.
Toilet customs emphasizing expected self-maintenance, privacy, and isolation.

Disregard of external stimuli. Task orientation.

During the reading of the story, the children grow quiet. They inch up and, with their mouths open, lean forward as the teacher reads. A child might stand up on his or her knees, point to the pictures, and comment on the story, "There are sure a lot of them," or "That's a *big* crocodile." When such comments are made, the teacher pauses, smiles, and sometimes asks them questions about the story.

Permitted mobility.

Spontaneity.

Nurturing. Indirect reprimands.
Reinforcement of task orientation and concentration.

When a child is distracted or restless, the teacher never simply says to be quiet. As one white female fidgets on the rug, the teacher pauses to say, "Ann, look at this big crocodile." Inevitably, the girl looks.

Event Transition 6

Care of the body. Recurrent administrative tasks. Responsibility training. Ranking. Regimentation. Lineality.

Nurturing. Accommodation. Care of the body. Order. Lineality. Waiting.
Implied lack of responsibility in children; children are deemed incapable of adult responsibilities.

Adult monitoring and supervision.
Recurring expressions of order, regimentation, and waiting.

Separation behaviors are ritualized.

Recurring adult preparation of the formal learning experiences.

11:15 A.M. At the end of the story the children smile, and the teacher tells them to stand up and stretch. The teacher and observer stretch with them. The teacher designates a black female to be leader of the line. She lines up by the aide, and others line up behind her.

The teacher tells the children to begin putting on their clothing, and she and the aide help with their outerwear. The teacher goes around to see that everyone is dressed properly. As the children line up by the door, a folded piece of paper informing parents that parent-teacher conferences are scheduled tomorrow is pinned to the coat of each child.

11:20 A.M. The teacher escorts the children to the buses and leads them down the hall to the main doors, holding the hand of the first child. The others follow in a near perfect line. When the bus stops, the teacher holds the doors open until they all pass through. When all are outside, the teacher leads them, single file, to the buses. All this time, the children laugh and play, yet no one is out of line. Most of the children loudly say good-bye to the teacher. The teacher smiles and says good-bye to them.

11:30 A.M. Midday break. Lunch.

1:00 P.M. The teacher is preparing activities as the children arrive from the buses. The students and the teacher exchange greetings.

The children take off their outer clothing, throw it into the closet, and mill around the room until the teacher tells them to pick up their coats and *hang* them on the closet hooks. The teacher says they will not go outside (recess) today because the aide is absent. Some children have brought books from home, and the teacher tells other students to look at the classroom books or finish their necklaces. Not all of the children immediately go to pick out books. Children just arriving do not hear the teacher's statement. Some children wander to the storage areas and begin playing with the toys, and the teacher tells them to get books and take their seats. A white female enters, tugs on the teacher's pants, and asks if she can go to the bathroom. The teacher says, "Yes." The girl flicks on the light switch and closes the door behind her.

Spontaneity followed by the denial of spontaneity. Emphasis on order and neatness.

Spatial separation of work and play.

Literacy training is reinforced. Task orientation and self-direction.

Spatial confinement. Order. Denial of self-generated activity.

Deference/permission requesting procedure.

Toilet procedures emphasizing autonomy and isolation.

Event Transition 1

1:15 P.M. The teacher says they may now start their play period, and they race for the toys. They do not make much noise, but they are very active and mobile, and there is constant movement in the room.

Both males and females clearly prefer the wooden toy trucks. While making what they term "engine noises," the children rapidly push the trucks around the room. Like the media stereotype of cowboys being pursued by Indians, they race the trucks in a wide circle around the room. The usual pattern is for a child to lean down, put both hands on the side of the toy, look up, and push the truck around the room. The teacher comes over to the observer and smilingly throws up her hands, saying that they do this *all* the time! After about five minutes, she stands in front

Temporal separation of work and play.

Compliance with quiet and order are class norms. Permitted mobility during play.

Valuation/manipulation of models of machine technology. Emphasis on mobility and transportation. These are values and preferences children bring to the classroom. Link between classroom culture and the culture of the larger society.

This is a self-selected, recurring activity.

Authority posture; the teacher controls the class by cessation of the activity.

In loco parentis concern with safety. The dialogue appeals to self-restraint and discipline.
Indirect regulation of conduct.
Morality norm of solicitude toward others is observed to be more ideological than actual.

Negative command. Appeal to self-restraint and the control of impulses. Compliance/obedience.
Passive aggression. Conscious violation of classroom norms. Manipulation of the rules. The teacher "lost." Competition.

Male (stereotypic) role behaviors and values. Emphasis on aggression, physical violence, and machine technology ("guns").
People often are unaware of the meaning of covert patterns in their own culture (Merton 1957:60–82).

Physical violence among males. Peer ranking. The popular stylized violence of the mass media with which the children are familiar.

of the room and, quietly but firmly, tells them to put the trucks away because they are running into each other and the tables. "What happens when you go too fast?" she asks from the center of the room. They all stop to answer her: "CRASH!" "Now, what would happen on the road if *everyone* drove around like that?" Several children start to mumble, pausing to think about her question. But before they can answer she asks, "What are some *good* ways that you can play with your trucks?" They make a few garbled comments. They have started to put away the trucks. The teacher says, "Let's see if we can make a road with the blocks." Obediently, the children try to construct a road from the large cardboard blocks.

Gradually, children creep back to the trucks. They glance at the teacher and then, when she is not looking, move closer to the trucks. A minute later, they are whooping and racing. This time, the teacher does not intervene.

The males dominate the trucks. Several other males run after them shouting, "I'm a bad guy . . . I'm a bad guy." One says, "I'm *really* a bad guy and I go POW! POW! POW! with my *gun!*" He points and jabs his finger at the truck he is chasing while making a sound like a gun. Exasperated, the teacher tells the observer that if she just left them alone they would do *nothing* all day but play shoot-em-up and race the trucks! She blankly stares at the observer. She does not, she says, understand their preference for these activities.

In the back of the room, two black males pretend to fight. One feigns the use of karate hand chops and side kicks. The teacher does not see them.

A large white male chases after the children racing the trucks around the room. He has a long stick from one of the construction sets and, using it as a toy gun, he runs after the trucks shouting, "POW! POW! POW! POW!" After a minute or so, the teacher intervenes, telling him, "Now let's see what else we can make out of this other than a gun." He looks at her and sulks.

Several more children (all male) go to the storage boxes to get the *larger* toy trucks. They seem to want to get into one of the larger trucks and have someone push them around. Many of the children, however, prefer to take one of the smaller trucks and push it around the room while making "engine noises." Periodically the teacher intervenes, with her mild, smiling voice, and tells them to *slow down*.

A white male playing on the rug is throwing cardboard boxes at another white male. The teacher goes over and stops him by saying that he might hurt someone. A black male races his truck around the room. He rears up to do a "wheelie like Evel Knievel does!"

At the round table, several children finish their necklaces. A white female helps another put on her necklace. The teacher firmly tells several boys playing on the rug: "Don't knock over each other's buildings!" and "Don't stand on the blocks!" The boys cease these activities when told to do so.

Several children whine, saying they want to go outside. The teacher ignores them.

An activity taking place at the round table involves trying to place varicolored blocks on a sheet of paper made up of randomly colored squares. At one of the long tables several children put together jigsaw puzzles of vari-

---

Manipulation of objects in games associated with skill and strategy. Continuing parodies of physical violence using machine technology.

Denial of physical violence. Negative command and discipline through cessation of activity.

Segregation by sex. Place/space coordination.

Peer ranking. Dominance-submission behavior.

Autonomy. Individualism.

Emphasis on safety.

Segregation by sex. Male physical violence, aggression, and peer ranking.

Discipline by appeal to solicitude/concern for others. Safety. Mass-media reference.

Contrast in male and female classroom activity patterns. Female solicitude and sociability.

Solicitude for others.

Emphasis on safety and care of the body.

Schooling as forced confinement. Students must learn self-discipline and control of emotions.

Place/activity coordination. Time/space coordination.

Activities emphasizing assemblage, coordination,

and the manipulation of objects.

ous animals. The teacher works with another group of children, who are making necklaces. They cut various shapes from pieces of paper and, in between lengths of white plastic tubing, string them together on a piece of colored yarn.

Permitted mobility.

Children move from activity to activity as the mood strikes them. A child might be at an easel painting one minute and at the modeling clay table the next. When a child wants to begin another activity, the teacher helps him or her get started. For example, if someone wants to paint she ties a plastic apron around the child's waist and puts a fresh piece of newsprint on an easel.

Neatness. Cleanliness. *In loco parentis* protection of clothing.

In preparation for Halloween, several children are cutting the insides out of pumpkins. The teacher asks if she can help with this activity, and everyone broadly smiles and says, "Yes!"

Required observance of national celebration.
Ritualized association of particular foods with particular events. Permission requesting.
Propriety.
Imitation of "cowboys/ Indians" stereotypes. Physical violence. Male emphasis on mobility, transportation, and technology. Imitation of/identity with machines.
Control through power of cessation of activity.

Several boys run around the room in a tight circle, each pointing an outstretched index finger at the other and shouting, "BANG! BANG! BANG! BANG!" Several other children, mostly male, have made a "road" out of the cardboard boxes and race the smaller trucks over them, making deep, growling, guttural "engine noises." The teacher looks up from her table and tells them to put the trucks away. The boys obey.

Compliance/obedience.

On their way to new activities, several children stop where the observer is sitting to say, "Hi, what's your name?" or "My name is Rachel, what's yours?" To get past the observer a white female quietly but firmly says, "Excuse me," because he was in her way. As she passes she says, "Thank you." At the rear play area, a black female and a white female are arguing, loudly, about who will play

Propriety ban on unpermitted touching. Autonomy.

Sexual segregation ex-

"Mommy" and who will play "Daddy." Neither wants to play the "Daddy."

1:45 P.M. A black female student aide comes into the room, and the teacher informs the observer that three fifth graders volunteer to help her. The children do not stop their activities.

Conditioning to task orientation and concentration.

A black male is crying because he cannot have all the blocks he wants. The teacher goes over to him, bends down, puts her arms around him, and says that if he wants to continue playing with the blocks, he will have to stop crying. Crying, he keeps saying, "I want my daddy . . . I want my daddy." A black male and a white female blankly look at him. Both call him a crybaby. The other children do not pay any attention to him.

Spontaneous expression of emotion followed by reinforcement for self-discipline and control of emotions.

Schooling as a process of "weaning" children (Dreeben 1968) from the family. Age/role peer expectations for control of emotion. Autonomy.

It is recess time for another class. Periodically, children peer in the outside windows, knock on the glass, and yell until an adult outside (an aide) yells for them to stop. They scamper off. The teacher briefly looks up, then goes back to work on her pumpkin. For the most part, the children do not noticeably react.

Spatial separation of work and play. Notice the lack of privacy in the classroom and the continual adult monitoring and supervision of the children. Task orientation and toleration of distractions.

A white male approaches the observer and half climbs up on his knee to share a story. Several other boys, both black and white, are on the rug carefully building vertical structures with the cardboard boxes. When finished to their satisfaction they back away, momentarily smile, then aggressively charge the cardboard boxes and, while laughing, knock them down.

Contact-seeking. Literacy training.

Spatial segregation by sex.

Male aggressive behavior.

Event Transition 2

2:35 P.M. The teacher says it is time to clean up and rapidly flicks the light switch on and off. The children immediately stop their

Nonverbal signaling—stimulus/response behavior.

pressed spatially. Sex-role stereotypes.

Compliance/obedience.
Place/item coordina-
tion. Order.
Housekeeping tasks =
responsibility training.
Compliance/obedience.
Place/item coordination.
Order. Task orientation.

play and begin doing what the teacher asks.
Several chairs are overturned, paper is on the
floor, dolls, cardboard boxes, and clumps of
modeling clay are strewn about the room.
There are specific places for all of the toys.
The children are assigned specific areas of the
room to clean up. There is no balking, and
they diligently perform their clean-up tasks,
methodically putting the materials away with
as much dedication as they exhibited while
playing with them. They place each item *exactly* where it belongs. Nothing is casually
thrown or tossed about but carefully and
slowly *placed*.

Order. Procedure.
Place/item coordination.
Neatness and order.

Event Transition 3

Care of the body.
Self-control. Toleration
of physical discomfort.
Withholding of affec-
tion fosters autonomy and
self-maintenance. Self-reliance is reinforced. Notice
the lack of peer support.

2:40 P.M. After cleaning up, the teacher
tells them to lie on the rug for several minutes
and rest, this time without blankets. The boy
previously mentioned again starts to cry.
Amid sobs, he complains that his stomach
hurts. The teacher does not go to him but
quietly says that if he would lie down for a
few minutes he would feel better. The child
does so but continues to cry for several minutes. No one pays any attention to him.

Event Transition 4

Differential rewards.

Competition. Peer
ranking. Order. Regimentation. Waiting.

Space as private prop-
erty.

Rotating housekeeping
tasks = responsibility training. (See Carroll 1982 and

2:50 P.M. Depending upon how quiet a
child has been, the teacher calls each one to
the sink to wash his/her hands. Half bouncing
up and down on the rug, the first child to be
called cannot contain her glee. Afterward,
they take specific places at the tables; the
teacher does not permit any other child to sit
at that child's place.

A white male and a black female are assigned to set the tables with paper cups and
napkins. A snack, consisting of orange juice

and cookies, is served. A child, invariably the quietest one, asks the blessing.

Several children ask for second portions. Pausing briefly, the teacher replies, "What's the magic word?" Softly, they murmur, "Please."

The teacher goes over to the boy who has been crying, embraces him, and asks if he is feeling better. She also asks a neighboring black female if her sister is better today.

After eating, the children are told to clean up, and without further instruction, they get up to put their waste in the basket.

3:15 P.M. After cleaning up, they take their places on the rug because the teacher is going to read another story. She reads from a book that a child brought from home. Several times the teacher repeats, "I'm going to make a *good* listener the leader of the line," or "I'm going to see who can be a *good* listener." The story is about the adventures of a monkey and a crocodile. While the teacher reads, the aide places the chairs upside down on the tables, then straightens materials and papers on the teacher's desk.

A black female is rolling on the floor and not paying attention to the story or the teacher. The teacher snaps her fingers, and the girl immediately crawls back into place. If the teacher considers the group too noisy, a "Shhhhhhhhh" with fingers placed to the lips is sufficient to quiet them. At the conclusion of the story, the teacher praises them for being

Douglas 1975:249–75 on food rituals in the United States.) Differential rewards and ranking. Ritual association of foods and supranatural sanction. Link between religion and education.

Denial of spontaneity by reference to formula/procedure for bringing about desired end.

Affection and nurturing as reward for self-discipline.

Nurturance. Solicitude.

Cleanliness, neatness, and order. Compliance. Self-direction.

Event Transition 5

Place/activity coordination. Status reflected in height differences (Leach 1976:53–54). Literacy training.

Competition. Ranking as reward for passive reception of knowledge morally reinforced.

Anthropomorphism/allegory.

The aide's work will help the janitor to clean the room. Emphasis on order, neatness, and cleanliness. Ranked tasks.

Nonverbal signaling. Stimulus/response conditioning.

Control through manipulation of emotions. Teacher praise as reward.

Event Transition 6
Separation procedures. Emphasis on continuing *in loco parentis* concern with safety and the care/protection of the body.

In loco parentis concern with care of clothing.

Ranking as reward. Competition. Lineality. Waiting. Physical violence. Discipline through spatial ranking. The idea of "first" and "last" is spatially expressed. Spatial positioning as a vehicle for (moral) labeling.

Adult monitoring and supervision. Emphasis on order, regimentation, and lineality.

good listeners. She smiles and "coos" at them, and they grin with pleasure.

3:30 P.M. The teacher tells the children to go to the closet and get their outerwear. The teacher and aide help several of them with their clothing. They tell them to button their coats all the way up because it is very cold outside. The teacher and aide pin small notes on their coats. A black female heads toward the easel as the teacher shouts, "Don't play in the paint when you have your coat on!"

Quietest children first, the teacher lines them up by the hall door. While in line, a black male hits a black female, and the teacher tells him to go to the end of the line. The observer comments that one might always be able to tell who were the "bad" children because they are generally found at the end of any particular line. The teacher replies, "Gee, you know, I never thought of that." She puts on her coat and leads them single file to the bus. There is a bold yellow line in the hallway about a meter from the wall, and everyone walks inside this line.

Preschooling initiates children into the nature of school and the process of schooling. Preschooling is preparation for the transitional aspect of schooling as rite of passage, and the early grades especially reinforce the physical separation of children from their families. Before any initiation, new recruits must be conditioned properly and prepared for the important teachings and learnings to come. At West Haven children are first physically isolated, then subjected to a series of personally transforming events and activities over which they have little control, the full meaning of which undoubtedly they do not understand. Beginning in kindergarten, recruits are sorted into subgroups and moved on for more specialized, advanced instruction.

The separation phase in the rite of passage sequence of schooling is seen in the fact that virtual strangers are enclosed together in isolated rooms for considerable periods of time. Preschool children intentionally are separated spatially from influences other than those occurring within the confines of this particular classroom. With only a few exceptions, the children in the room have no kinship relationship either to the adult teacher or to one another. Preschooling exhibits the initial parental surrender of children, their spatial confinement, and instruction by nonkin personnel. This situation is not unique. In many societies, initiation begins with the physical separation of children from their families and households. Unlike West Haven, though, adults charged with the initiation of children customarily are elder kinfolk; the society's education system overlaps its kinship system (Cohen 1964:54–99). Among the Tiwi (Hart and Pilling 1960) of Australia, for example, elder male relatives of pubescent boys unexpectedly and suddenly appear one day literally to drag the children from their mothers' arms. They take the boys into the brush, to secret places, for a series of initiation rites. During this time, the boys are taught how to be "men." Their separation from the household, and especially from their mothers (Eliade 1958:50), is apparent. Similarly, around the time of puberty Hopi boys and girls are taken from their households (Eggan 1956). Physically removed by elder relatives, they are taken underground into *kivas* for their initiation ceremonies. In each of these cases, initial rites of separation and the subsequent physical isolation of children intimately are associated with the process of education.

A distinguishing feature of American schooling, in contrast with other forms of education, is that the people involved normally are not related by kinship. The initiators of children (teachers) are certified by the state rather than by local kinship groups, which merely select the ones certified. Local kinship groups (relatives of the children) customarily do not have the power, as they do in other types of societies, to determine directly what is taught to their children or who will teach it. Spatial isolation and the comparative absence of kinship ties among schoolchildren reinforce the ascribed power and authority of the nonkin initiator (teacher). When brothers and sisters are in the same classroom, they rarely are permitted to sit together. It is unusual for a parent, or an adult kinsperson of a child, to be in the classroom for significant periods of time. Similar to adult, bureaucratic workplaces, public schooling orients children to a system of normative social relationships not based on kinship. Kinship and descent are not principles around which American society is organized, and this is reflected in the society's national educational system. Children in public schools learn to establish ongoing relationships with strangers. In preschool, children are eased into the reality of this relationship norm by being permitted to interact with one another much more than they will be permitted to do in later grades. As potential students, children must embrace the school's normative pattern of social organization and relationship. Most of the continuing resistance to teacher control that is expressed primarily during the middle grades will come from students who continue to retain strong quasi-kinship peer relationships with one another. Success in the sociocultural world of the classroom, however, will come only to those who learn to behave autonomously. Deference to nonkin adult strangers, acceptance of a lack of privacy, acceptance of the arbitrary orders of unrelated and unfamiliar strangers, and continual teacher surveillance and monitoring are some of the overt and covert social and cultural lessons students are expected to learn during the initial stage of schooling.

If school classrooms are small societies, then the preschool classroom is more autocratic than egalitarian. Children are expected to accept teachers as the sole authority in the classroom. Teachers reserve the legitimate right to control conflict; they administer the rules and regulations to which a captive client student population is expected to conform. Whether making classroom decorations or organizing reading groups, teachers control the flow of energy and labor in the classroom as well as the distribution of strategic classroom resources, including the important apportionment of food.

During preschool and kindergarten there is ongoing classroom emphasis on *in loco parentis* behaviors, such as nurturance and accommodation by the teacher; these behaviors disappear gradually during the early and middle grades. *In loco parentis* behaviors ease the social and cultural shock of the child's initiation into classroom ways of life, as does the preschool scheduling of half-day classes. The predominance of female teachers in the early grades provides children with an initial affective adult initiator. Females in our society customarily still are associated with primarily affective characteristics such as nurturance, solicitude for others, tolerance, and other-directedness, whereas males customarily still are associated primarily with more instrumental, task-oriented activities. The preschool teacher exhibits physical and personal characteristics (stereotypically) associated with "mother." She is portly and cherubic. By temperament she is outgoing and warm, and by nature she is affectionate. Her manner is nurturing and compliant, and she is thus well suited as a surrogate mother, an affective frame of reference, for children first coming to school. Constituents at West Haven recognize this need for nurturing, and the *Paraprofessional Handbook* states:

> For many [students] this is the first time they have been separated from their mothers [not fathers!] for all day almost every day. This plays an important factor in what they are going to do. Again, for the first time youngsters are faced with a new adult and they must obey. This new adult is probably a woman. His mother being a woman, an adult, probably resembles the teacher—the child will react to her like he did to other women. He will treat the teacher as he treated his mother.

The only male teachers in the elementary school are in the upper grade classrooms. There, male teachers provide a frame of reference orienting children to the more instrumental aspect of secondary schooling.

Other classroom events and activities ease the required physical and emotional separation of children from the outside world. In West Haven elementary school classrooms, meals are served and taken in a (stereotypic) family-style manner. Customary American food habits are reinforced, and 17 percent of preschool classroom time customarily is devoted to food and meals (see Figure B-1, Appendix B). Eating together in the classroom reinforces the incorporation of children into a new social group (Van Gennep 1960:29), and initiation ceremonies and rites of passage customarily include instruction in food handling (Eliade 1958:14–15). Considerable preschool attention is given to the physical care and protection of the children. Just as their mothers undoubtedly bundled the children up to ship them off to school, their surrogate mother nonkin teachers do the same in shipping them back home. The children, in each case, are cared for by females. Paralleling the wider culture, more contact is permitted between adult females and children in the classroom than between adult males and children. More physical contact occurs between teachers and students in the early grades than in the later grades. There is little physical contact between the children, especially the male children, and male teachers as observed in the upper grade classroom sessions. Finally, 47 percent of observed preschool classroom time is devoted to play (see Figure B-1, Appendix B). Permitted play seduces children into forming affective bonds with the school. A stated goal of the educational system at West Haven is to get children to *want* to come to school. Play is enjoyable to these children and involves permitted exploration of the sensate preschool environment. Teachers hope that children, by association, will come to find classroom life enjoyable. The association of classroom life with play is permitted in the pregrades but is sharply curtailed along with other separation shock-reducing tactics as children continue their early grade initiatory passage.

Classroom sociocultural systems exhibit a core norm and value orientation; that is, there is a predominant event and activity pattern to routine classroom life that is of social and cultural consequence. A great deal of activity takes place throughout the average preschool classroom day, but in most cases only a few core social and cultural traits underlie that activity. For example, the preschool sessions primarily condition for student adherence to the norm of classroom order (1), a composite norm that continues to be expressed on many grade levels in the elementary school. The broad category of order includes recurring classroom session emphasis on temporal and spatial coordination (3), routine housekeeping tasks (6, 10, 33), ranking (2), the reinforcement of student self-control (7), compliance and obedience (11), regimentation (18), coming to attention (61), and waiting (21).* Preschool session events and activities emphasize the initial ordering of student-to-student and student-to-teacher patterns of relationship fundamental to the on-going way of life of the classroom as a society. The ordering and ranking (2) of events and activities generate predictability in classroom life; routinely, rest follows play, story time comes after meals, and so forth. The sequential event and activity structure of the preschool day orients children toward, and conditions them for adherence to, the pattern of school society.

The social system of the classroom expects norms for behavior not merely to be obeyed by students but to be internalized by them as well. Denial of spontaneity, for example, conditions for the control of impulses (Henry 1959), and the self-indulgence children often bring to school is harnessed by the teacher's often gentle nudging toward the classroom norm of self-control (7). The sociocultural system of early and middle grade classrooms makes a distinction between those children who have internalized customary classroom norms ("good" students)

---

*The numbers in parentheses refer to corresponding numbers in the statistical summaries of preschool features in Figure C-1, Appendix C.

and those who have not ("problem" students). The classroom emphasis on order and proper social relationship customarily accompanies a ban on self-expression and self-generated activity. Student mobility (13), for example, increasingly is permitted only at the teacher's discretion. Figure C-1, Appendix C, lists very few high-ranking preschool features such as literacy training (27) directly bearing upon academics. The initial lessons of elementary schooling are attitudinal and behavioral.

Many of the features isolated in the preschool narratives are associated with the modification and classroom channeling of values and behaviors children bring to school. The culture and society of West Haven, in particular, and of the contemporary United States, in general, affect children long before they arrive at the doors of school classrooms. The link between school and society is maintained as much by schoolchildren as by schoolteachers. There are, for instance, many incidents of violence (9) occurring in the preschool sessions. The mass media influence the stereotypic forms through which violence in the classroom is expressed: guns; cowboys and Indians; kung fu and karate. The teacher spends a great deal of time trying to counter the expression of these stylized forms of violence the children bring into the classroom. The school does not cause competition, individualism, consumerism, violence, or the desire for mobility; these are core features of the society and culture of which public schools are a part.

The preschool emphasis on neatness (6) and cleanliness (10) reinforces behaviors and values predominant in the wider culture and society outside the school (DuBois 1955; Henry 1957; Miner 1956). Initiation ceremonies customarily are marked by rigid adherence to special forms of dress and decoration (Wax and Wax 1965). Neatness and cleanliness are stressed in public school classrooms other than at West Haven (Leacock 1969:210), but these sartorial sanctions go beyond a basic *in loco parentis* concern with presentability. The specialness of classroom spaces requires that children be kept clean, neat, and orderly for participation in them. The West Haven *Elementary School Rules and Safety Reminders* booklet warns that "any student who comes to school without proper attention having been given to personal cleanliness or neatness of dress, may be sent home." Standard entry procedures emphasize the ritual preparation of classrooms. Teachers, and sometimes aides, carefully prepare each classroom for a series of precise activities analogous to preparations for a religious ceremony (Van Gennep 1960:65). Just as removing one's hat in church is a ritual procedure signaling respect, so too is the removal of "dirty" protective clothing a literal shedding by students of some of the profane vestiges of the outside world (Van Gennep 1960:33). Children have to learn that entering classrooms involves a precise, ritual procedure (46). Preschool session children spend 13 percent of their time on entry and exit procedures (32) (see Figure B-1, Appendix B). Nothing angers teachers more than "disrespectful," often spontaneous, student entry and exit procedures—students not removing their hats or boots and other similar behavior. Succeeding classroom narratives reveal teachers standing by the hall door, literally guarding the classroom threshold, so as better to monitor student entry and exit procedures. Running in and out of the classroom is "disrespectful." Participants are conscious of the classroom as a special space, and "good" students adhere better to this behavioral norm than do "poor" students, who make known their feelings about their place in the classroom social system by violating the sanctity of the classroom with consciously inappropriate behavior. Standard exit procedures from the classroom continue to emphasize neatness, order, and cleanliness. Upon leaving there always occurs, or is supposed to occur, the precise rearrangement and ordering of the classroom by participants. The classroom remains a special place through which the often rowdy students pass. Students are expected to keep the classroom (not the toilet, playground, or lunchroom) neat, clean, and orderly; they are conditioned to accord the classroom deference and respect. Students can be punished by excommunication from the school for sartorial and behavioral impropriety in classrooms.

The predictable sequencing of major activity and event segments subtly conditions children for adherence to classroom norms of order (1) and procedure (32). Children are expected to associate classroom life with the characteristic form of the occurrence of particular events and activities. One eats a meal in the classroom just as one eats a meal at home, for example, but in the classroom one does not eat a meal at any time or in any place. Classroom meals are eaten at a table after the rest period, and snacking is never permitted in classrooms although it may or may not be permitted at home. The society and culture of the classroom are manifested to children as a spatial/temporal process, and learning the form and pattern of schooling initially means learning the proper coordination of a host of activities in their proper sequence (3). The major events that constitute preschool sessions are particulate and summarized in Figure B-1, Appendix B. Classroom events, and the activities they include, tend to exist separately in time and in space. For example, eating is separated spatially and temporally from play. Rest is separated spatially and temporally from reading: "He is required to do certain things at certain times by this new adult when he does not want to. He must sit down and listen to a story when he would rather put together a puzzle. Having to do something that is not his choice will probably become his number one frustration" ([West Haven] *Paraprofessional Handbook*). At West Haven there is a time and a place for everything, and everything has its *separate* time and its *separate* place. One is not supposed to talk while eating. One should not play while stories are being read. The organization of classroom life conditions children to adhere to the precise coordination of events and activities at certain times and in particular places (3).

Themes of confinement, separation, and isolation are expressed not only in the physical and organizational features of the preschool classroom but in the manner in which children are expected to relate to one another as well. Preschool classroom sessions place normative emphasis on student autonomy (5). Autonomy is a form of isolation; the separation is between oneself and others. Classroom autonomy is expressed in preschool children being conditioned to adhere to sociocultural patterns of eating from separate plates (25), going to the toilet alone (57), and bearing increasing responsibility for the control of their own bodies (7). The spontaneous clustering and grouping (8) exhibited here are squelched during the middle grades when children group themselves and are grouped with respect to sex (29) and color, furniture arrangement, differences in adherence to classroom norms and values, reading ability, and other subtle factors. The ideology as well as the fact of individualism and autonomy are core American values (Henry 1966; Hsu 1972; Shimahara 1975), though I found it sad to watch children learning classroom behavioral norms and values well enough to apologize when they bump into or merely touch one another or when they curl up alone, fetuslike, on the rug while taking a nap. Preschool children are oriented to education, schooling, only occurring during the day. At the end of the school day, classroom settings are abandoned and customarily remain unused until the next morning. In nonschool settings, though, teaching and learning are both diurnal and nocturnal and informally occur at any time or in any place, especially within a child's home and family. Children are conditioned to make the association between the school, as an exclusive and special setting, and "education."

The very act of going to school means learning to coordinate (3) the two properly (not being "tardy") in space and time.

This major theme of coordination pervades succeeding classroom narratives as well as the wider national society and culture of which the school is a part. In modern societies such as our own, the clock on the wall is as omnipresent as it is in every classroom in West Haven Elementary School. Time itself, national time reckoning, is a subject for classroom study. Students are expected to know the day's date, number of months in a year, number of days in a month, and so forth. Wristwatches are student status items at West Haven. Local time reckoning, though, often conflicts with national school time reckoning. As recently as the 1960s at West Haven, there was parent/school conflict over males (especially) irregularly attending school because their parents expected them to help with family agricultural work. Adhering to the pattern of schooling and classroom life involves the initiation of children to the bureaucratic principle of order (1). The coordination of events and activities in time and space, by clock time, is crucial to the orderly functioning of both schools and society. In preschool and kindergarten children are exposed to and conditioned to adhere to the form of public schooling and classroom life, itself an important nonverbal message, before the initiatory transmission of further social and cultural information.

KINDERGARTEN: BECOMING A STUDENT

The preschool teacher keeps file cards on which she records each child's progress and achievement. For each relevant set of classroom activities, she records how well each child performed in meeting her lesson plan objectives. Evaluations are both subjective and objective: "Doesn't listen to story"; "Very quiet"; "Loves to use crayons. However, she only puts a line down for each color and then is finished"; and so on. These cards, covering a wide range of classroom behaviors, attitudes, and skills, are part of each child's permanent school record.

Two groups of kindergarten students are formed on the basis of preschool evaluations. Kindergarten literally means *children's garden*, but at West Haven the garden aspects of this grade are muted by the emergence of a new principle of school and classroom organization: stratification, the division of a social group into internally defined inferior and superior subgroups. Termed "tracking" at West Haven, the homogeneous preschool student group is ranked, divided, then placed in different kindergarten rooms. The schooling of these two ranked subgroups of children, termed "high" and "low," occurs in different classroom spaces, designated as "high" and "low" classrooms. The classroom spatial separation between the ranked subgroups of children in kindergarten is important, and the spatial separation of kindergarten children into different rooms makes their different status and rank more distinct. Succeeding chapters compare observation samples of both so-called "high" and "low" sessions and highlight similarities and differences in the classroom experiences of each group of children.

The north wall of each kindergarten classroom borders the covered walkway spanning the front of the building. Half of this wall is glass, often covered with drawn drapes to maintain privacy. The east and west walls hold full-length blackboards (actually, they are green in color). Kindergarten classrooms are "self-contained," as they are termed; that is, the east wall contains a bathroom as well as a child-size water drinking fountain and sink. Children are presented with few reasons to leave the room during the day. The south wall contains the hall door and classroom closets, and it faces the playground. These walls contain floor-to-ceiling safety-tempered windows, permitting an abundance of light in the rooms. Below the window area and to each side of the hall door is an open shelf storage area spanning the length of the wall; toys, games, and other classroom paraphernalia are stored here. Both kindergarten rooms contain movable bookcases, overflowing with children's books, at times serving as room area dividers. Each room is painted green with light gray ceiling and floor tiles. The floor rugs are deep green. Both rooms are bright, airy, and spacious, and contrasting textures and visual stimuli lend warmth to the environment. Similar to the preschool classroom, each kindergarten room is sensate and stimulating, and an abundance of objects beckon to be touched and explored. The environmental seduction continues.

There is more furniture in each kindergarten room than in the preschool room (see Figure 4). There is a corresponding decrease in the amount of unrestricted classroom space available for movement and exploration by the children. Furniture is spread widely around the room. The greater number of separate pieces of furniture, and their diffuse spatial placement, discourages spontaneous mobility. The kindergarten pattern of furniture placement further reinforces the clustering of children in particular classroom spaces. Children spend more class time at their desks than in preschool, and the classrooms physically and spatially reflect the emphasis on task orientation predominant in the kindergarten curriculum. Tables (A_4) are pushed together to define settings conducive to interaction-oriented classroom events and activities; group work projects are carried out on these pushed-together tables. The teacher and teacher's aide routinely take small groups of children to the two circular tables (A_3) for special reading instruction.

The spatial separation between student and teacher (A_1) desks increases, and the teacher's desk assumes a prominent, high-status spatial position in the classroom. The teacher's desk and the spatial areas immediately surrounding it customarily are not shared with the children. Explicitly defined is the public, low-status space of the children's designated classroom area and the more private, high-status space of the teacher's designated classroom area. The floor rug (B), although smaller and not as prominently placed as in the preschool classroom, is present in each kindergarten classroom and continues to be a spatial focus for group activities such as reading lessons, play period games, and the use of toys. The children are still playing, but they are working more, and this change is reflected physically in the smaller size of the kindergarten floor rugs.

The visual and physical emphasis in both kindergarten classrooms is on the display of animals exhibiting anthropomorphic qualities of human speech and personality, on numbers, and on the elaborate and prominent illustration of national holidays. One classroom is personalized with the children's (abstract) artwork hung on a string strung directly in front of the outside window. There is a large commercially produced EXIT sign by the hall door. On the other side of the door is a large commercially produced calendar next to which is a bookcase crammed full of commercially produced children's books. Above the bookcase is a sign saying WET PAINT. The room visually reinforces literacy in general and the (national) English language in particular. Large alphabet letters cut from multicolored crepe paper are taped to the wall. Small letters above the blackboard on the north wall spell out the alphabet. Taped to another blackboard are posters exhibiting the numbers one through fifty. Small posters depicting prancing squirrels are taped to the wall above another blackboard; the smiling squirrels illustrate the concepts of behind/in front of, over/under, up/down, left/right, off/on, in/out, and closed/open. Most of these visual references condition for the children's adherence to a lineal, segmented conception of time and space. Letters and animals spelling out the month of N-o-v-E-M-B-E-R

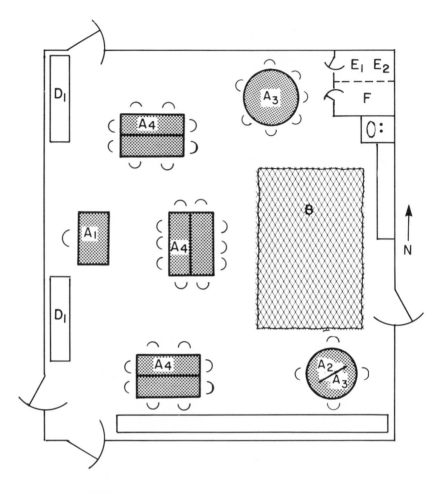

Figure 4. A Kindergarten Classroom

Legend

A_1 = teacher's desk	B = floor rug
A_2 = teacher aide's desk	C = chair
A_3 = classroom activity desk	D_1 = bookcases/storage areas
A_4 = student desk	E_1 = teacher's closet
	E_2 = students' closet
	F = lavatory

are taped to the rear wall in one room. A calendar, on which each day of the month is represented by a small square, is taped to the wall near the hall door. A small papier-mâché turkey, on which each day of the month is printed, is pinned to an appropriate square. Other papier-mâché turkeys are hung on a cord strung in front of the outside window.

National holidays and national origin legends are emphasized visually and physically. On the hallway wall in the first kindergarten room, a bulletin board displays a scene of a Native American powwow. Clad in deerskin, naked to the waist, and wearing feathered headbands, conspicuously red-skinned Indians dance around a fire. Adjacent is a similar scene of prancing Native Americans dancing with smiling white children. Sitting at a log table amid remnants of a meal, Native American and white elders smoke a long wooden pipe. In the second room, a large papier-mâché turkey is taped to the front blackboard. Adjacent to it is an elaborate commercially produced poster of a contemporary Thanksgiving dinner scene. A portly white man, holding a knife and fork, stands over a steaming platter of turkey and cranberries, and a broadly beaming matronly woman, wearing an apron, sits at the opposite end of the table. Two well-scrubbed, freckle-faced children sit facing the viewer. The boy wears a striped T-shirt, and a rumpled baseball cap casually hangs on the post of his chair. The girl has blue eyes and pigtails. A beagle puppy, his tongue lolling with anticipation, peeks out from under the table. Taped to the closet door is a student-made drawing of a cornucopia from which flows an indeterminable array of foodstuffs. On either side of this river of food are a boy and girl, with upraised hands and open mouths, jumping and shouting with glee. These seemingly unobtrusive displays visually promote and condition students for adherence to, among others, the following social norms and cultural values: the ideological primacy of the nuclear family, traditional age and sex-role divisions, an assumption of Anglo-American sociocultural hegemony, expected male superiority, material well-being, neatness, cleanliness, order, private property, and conspicuous consumption. Kindergarten children are bombarded with visual messages reinforcing national symbols and images, myths, and legends.

The first teacher we will meet is a frail, nervous white female in her mid-twenties. She has been at West Haven for three years. Her assigned aide is a middle-aged female of Spanish-speaking descent. The teacher of the second class, a stout white female in her mid-forties, has been at West Haven for seven years. Her aide is a white female, also in her forties. Students are five and six years of age. There are twenty-four students in the first (low) class: five white males, six white females, six black males, and seven black females. In the second (high) class there were twenty-three students in the sessions observed: five black males, six white males, four black females, and eight white females.

A Low Classroom Session

8:45 A.M. Both the teacher and aide arrive before the children and arrange materials for the day's activities. Children come in from the buses in small clusters, rarely alone. The teacher and aide help remove their clothing and help put the clothing in the closet.

> Adult supervision/monitoring.
> Peer coaction lessens with increasing classroom emphasis on autonomy.

9:05 A.M. The children take their seats and begin individual activities. The teacher tells the class to work on "sets." This activity consists of identifying sets of things: one-to-one matching, the joining and separating of sets of things, and the like, and students gain practice in measuring quantities. The teacher goes around the room looking at their work and says, "I'm not happy with the sets you have been finding. Let's look for some others." The teacher uses the term "Honey" quite a bit, speaking in a high falsetto voice while drawing out her vowels. Many of the children are having difficulty with this activity, and the teacher says, "You don't have to continue with these sets if you don't feel like it. You can come back to them later." Most of the children cease this activity and go to another.

> ### Event Transition 1
> Student self-direction.
> Location in "personal" (Sommer 1969) space.
> The nature and organization of reality as segmented/particulate (Lee 1950).

> Indirect command.
> Please-the-teacher approach through manipulation of emotions and "baby talk" (Henry 1955).
> Student-centered activity. Accommodation. Emphasis on finishing (Goetz 1976:40).
> Permitted spontaneity. Personal choice.

Most of the children are working on a cutting-and-pasting activity. The teacher and aide have placed a pile of newspapers on one activity table and a scissors rack and paste on another. The children cut groups (sets again)

> Assemblage activity.
> Place/activity coordination.

of items out of the newspaper and paste them on sheets of white paper.

The children work individually in separate chairs regularly spaced around the desk. They pause frequently to look at the work of other students and to show one another the pictures they cut from magazines. The teacher intervenes to ask, "Are we playing or working?" Most of the noise is laughter, but after the teacher's admonition, the children become quieter. The children show the teacher their work, and she immediately corrects any mistakes they have made. If they do not have "matching items," they have to start over. Occasionally and in a frustrated manner, the teacher grabs a paste brush from a child and shows that child how to do it as she would like.

Several children get up to show other children their work. The teacher is looking at the items a white male has cut from his paper. He counts them for her, going from right to left, and the teacher immediately and firmly tells him to count from left to right. He begins again. A white female whines that another child is in her chair. The teacher tells the errant boy to get up. He does, and the girl sits down, smugly.

9:45 A.M. The teacher tells the children they are "good listeners" and "good workers" and rewards them by passing out small pieces of peanut brittle. The children are told to get ready for a story and, without being told, they line up by their desks. They are told to sit down, then the teacher stands in front of the room and reads a phonic poem. Each charac-

---

Autonomy. The spatial separation of children during work periods.

Spontaneous peer interactions are negated. Stress on autonomy. Distinction between work and play.

Deemphasis of peer interaction and emphasis on the teacher as focus of classroom interactions.

Emphasis on mastery. The idea of "right" and "wrong."

Role learning by following an instructional model.

Spontaneous mobility. Demonstration/proof.

Emphasis on procedure, sequence, and lineality. Mastery norm. Stress on individual responsibility for performance.

Proprietary rights. Private space as property.

Event Transition 2

Task orientation and concentration norm. Work.

Food as reward for work. Controlling the distribution of food is a powerful political act.

Regimentation norm is internalized. Sitting down is voluntary ordering and confinement. Continuing ma-

ter in the poem is represented by a sound. Prominent in the poem are a Mr. N. and a Mr. M. The teacher periodically holds up the book so they might see the pictures and frequently asks them who each character is and what he sounds like. She sounds out the word with them, saying, "Mr. M. Mmmmmmmmmmm as in mmmmmmmmmmilk." The children are excited by this activity and shout out the answers before the teacher acknowledges them. The teacher tells them to be quiet, pausing briefly to reinforce the message, and to respond only when asked.

> nipulation of space to emphasize teacher authority and powers of control.

The children fidget in their chairs, and one child enthusiastically jumps up in response to a question. The teacher tells him to sit down. She frequently tells children to sit down and/or not talk out of turn.

> Spontaneous behaviors are controlled. Deference to adult (higher rank) authority. Emphasis on following procedure.

> Again, there is a denial of self-generated movements. The teacher has the power of confinement. Children must follow sequence and procedure.

Event Transition 3

10:00 A.M. The teacher begins a tracing exercise. The children work at their desks. The teacher passes out a sheet of paper and a pencil to each child. A white male loudly complains that his sheet of paper is "used," but the teacher does not respond. As the teacher passes out the pencils, a black male grabs a pencil from the can before she can give it to him. She quickly snatches it back and gives him a hard, cold look as if to say he should know better. She slowly hands him the pencil.

> Rote. Following models.
> Autonomy. Adult distribution of strategic resources.
> Value of "newness" (Henry 1963:15–22).
> Classroom materials are not reused (emphasized consumption).
> Restraint, self-control, and waiting are reinforced.

The children practice drawing letters, and the teacher loudly admonishes them not to hurry. She repeats the message several times, cautioning them to take their time when printing. Several children are talking, and the teacher says, "Shhhhhh," telling them to be quiet while working. The children trace over a

> Literacy training.
> Procedure norms stress individual task orientation and concentration. Quietness means that autonomy is in effect, and peer interactions ought not to occur.

large *N* with arrows drawn on it, to indicate which lines are made first:

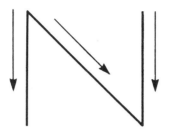

Rote procedures. Mastery—right/wrong. Conformity, following models, and adherence to established procedures are stressed. Lineality and sequencing are reinforced.

Denial of spontaneity.

The lack of personal responsibility for materials is age/age-grade-related.
Peer (student/student) competition is reinforced.
Waiting. Pleasing the teacher. Denial of spontaneity. Children must learn to control their bodies and their emotions (Henry 1959).
Permitted movement within spatially confined areas.
Mastery incentive by pleasing the teacher.
Public display of differential praise and rewards reinforces peer competition and ranking.

They are reminded to print from left to right. A black male traces over the arrows as well, and the teacher sternly tells him to do only what she asked: to trace only over the letter. While the boy attempts this, she stands directly over him. Departures from the teacher's instructions are frequent, and to the class as a whole, the teacher says that they are not doing as she asked. For instance, they should *trace* letters only and trace them only *from left to right*.

10:15 A.M. The previous materials are collected and math workbooks passed out. Working with the class as a whole, the teacher asks, "Who knows the answer to this one?" and waits for hands. As the books are passed around, the aide says, "I like it so much when James patiently waits for me to pass out the books." In anxiously wanting her book, the black female got out of her seat. Students are frequently admonished to sit down. Children climb up on their seats and lean into their work, and the teacher permits them to do so. As they work on their problems the teacher and aide reward desired responses by saying, "I *really* like the way you did this one." Occasionally they hold up the paper for the class to see.

Two black females are arguing and feign hitting each other. One is not giving the other enough room at the table, and she feigns a karate hand chop to the offender's neck.

Physical violence over space as personal property. Stylized media violence is familiar to, and valued by, the children.

The aide tells a white male not to write on or mark the tabletops. Another child is told not to make any more figures in the workbook than asked for. A black female is out of her seat rolling around on the floor, and she is told to get back in her seat.

Cleanliness norm. A ban (manifest) on personalization of property/environment.

Denial of spontaneity. Spatial confinement reinforces classroom norm of self-control.

While the teacher and aide are not looking, a black male snatches some crayons from a neighboring student. When the white male looks up to protest, he gives a cold, menacing look. Then, as if for just looking up, the black male hits him on the shoulders. The boy does nothing. The black male then feigns a karate kick and muffled scream while hitting a white female sitting next to him. The girl makes a "please stop" face but says nothing.

Property theft.

Peer (male) nonverbal threat gestures/ranking. This boy does not use actual physical violence to establish a dominance hierarchy.

Event Transition 4

10:45 A.M. The activity session ends. The children are told to take their regular seats. The teacher passes out a small piece of candy to each child. The children are supposed to rest for a while. They put their heads down on their arms folded across the tabletop. There is quite a bit of fidgeting. The chairs are cold and hard and uncomfortable.

Attention position.

Adult distribution of food/control of classroom resources. Care of the body.

Toleration of physical discomfort is reinforced. Self-control of body and emotions is required for participation in classrooms.

Event Transition 5

11:00 A.M. When the children have rested and remained quiet to the teacher's satisfaction, they start a series of game activities. By the name of the color assigned to their par-

Deference to authority.

Differential ranking

and reward to reinforce classroom norms.

Machine technology. Denial of spontaneity. These games condition for following orders in general and classroom procedure in particular.

Spontaneity and self-generated impulses are managed by the emphasis on order and following procedure.

Children have yet to internalize these classroom norms completely.

Physical violence. Adult norm stressing physical and emotional restraint. Spatial confinement as punishment. Appeal to self-discipline.

Control by power of cessation of classroom activity.

Regular rotating leadership role = responsibility training.

Strategy games involving pursuit, aggression, and competition. The game has a lineal sequence of beginning, middle, and end and exhibits an outcome marked by "success" or "failure." Emphasis on predation and autonomy. The peer group is divided against itself. Again, there is an emphasis on "winners" and "losers." Exposure to public display and ridicule.

ticular table, and implicitly by how quiet they have been, children are called to begin a game. They imitate the actions and sounds of animals as the aide plays the phonograph. Both the aide and the teacher stress that the children must follow directions and instructions. They are told, "Go around the table" and "Stop when the record stops" and "Listen . . . you show me that you want to do this by doing it as you are supposed to." Though there is individual interpretation and elaborate variation on the teacher's instructions, most of the children follow her directions. They improvise on her instructions; the teacher and aide intervene in getting them to do as they would like. There is considerable laughter from the children. One black male is running around imitating an animal while using karate side stances. The teacher says, "Please be a gentleman," and to several recalcitrant children, "If you don't want to play, stay at your tables. Don't complain." They become very energetic and boisterous. In response, the teacher changes games.

Sitting on the rug, the children form a large semicircle. To start the game, a child is picked by the teacher. This child gets up and runs around the outside of the circle. He says, "Ahhhhhh," and holds his hands above the heads of the other children. Suddenly he says, "Choo!" dropping his hand to tap the head of a female. Gleefully, she jumps up and laughingly chases him. If she can tap him, she can sit back down. If not, she has to continue around the circle while the first child gets to sit down. More often than not, they do not catch each other.

In the next game, the children stand up,

holding hands, to form a circle. The teacher
tells them to hold their locked hands up in the
air. Then several children, called "mice," run
in and out of the upturned "maze" until she
gleefully shouts, "Lower the trap!" and the
children quickly drop their arms around those
not quick enough to escape. As the "trap"
falls, everyone shouts with glee. The children
scream with laughter and enjoyment. The
children "trapped" inside do not laugh. Those
"caught" have to sit on the floor in the center
of the circle. They play this game several
times. When they become too noisy, the
teacher tells them to stop. The teacher says
they have to stop because they "don't want to
do it right. The mice at the center did not sit
quietly on the floor."

Denial of spontaneity
through power of cessation
of activity. Emphasis on
classroom norms of order,
quietness, and passivity.

The next game is called Farmer in the
Dell. The children hold hands and slowly go
from left to right in a large circle. One child,
chosen by the teacher, stands alone in the center of the circle. The person standing alone
chooses people to join the center and represent various animals and people such as a
nurse, a farmer, a cow, and a mouse. This continues until all the categories are exhausted
and most of the people are in the center.
There are always a few children not chosen.
The class response to this game is less enthusi-
astic than to the game in which they "trap"
each other. At the end of this activity session,
the children are told to go back to their seats,
"Quietly . . . like mice."

Emphasis on au-
tonomy. Divison of the peer
group against itself. Competition.

Peer ranking and com-
petition. "Success/failure"
receives public display.

11:30 A.M. Recess.

Event Transition 6

12:00 P.M. The aide leads the children
back to the classroom. Once inside, it takes
some time for them to quiet down. The
teacher says, "Turn off the outside voices!"

Adult supervision.
Different voice levels
and patterns of interaction
associated with work (in-
side) and play (outside). Ex-

pected self-maintenance (toilet). Waiting. Regimentation.

Passive-aggressive norm violation.
Continuing physical violence and peer ranking.

Intraclassroom sub-grouping and labeling by space and territory. Control by appeal to self-discipline.
Passive resistance. Low sessions spend more time on behavior modification and the children's adherence to classroom norms and values than do high ones. The children are testing and manipulating authority.

The children hang up their coats, and, if they must, line up to go to the bathroom. Then they are told to line up to wash their hands in the sink. A student drops his towel on the floor, looks at it, but does not pick it up.

A black male is hitting a black female. She hits him several times, after glancing over her shoulder to see if the teacher or aide is watching. Boys scuffle with each other much more than with girls, though girls occasionally scuffle with boys.

The teacher is angry. The tone of her voice is strident and menacing. "Table three," she intones. "What did I ask you to do?" The noise level drops. Several of the children, though, continue to murmur and snicker under their breath. After a few minutes, the noise level creeps up. Again, the teacher is visibly angry. She stands in the center of the room with her hands on her hips and loudly and angrily says, "You children know how we prepare for lunch!" The noise level drops to zero. When she turns her head, several children snicker and murmur under their breath. She does not hear them. When she turns back to the class, they immediately are quiet.

Event Transition 7

Food handling/distribution by adults. *In loco parentis* nurturing functions. Food rituals stress waiting and the control of emotions.
Illegal use of prayer in schools.
Monitoring and reinforcement of food norms. The ritual sequencing of foods and the control of student movements and emotions.

12:10 P.M. The teacher and aide set places in preparation for the noon meal. Another aide brings the hot lunch cart to the outside door. In setting their places, the teacher tells them not to touch the food or utensils until she directs them to do so. After the food is passed out, the teacher picks a white female to say the blessing: "God is good, God is love. Let us thank him for this food. Amen." Then the teacher tells them to eat slowly and walks around the room watch-

ing them while they eat. The children drink
milk with straws and eat bread with their
hands. Otherwise, they use plastic utensils.
The teacher tells them to eat their meat and
potatoes before their fruit and cookies. A
white female balks and says she is not hungry.
The teacher tells her to eat now because she
might be hungry later. Whining, several children complain that they do not like the food.
The teacher ignores them. She quiets them by
calmly saying she will put their names on the
board. When they do not respond quickly
enough, she calls out individual names in a
stern, level voice—then glares at them for a
second or so. A black female gets up to get another straw, and the teacher admonishes her
for not first raising her hand. When they finish eating, the teacher dismisses them, by tables, to throw away their waste. They return
to their desks and, without being told, put
their heads down on their folded arms. Returning to his seat, the previously mentioned
boy hits another boy on the back. The boy begins crying and pleads with him to stop. The
observer thinks the teacher does not see the
incident because she does not immediately respond. Smugly, the boy saunters to his seat.
After a moment the teacher gets up, goes to
where he is sitting, and quietly says, "Well, I
guess people who hit other people can't go to
music class." The boy bursts into a tantrum.
He cries, flails his arms, spastically jumps up
and down on his seat, pounds his fists on the
table, and screams. The observer is stunned.
Yet the other children nonchalantly look up,
then quietly go back to their work. The boy
continues his tantrum for several minutes.

Denial of spontaneity/
whim. Linear concept of
time.

Public ridicule/censure
as control mechanism.
   Control/dominance by
nonverbal threat gesture
(Campbell 1974:313–15).
Deference to authority must
precede each movement.
Cleanliness, neatness, and
order.
   Internalization of procedure. Attention to position.
   (Male) physical vio-
lence and dominance behavior.
   Beginning of a class-
room pattern of both pas-
sive and overt aggression
toward/resistance to classroom norms and values by,
especially, black males. In
this instance, the teacher exercises control through the
power of cessation of ac-
tivity and confinement.

Emphasis on au-
tonomy. Lack of peer sup-
port.

Event Transition 8

12:20 P.M. The teacher prepares the class for the trip to the music room. Other children get into line as the previously mentioned black male grows silent and begins to pout. Loudly and belligerently, he says he, too, is going and walks straight to the front of the line forming by the door. The teacher, very calmly, tells him to sit back down. Sullenly, he leaves his place but goes to the back of the line. The children file out the door. When he gets to the door, the teacher calmly tells him that he cannot go. She stands in front of the door. Again, he bursts into a tantrum, this time more violently. The teacher has to restrain him. He attempts to strike her. He cries and throws himself against the teacher in trying to get out the door. His anger and energy and pain are intense, and the observer grows tense, then gets up to help the teacher. Struggling with the child, she asks if he will take the students to the music room. The observer runs after the line of children already halfway down the walkway. At the front of the line, the observer grabs the hand of a white female and asks her if she will help him. She smiles and nods her head. Several of the children begin taking advantage of the situation by "cutting" to the front of the line. The observer sees them but is afraid to stop the line to correct them. From the front of the line, it looks as if he is leading a hundred wiggling bodies. He asks the girl holding his hand if she knows where the music room is, and she quietly nods her head. The observer asks her if she will lead them there. She nods her head. At the building entrance, the observer holds open the door for the children. A boy at the end of the line solemnly tells him that two other boys "cut" the

The themes and traits exhibited here occur in the wider society and culture (Schwartz 1975).

Emphasis on control and composure under stress.

In this incident, there are several conscious student violations of sequencing, regimentation, and classroom ranking norms.

Students must be unline. The observer frowns. After making certain they are all in the room and the music teacher does not need him, the observer races back to the kindergarten room. The observer, expecting chaos, finds the boy quietly sitting in his chair. The teacher smiles as the observer stumbles through the door. She is working on some papers at her desk. The observer is sweaty and tense. Fumbling, he asks if she needs any help. The teacher smiles and almost laughs. She pauses to say, "No, thank you," and goes back to her work.

der *in loco parentis* adult supervision at all times. Continual monitoring.

Event Transition 9

1:10 P.M. The aide brings the children back from music, and they hang up their outerwear and take their seats. They carry manila folders with their names on them, and before the teacher can collect them, a black female gets out of her seat. Immediately the teacher shouts for her to sit back down. The girl tells the teacher that her folder had dropped to the floor. Then she sits down. For several seconds they maintain eye contact and glare at each other. The teacher mumbles to the observer that she does not like "people getting out of their seat without permission and that they will have to learn to stay in their seats." She is angry. For several minutes, behind the teacher's back, the girl glares at her.

Adult supervision/ monitoring. Expected self-direction. Neatness. Attention position.
    Autonomy. Individual accountability.
    Spontaneous movements = no deference (handraising).

    Passive aggression/ threat gesture. The girl bypassed required deference to teacher authority to control bodies and movements.

Event Transition 10

1:25 P.M. The children are told to get their blankets and lie down on the floor and rest for a while. They scatter around the room and maintain at least a meter's distance between each other. The teacher takes piles of blankets from the closet and goes around to cover each child. She tells the wigglers to

    Care of the body. Continuing emphasis on autonomy and isolation.
    Nurturance. Care of the body.
    Self-control. Self-discipline.

Toleration of discomfort. No spatial movement.

"stay in your places." Most of the children are sound asleep, snoring. Two are lying staring abstractly at the other children, while the rest are fidgeting, rolling around on their blankets, or complaining about being cold.

Event Transition 11

Neatness and order. Place/item coordination. Attention position.

Space/activity coordination. Spatial separation of work and play.
Orientation toward national celebrations/legends. Punishment by removal from group and spatial isolation. Public display of personal information.

2:30 P.M. The aide awakens the children and tells them to put their blankets up and to take their seats. Most are half asleep.

When the children are seated, the teacher calls them, by tables, to sit on the rug in preparation for a story. They sit in a tight semicircle around the teacher as she begins reading. The story is about one family's Thanksgiving dinner. A black female is fidgeting. Suddenly the teacher yells for her to go to her seat if she cannot behave. To the observer, and in front of the children, the teacher says that "Jill has been upset all day. The first thing she told me this morning was that they came and took her Daddy to jail yesterday." The teacher sighs, and her shoulders sag. She says she tries to tell the children that policemen are helpful, especially when mentioned in the stories they read, but "to no avail." She stares into space for a half second, then continues reading. The girl sits quietly in her chair and very gently sucks her thumb.

Disparity between classroom ideology and outside reality illustrates that the cultural values promoted in the classroom in many cases are idealized.

Event Transition 12

Attention position.
Differential ranking by subgroups. Internal division of the student peer group.

This commercially produced book assumes that

3:10 P.M. At the conclusion of the story, the teacher tells the children to take their seats. When they are seated, she tells them, by tables, to get their coats and then take their seats. As two black females put on their coats, the observer hears them comment on the function of the person reading the bedtime story to the child. The teacher had held the book up for them to see a particular scene. One girl did not know who that person is, and the other girl says, "He's a father." The girl simply says, "Oh," and they continue putting on their coats.

the two-parent nuclear family is normative.

3:20 P.M. Each child is told to place his or her chair upside down on top of the table. The teacher lines the children up by the door, then takes them to the bus. The children walk inside the yellow lines on the floor. The aide remains to pick up stray pieces of paper and straighten the room.

Requiring housekeeping tasks = responsibility training. Regimentation, lineality, and order. Adult monitoring/supervision. Neatness, cleanliness, and order.

A High Classroom Session

8:45 A.M. Arriving from the buses in small clumps, the children quietly enter the room. They hang their coats in the closet. The teacher removes a splinter from a boy's hand, then praises a girl for a new coat and another for a new pair of boots.

Quietness and order classroom norms are internalized. Newness and consumerism are reinforced. Differential public praise. High sessions exhibit more student/teacher contact and interaction than do low sessions. Order and quietness.

The teacher tells the children to get books from the racks near the door, take their seats, and begin reading. Quietly, they do so.

Event Transition 1

9:00 A.M. The teacher and aide prepare for a story, and the aide sits on a chair within the rug area. Each table has a number, and by that number, all of the children at that table are told to sit on the rug. They cluster quietly in two parallel rows in front of the aide. When they are grouped to her satisfaction, the aide begins reading. The story is about the adventures of a rabbit. The aide holds the book so they can see pictures of the various animals.

Height reinforces status. Ranking and differential grouping. Internal subdivision of the student peer group. Regimentation and order.

Anthropomorphism often accompanies subtle moral lessons (Henry 1960).

The observer sits on the rug with the children. Despite the rug, the floor is hard

Order and self-control. Toleration of discomfort.

and cold, and the observer is uncomfortable. Noise and body movements, though, are very low. Unlike the observer, the children tend to remain in one spot when they squirm and fidget.

9:10 A.M. The teacher is doing paperwork at her desk but suddenly gets up and leaves the room. Although the door closes with a loud BANG no one looks up. When the teacher returns, there is another sharp BANG as the door closes. The teacher clumps across the room and drops a pile of materials on her desk. She opens and then closes a desk drawer. Finally, there is a sharp, ragged scrape as she draws out her chair to sit down. The children are not distracted.

When finished reading, the aide does not solicit comments about the story but instead asks questions about the children's weekend activities. The aide leans toward the children as she talks to them. As she does, they fidget and turn away.

The aide is saying, "Oh, Jean."

Jean jumps at the sound of her name.

"Where'd you get your boots, Jean?"

Jean does not answer. The aide moves closer.

"I notice you got new boots on. Where did you get your boots?"

Jean does not answer.

"Did you go to the store with your mother?"

Jean nods her head.

"You did! I think they're pretty."

Jean makes no response.

"I-can't-hear-you," says the aide, in a sing-song voice.

"Can you hear what she is saying?" The

Margin notes (left column):

Self-restraint.

Task divisions of labor. Student toleration of external stimuli. Task orientation and concentration.
Higher ranks/status constituents are permitted mobility outside the room.
Classrooms are noisy environments. This noise conditions for the norm of self-control and restraint (Henry 1963).

"Show-and-tell." Public display of personal information.
Self-control of movements.
Denial of spontaneity. Submissive posture.

Emphasis on consumer items and newness.

Not "father"; sex-role stereotyping.

Physical attractiveness and clothing in females is reinforced. Sex-role stereotyping.

aide looks to the back of the cluster. There is
no response.

"Sandra?"

Sandra puts her finger in her mouth and
imperceptibly leans away from the aide.

"No?"

A black male starts to say, "I did!" and is
cut off by the aide with a stern, cold look.

"I'm talking to Sandra right now." She
holds his gaze for a second, then returns to
Sandra. The boy shrinks back into his spot.

The aide addresses the children as a
group, signaling the end of this activity.

"OK. You've been pretty good listeners
so far. . . . What month is it?"

At this question, swarms of hands flagel-
late like seaweed. If one child is called upon
and hesitates for the least amount of time in
responding, other children try to attract the
aide's attention. As the aide points her own
outstretched hand about while deciding who
to acknowledge, the children's hands follow
her like magnet filings.

"Johnny?"

"September!"

"Oh," says the aide dejectedly, "that's the
first month that you come to school. That's
when we came to school . . . September . . .
Harrison?" Indistinctly, Harrison mumbles
something. "Hmmmmmm . . . ah, Arthur?"

"November!"

"RIGHT!" the aide loudly exclaims to indicate her pleasure.

"It's November! What holiday is in November?"

"THANKSGIVING!" they respond in unison.

"Right . . . Thanksgiving. We'll have to
remember that. That's good. Ah, what people

Denial of spontaneous,
out-of-order expressions.
Emphasis on procedure and
waiting.
Nonverbal threat ges-
ture. Submissive posture.

Recurring dominance-
submission behavior. Adult/
teacher must maintain high
rank/status.
Value of compliance.
Time socialization.
Peer competition for
permission to display
knowledge.
Pleasing the teacher.

Linear time orienta-
tion. Time/activity coordination.

Teacher's pleasure as
reward.

Orientation toward na-
tional celebrations. Time/ac-
tivity coordination. Reinforcement of national origin
legends.

do we talk about on Thanksgiving? Or have we talked about? Arthur?"

"Uh . . . Mr. F.!"

"Noooooo," she slowly says, making a mock face of displeasure, tightening her facial muscles and lowering her eyebrows. "I'm not talking about the people at Thanksgiving. You know, they celebrated and ate together. . . !"

"Turkey."

"That's the food they ate. Yeah."

"Turkey. It tastes good."

"Yeah, OK. Well, let me ask something else. What people have we talked about?"

"The Pilgrims."

"The Pilgrims!" The aide's voice rises as if indicating that the child should continue. She is pleased with her response.

"Right, the Pilgrims and the Indians. They all ate together on Thanksgiving. And they did eat turkey . . . OK. Ah, yesterday . . . was Sunday and today is. . . ?" The aide pauses on a rising intonation. The children do not immediately respond.

"Wednesday," volunteers one male.

"Noooooo," replies the aide, drawing out the vowel, "not Wednesday."

Hands are raised.

"Jamie?"

"MONDAY!"

"RIGHT!" the aide loudly replies. The teacher wanders over to the group and asks the aide who is the leader of the day. The aide says that she thinks it is Colette. She asks Colette if she has had a turn, and Colette says yes. The aide says that Lloyd had his turn so that it must be Arthur's turn. The aide pauses, as if waiting for the teacher to say something else. The teacher does not say anything but stands at the edge of the rug looking on. The

---

Teacher's pleasure as reward.

Right/wrong mastery.

Ritualized association of particular foods with particular ceremonies/celebrations.

The state Board of Education requires that time be devoted to the discussion of national celebrations. Conditioning for participation in national-level culture.

National time scheduling.

Again, right/wrong classroom norm is associated with the teacher's emotional state. Emphasis on pleasing the teacher.

Rotating administrative tasks and responsibility training.

Emphasis on classroom order and procedure.

Ranking. Deference to teacher as final authority.

aide continues her activity. "Today is the eighteenth. Ah . . . Troy! You're our leader today so will you go over and pull off one of the numbers from the calendar over there. And tables one and two, will you take your seats please. Tables *one* and *two*."

Rhetorical request but an implied command.
Differential student grouping and ranking.

Event Transition 2

9:30 A.M. The children immediately do as they are told, and there is little talking and little undirected movement. A white female, slow to respond, merely sits in the nearest seat. The aide responds stridently and harshly: "Patricia, what table do you sit at?" The aide glares at the child. Offhandedly, yet in front of the children, the teacher says to the aide that they have not yet learned their numbers. The tone of her voice expresses disappointment. She is saying, "Let's go—where do you sit, Troy? OK, tables one and two!" The aide's voice is harsh, stern, and commanding; the implication is that they are doing something wrong. The children quicken the pace to their seats. There is no slacking or back talking. At this point, the teacher tells the aide to go out and get change for the lunches. When the aide leaves, the teacher assumes direction of the children. The teacher is saying, "OK, Nancy, I want you over at this table here, OK?"

"All right," says Nancy.

When they are seated, the teacher says, "OK. We've been pretty good listeners. Now, people in the middle, you can get something to play with." There is a noisy, semifrantic scramble as they dash to the storage area.

"*If* you play quietly," the teacher intones. "Let's use our inside voices."

The teacher divides the room into three areas, and folding dividers are put in place.

Compliance/obedience. Self-restraint. Order.

Regimentation. Ordered placement in space.

Public ridicule as a control mechanism. Expected self-direction.

Depersonalization. Regimentation and order. Public ridicule. Compliance/obedience. Hierarchical ordering of authority. Ranking. Continuing emphasis on order and regimentation. Ongoing observations find the teacher spending time on giving orders.

Concentration and compliance are reinforced. Differential grouping/ activity organization. Spatial separation of work and play, an important pattern continually repeated in the classrooms. Appeal to self-monitoring. Spatial separation of work and play.

There are three tables on which are spread specific materials and activities. The middle table is the one on which several of the children are playing with toys brought from the storage area. Returning with the lunch money, the aide begins a memory drill at another table. The teacher goes to the third table and begins a tracing exercise.

The writing exercise consists of instruction in tracing letters, and the children work individually. The teacher praises their straight lines, starting a line from the top rather than vice versa, and correctly holding their pencils. She frequently uses phrases such as "Good workers," "Beautiful," and "Write nicely."

The children at the middle table are noisy in playing with the toys. The teacher looks up to say, "I have real nice workers in the middle. They are quiet." The noise from the middle table increases, and at one point a black male says, "Shhhhhh" to the others, who then glance in the direction of the teacher, but she is not looking at them. They become quieter.

In one corner of the room, a quiet girl plays with the doll house. A boy plays with one of the toy trucks. Several other males, both black and white, have made a ramp out of some wooden blocks and are pushing the trucks over them. There are sporadic arguments concerning who gets to play with what toys, when, and who gets to play with what first. As they finish playing with one toy, and without being told, the children very carefully and methodically put it back in its exact place before taking another. The teacher is telling a cluster of boys, "Be careful with those toys. Somebody might get hurt by them." The boys

---

Students are beginning specific academic tasks (work). Emphasis on rote learning and following models.

Autonomy.
Procedure.
Right/wrong mastery.
Differential public praise and ranking; differential distribution of rewards from the teacher (subjective basis).

Students are permitted to play in groups but must work individually.

Pleasing the teacher. Guilt as a control mechanism.

Peer monitoring assumes the internal division of the peer group and the internalization of classroom norms and values.

Spatial reinforcement of sex-specific activities. Sex-role stereotyping.

Machine/industrial technology.

Property disputes. Ranking.

Place/activity coordination and neatness and order norms are internalized.

In loco parentis concern with safety. Solicitude for others. Care of the body.

The primary status/rank of work is reinforced. Nonverbal threat gesture forces compliance.

energetically fling the trucks across the ramp. In a stern voice the teacher says, "I've told you several times about this noise. It is getting too loud for us to work." She glares at the offenders. They become quiet.

10:00 A.M. Standing up, the teacher says, "People . . . time to change. Switch tables." A group of boys and girls goes to the play table while other groups go to different supervised tables. Children do not run from table to table but line up by the dividers, wait until the table is free, then proceed in single file.

Authority posture.

Sequential/lineal ordering of activities.

Waiting. Self-restraint.

10:10 A.M. Without knocking, a secretary enters with a notice from the office. She goes across the room and hands it to the teacher. The children do not look up from their work.

Right of trespass. Final authority is the administrative sector (nonkinship authority). Task orientation.

10:30 A.M. The teacher says, "Time to switch," and each group goes to another table and another activity.

Time/activity coordination.
Place/activity coordination.

The aide writes out exercises on the board as the children watch. While the children respond, she stands directly over and in front of them. Demanding a precise answer, she unblinkingly stares them straight in the eye and demands that they exactly follow the model she has worked out on the board. She frequently asks, "Do you understand?"

The board reinforces learning from a model by rote. Demand for proof/demonstration. Right/wrong mastery. Obedience training.

The aide uses a wooden pointer to indicate numbers on the board and occasionally to tap children on the shoulder to get their attention. She tells a boy, as a reprimand for not paying attention, that he will have to stand near the outside door "all during recess." Then the aide harshly asks, "Julie, do you want your name on the board?"

"No," whispers Julie.

"Well," says the aide, "you will, unless you settle down."

Physical violence. Emphasis on concentration and task orientation. Confinement and denial of spontaneity as punishment. Public display and ridicule as control mechanisms.

Passive resistance behaviors. Unlike low ses-

sions, high-session children do not engage in direct forms of defiance (Henry 1959).

As the aide drones on, a white male intently watches two flies scurry across his desk. Children look at the board with glazed eyes as if daydreaming, their lips slightly parted.

Event Transition 3

Use of height as an authority position; nonverbal sign of status.

Expected self-maintenance.

Autonomy.

Order.

Compliance and obedience.

Propriety norm is internalized.

11:00 A.M. The teacher stands up to call this activity period to an end. The dividers are folded and stacked against a wall. The teacher tells the children to go to the bathroom if they have to, but to go one at a time. Several boys run for the door, and the aide yells, "Walk—don't run!" The children slow down. As she goes into the bathroom, a white female leaves the door slightly ajar. Another white female silently closes it for her.

Event Transition 4

Expected self-maintenance.

Order and quietness classroom norms are internalized.

In loco parentis concern with protection of the body.

Readiness position. Adult monitoring.

Some students wear less clothing than others, an observed basis for peer ridicule.

Internal division of stu-

11:15 A.M. The children are told to put on their coats, and they do so by themselves. The teacher and aide encourage them and help only when necessary. In no appreciable order, the children go to the closet. There is no pushing or shoving. Finally, the teacher takes great pains to check that the children are properly dressed. She praises them for having their coats buttoned and for having their gloves on and their boots zipped. "Don't go outside without your mittens and boots!" she intones.

When dressed, the children take their seats. The teacher again goes around the room checking to see that they are dressed to her satisfaction. "Don't wear tennis shoes in the winter!" the teacher yells to a female. "You should only play on the blacktop [the tar-covered driveway] with these tennis shoes." She tells the aide to make sure that the girl does not play on the dirt areas while outside. She is upset that the girl is wearing tennis shoes in the winter.

dent peer group with respect to differences in clothing and dress.

The teacher picks a white female to open the outer door. The girl goes to the door and props it open with a wooden block. Intense sunlight floods the room. The teacher tells the children to line up by the door. She dismisses them by tables, the quietest table first. Several times she shouts, "No running! No running!" When they are lined up to her satisfaction, she dismisses them. They let out a joyous whoop and go bursting into the sunlight.

Rotating housekeeping tasks.

Lineality, order, and waiting.
Ranking and differential reward as control mechanism. Order. Self-restraint.
Self-restraint and order are expected until the children are outside.

11:30 A.M. Recess.

Event Transition 5

12:00 P.M. The aide leads the children back into the room, and they immediately take off their coats and put them in the closet. The teacher says, "Be careful with your clothes when you are around the paints [the painting easels by the door]."

Adult monitoring.
Procedure norm is internalized. Neatness and order.
The value of cleanliness and protection of clothing are reinforced.

Event Transition 6

12:15 P.M. The children take their seats as the teacher and aide prepare for the noon meal. The teacher provides each child with a napkin and plastic spoon. She gives each child two cookies, but they do not immediately eat them. Through the hall door, the aide wheels in a hot lunch cart. The teacher gives each child a plate. The food is distributed in no apparent order, and when all have food, they begin eating.

Recurring adult handling of food; distribution of strategic resources.
Food norms are internalized. Self-restraint. Waiting. No food sharing. Autonomy. Though required, some teachers do not say grace.

The teacher tells them to put their spoons on the counter and to throw their waste in the basket when finished. The children then go over to the book rack to pick out books.

Cleanliness and neatness. Expected self-maintenance. Literacy training.
Value of books. Neatness.

Indirect reprimand—appeal to self-control.
Direct command and compliance by deference/submission posture.
Expected self-maintenance.

More complex scheduling here. Permitted mobility outside the classroom. High ranking and permitted mobility as reward.
Obedience training.
Regimentation, lineality, and order.

"Don't set your books on a wet table!" the teacher says. As the noise level increases, the teacher quiets them by saying that "you are noisy as Mr. N. and his noisy nose!" This admonition has no effect, and several minutes later the teacher has to say, "All right, you are too noisy. Put your heads down." Her voice is level yet emphatic, and the children obey. As the noise level lessens, the teacher tells them to put up their books and to put on their coats.

The children are going to the music room (see Figure 2). Both the aide and the teacher pin pink squares of paper, with the child's name on them, on the front of each child's coat. Quietest first, they are dismissed. Before starting, the teacher tells them to listen and to follow her instructions. The children, like shrunken boxcars, weave to the music room in a near perfect line.

Event Transition 7

Adult monitoring.
Expected self-maintenance.
Differential grouping of, and spatial isolation between, (ranked) student groups.

1:10 P.M. The observer brings up the rear as the teacher leads them back to the kindergarten room. Coats are taken off and hung in the closet. The teacher separates the children into two sections, and a folding divider is put between them.

The teacher begins an association exercise. To her group, she holds up a series of large, well-worn plastic cards, on which are pictured various foods.

This segment illustrates explicit food training and an emphasis on commercially prepared foods. Consumption, rather than production, of consumer goods in a market economy is reinforced.

"When," she asks, "is it time to eat *this* kind of food?" She holds up a card. The children quickly answer. Or the teacher asks, "When you get up in the morning, are *these* the kinds of things that you should eat?" or "When do you think your mother would like you to eat *this* ice-cream cone?" Some of the foods shown are bacon, toast, cereal, eggs, orange juice, potatoes, soup, cake, ice cream, cookies, jello, french fried potatoes, tomatoes, rye bread, lamb chops, macaroni, ears of corn, and a baked ham.

Particular foods in ritualized association with particular times and activities. Mother in association with food handling is sex-stereotyping.

A white female is looking at the activities at another table. The teacher turns to her and says, "You're being rude. You're not listening." The teacher asks the children to associate the various foods with specific meals. They do not make the associations the teacher wants. One black male, for instance, wants to eat cookies for dinner. The teacher makes the following associations for them: breakfast: bacon, toast, cereal, eggs, and orange juice; lunch: hamburgers, french fries, sandwiches, and hot dogs; dinner: baked ham, beef, carrots, potatoes, and green beans; snacks: cookies and Kool Aid (a commercially prepared drink); dessert: Jello (a commercially prepared food), pies, cupcakes, cakes, cookies, and ice cream.

Emphasis on concentration and task orientation. Compliance and obedience.

Consumption of food occurs during three specific periods and one irregular period of the day. The number three is a recurring theme in American culture (Dundes 1968:401–29).

Event Transition 8

1:45 P.M. Standing up, the teacher says that anyone needing to use the bathroom should do so. Several do. There is no shoving or pushing. Each child waits his or her turn. The folding dividers are put away. They have recess now, and the teacher and aide help, when necessary, with their clothing.

Authority position. Expected self-maintenance.

Internalization of classroom order norm. Waiting norm. Procedure. Expected self-maintenance.

"Rita," the teacher says, "I don't like it when you put pins in your mouth, honey." The children are lined up by the outer door leading to the courtyard and playground. The teacher props open the door. The winter sky is a cloudless cobalt blue. When dismissed, the children charge out into the sunlight and the snow.

In loco parentis concern with safety and care of the body.

Regimentation and order. Spatial separation of work and play.

Event Transition 9

Neatness and cleanliness.

Adult handling and distribution of food. Regimentation. Cleanliness and neatness.
Religious ritual within the educational subsystem.
Denial of spontaneity. Emphasis on ritualized procedures.

1:45—2:15 P.M. Recess.

2:15 P.M. Before they come inside, the aide tells the children to clean the snow off their coats and boots. They make a sport out of this activity, and before long there is a giggling mass of feet-stomping children outside the door.

The teacher sets places for another meal. After coats are hung, each child is directed to a specific place at a specific table, and napkins are laid down. The meal consists of milk and cookies. Everyone says grace, but the children do not begin eating until the teacher tells them they may; then they eat in silence. The teacher is quietly telling a white male that they all know they are supposed to stay in their seats until everyone is finished eating. The boy got up to put his waste in the basket. He returns to his seat and silently watches the others.

Event Transition 10

Neatness and cleanliness. Reinforces consumption of new items; old items are not washed and reused.
Care of the body. Personal property reflecting potential for status, rank, and prestige differences.
Regimentation and the ordering of spatial relationships.

Autonomy. Order.
Recurrent pattern of children not touching one another. Autonomy and individuation.
Notice the passive ag-

2:25 P.M. After each child has finished eating and they have carried their waste to the basket, the teacher tells them to get their blankets and lie down on the floor for a while. From storage boxes labeled with their names, each child pulls out a blanket. Some are more elaborate, newer, and larger than the others. The teacher takes quite a bit of time showing each student where she wants him or her to lie down. "Walk," she is saying. "Walk—don't run!"

Eventually, they are widely scattered all over the room. Some are permitted to crawl up behind the teacher's desk. Many prefer the corners of the room.

Many of the children balk at this rest period. They do not want to rest, and they do

not like the places where the teacher tells them to rest. There is complaining and whining, but no one back talks the teacher. Instead, they pout. To the observer, the teacher says that she keeps a paddle and "knows how to use it." The tone of her voice conveys that she is concerned with the impression that all this whining is making on the observer. The children nap for a while, and the observer and teacher informally chat.

gression. Children remain in their places. Compliance.

Control by threat of physical violence. Legitimization of violence.
Value of order and control. Compliance. Passivity.

Event Transition 11

2:45 P.M. Several of the children are roused by the teacher to begin work on individual exercises. To the observer, yet loud enough for the children to hear, the teacher is saying that these are the "slow ones" who require special attention. The teacher takes them to her desk and continues the counting exercises begun earlier. The aide is rousing other children, who begin work on the tracing exercises begun earlier.

Differential grouping and ranking. Public display and ridicule. Differential prestige exhibited. The student peer group is differentiated internally and ranked.

Event Transition 12

3:20 P.M. The work groups are dismissed, and the remaining children are awakened. The teacher prepares the class to leave. The "good workers" are called, by name, and go to the clothing area.

Different groups of kindergarten children are having different classroom experiences.

3:25 P.M. The children have on their coats, boots, and gloves. The teacher checks to see that they are properly dressed. They line up by the hall door in the order in which they were called to put on their outerwear.

Care of the body. Adult monitoring and supervision. Ranking and regimentation.

3:30 P.M. After putting on her coat, the teacher takes the children to the bus. In a single file, they walk inside the yellow line on the hall floor. The aide remains to pick up stray

Adult monitoring and supervision. Regimentation and order.
Ranked task divisions of labor. Housekeeping

tasks. Neatness, order, and cleanliness.

pieces of paper from the floor and to put the chairs upside down on the desks. When finished, she too leaves.

During kindergarten, children are exposed to several ongoing themes important in classroom society and culture: differentiated grouping, ranking, and a formal curriculum of instruction. Subtle sociocultural conditioning continues, but children face the reality of differing classroom experiences occurring in different areas within each room as well as spatially occurring between different rooms at the same grade level.

The pattern in the kindergarten sessions is for a large number of features to occur only a few times, while a small number of features occur more frequently. For both the low and the high sessions, the smaller number of features occurring with greater frequency roughly are similar (see Figure C-2, Appendix C). Order (1/1), for example, is ranked high in both the low and the high classroom sessions; student self-control (3/3), autonomy (2/13), emphasis on procedure (4/5), ranking (5/2), denial of spontaneity (7/9), and neatness (12/8) frequently occur and also are fairly stable for both sessions.* These features are associated with a continuing early grade emphasis on the modification and control of student behavior. The following sentences appear in one teacher's grade level lesson plans and goals: "Given situations in which gratification must be delayed, student will display appropriate classroom behavior [has to wait for recess]" and "must demonstrate increased ability to accept imposed delay and to regulate daily schedules, room arrangements, adults, etc.—and changes in routines." Core classroom values and norms are those behaviors, ideals, and physical objects that the teachers consciously work to get the children to acknowledge and adhere to.

There are stark differences, however, between low and high kindergarten sessions. The same features and themes exhibit a markedly different classroom emphasis. Violence, for example, is ranked (9) in the low session and (51) in the high session. The low kindergarten session in this

*The first number in the parentheses refers to features in the low session, while the second number refers to corresponding features in the high session in the statistical summaries in Figure C-2, Appendix C.

respect is more akin to the sociocultural aspects of preschool. The high session children are compliant (4), and their greater emphasis on task orientation (42/20) and regimentation (16/6) are signs that they are conforming to the classroom culture and society. High sessions exhibit a high degree of adherence to established classroom norms (7) compared with the low session (57). There is more concern with the care and protection of high session (15) than of low session children (28). The lack of nurturing and touching between the teacher and children in the low session is evident. The low session teacher has less status than the high session teacher, and she feels saddled with "problem" children who, as she puts it, are not "doing as well" as the high children. She explains the low classroom performance of her students by reference to the "deprived condition of their home life." The children, she says, are not read to at home, not frequently spoken to, and not told stories; their parents, she says, are not concerned with their performance in school. She points to a group of children, says that some are just "slow," shrugs, and asks me what one can expect. This teacher does not expect anything of the children. Many of the children are aware of her attitudes and resist her. The sociocultural system of the classroom will continue to reward "good" children with more effective, supportive contact with the teachers.

Public schools are ranked and stratified, reflecting the national sociocultural system of which they are a part. A classlike and castelike pattern structures public school systems (Ogbu 1974, 1978). Schooling is class-based to the extent that social positions in the classroom are achieved, ostensibly, on the basis of standardized test scores. Student subgroups then are ranked hierarchically (low/high) and differentiated spatially both within and between classrooms. Schooling is caste-based to the extent that once on a particular track, no matter how hard he or she works, a child's mobility from one track to another increasingly becomes difficult if not impossible. The structure of the educational system at West Haven conditions for political socialization (Ehman 1980) into the ranked and stratified structure of the wider social system (Bourdieu 1973b; Bowles and Gintis 1976; Ogbu 1979). These sociopolitical realities affect the children; for example, their plaintive desire for "nice clean" houses and two-parent families. A 1970 state evaluation rated one-third of the housing in West Haven as "substandard," one-third "seriously deficient," and one-third "basically sound." Mobile homes, so-called "trailers," comprise 22 percent of the housing in West

Haven. We learn that some of the children's parents have been in jail and that several of the children have had negative experiences with the police. Much like the issue of classroom violence in preschool, the kindergarten teacher glosses over the more sociopolitical aspects of the children's lives. Political matters, especially, are delicately skirted if not avoided. The view of the world promoted by these elementary school classrooms does not dwell on contradictions, and challenges to the harmonious world view of the classroom are met with swift teacher reprimand. School classrooms mirror the wider society and culture, but they do so on differing levels. Much of the overt content of classroom life reflects social and cultural ideals, while the structure and covert context of classroom life reflects social and cultural reality.

The social and political control aspects of kindergarten classrooms, the high sessions in particular, are associated with ordering participant relationships for more effective productive activities. The high session spends almost 50 percent more time on work-related activities than does the low session (see Figure B-2, Appendix B). Effective production demands that student spontaneity be controlled. In the classroom and in the wider society, work-related skills in task orientation and concentration (42/20), following directions (49/4), and self-reliance and maintenance (66/11) are important (see Figure C-2, Appendix C). Children in the high sessions gain more exposure to, and practice in, these important work-related skills than do children attending low sessions. Long after these traits have been adopted by the former, the latter continue to exhibit lack of adherence to them. Some teachers consider it natural for high session children to exhibit different work patterns than low session children. Rank in school becomes an expression of personal value and worth, and early grade teachers assume that high session children work more because they are higher. The increasing physical limits on movement in the classrooms help reinforce in children the task orientation (42/20) of work. Autonomy (2/13) and expected self-direction (40/65) are expressed and reinforced spatially. The ritual ordering of classroom behaviors associated with a formal curriculum (10/37) lends a quality of specialness to the instruction. The low classroom sessions spend slightly more time on their entry/exit procedures than do the high sessions (see Figure B-2, Appendix B). The continuing pattern is for high sessions to adhere better to customary classroom norms than low sessions. The high classroom session did not take a play period and spent about half as much time as did the low session on stories. In the manner of a self-fulfilling prophecy, the teacher says she gives more recess time to the high session children because they work harder. Play is a reward for work, but work contains more classroom success-related features than does play. High session children gain more exposure to behaviors and attitudes important to success in future West Haven classrooms. The teacher does not internally subdivide low session children into specialized, so-called ability-based reading groups, nor does she reinforce specific curricular tasks as does the teacher of the high session. High session children gain practice adjusting to the differentiated social organization characteristic of schooling as a whole.

Low session children spend a considerable amount of classroom time playing games, but games such as Farmer in the Dell and Three Blind Mice involve much more than play. Through these games, children learn about intricate social relationships (Polgar 1976; Roberts and Bush 1959). Games of strategy, such as Farmer in the Dell and Three Blind Mice, are goal-oriented and involve competition between opposing players for the following purposes: "winning," practice in the giving and taking of orders, leading and following, deference, obedience, decision making, and manipulating one's social position and rank vis-à-vis others. The classroom narratives show girls almost exclusively playing with dolls and boys almost exclusively playing games involving physical skill. At a certain age, children are not supposed to play certain games because they might appear childish, and during the middle grades classroom games and free play disappear. Games and play are more than entertainment (Sutton-Smith 1977); in the classroom, they function as vehicles for social and cultural conditioning. Their disappearance in the middle grades means that other, more subtle vehicles come into play by which major social and cultural classroom themes indirectly are expressed and reinforced.

Compared with preschool, 50 percent less kindergarten classroom session time is spent on entry and exit procedures, 66 percent less time on the taking of meals, and 40 percent less time in formal play situations. In addition, the kindergarten curriculum includes music and art sessions that take children outside the classrooms and permit them to explore the school complex (35/42). Compared with preschool there are more specific tasks children must satisfy, and these tasks account for 24 percent and 46 percent of class time, respectively, for low and high groups. A formal curriculum of instruction is associated with strict student behavior and performance criteria. Attention, concentration (42/

20), and following orders (50/20) are required from the children. Demonstration and proof of competence (51/55) are required, and the classrooms are settings for perpetual teacher surveillance (6/16). Knowledge and skill must be demonstrated to be legitimate. Even though one might know an answer, one must compete (11/39) with peers for the right to display that knowledge and skill (15/34) to the teacher. This way of life, as a cultural system, does not prize self-knowledge or extensive contemplation. Knowledge and skill are valuable only when and if they are exhibited and used. Teachers convey required information en masse. This mode of knowledge transmission is associated with student responsibility and individualism (2/13). To survive the demanding sociocultural system of the classroom, children are conditioned to take care of themselves rather than to take care of one another.

Kindergarten also introduces children to the idea of associating education with a formal curriculum of instruction, primarily learned by rote (Cohen 1970; Watkins 1943). There are required classroom subject areas to which children are exposed: reading and writing, mathematics, music, and art. Each teacher, along with the principal, writes a classroom schedule for the manner in which these required subject areas are to be implemented. The teachers and the principal feel that nine weeks is the longest period of time children can be expected to concentrate on one set of subjects. The formal curriculum of instruction is based on recommendations from the state Department of Education. State recommendations set minimal local school expectations of standards for student achievement. Local school systems, such as West Haven, must adhere to these minimal standards or lose state funding and/or certification. West Haven has to file yearly reports to the state Board of Education indicating the manner in which it adhered to these recommendations; the school must indicate the number of hours, as well as the nature of the classroom events and activities, devoted to instruction in reading, writing, and mathematics. West Haven constituents take these requirements very seriously. The school community wants to expose children to the knowledge and skills prerequisite to success in the wider society; teachers, especially high session teachers, as a consequence spend more than the minimum recommended time teaching basic academic skills.

The formal curriculum of instruction is generated at the supralocal state/national level and is not decided in West Haven. State departments of education follow guidelines on curricula and instruction issued by federal education agencies. What is taught at the local school level, for the most part, is suggested at state and national administrative levels. Curricula generated at the state/national level tends to standardize the knowledge and skills characteristic of local school classrooms. As a consequence, subjects and bodies of knowledge important to local communities customarily do not receive the formal recognition and status ascribed to those deemed important by the nation state. West Haven, as a local school community, is highly congruent and in accord with state directives. The school also is doing exactly what most parents, both black and white, want it to do. Many local school districts, however, bitterly fight the imposition of what they consider outside knowledge being brought into their schools. There is potential for conflict between people and their schools, especially when the two are not socioculturally congruent (Moore 1976; Rosenfeld 1971; Spindler 1974). The mass-produced images and symbols of Thanksgiving displays in West Haven's Elementary School classrooms stress a normative orientation toward a nuclear, neolocal family structure, which may or may not be at variance with the normative family structure of the local school communities in which such posters are found. Amish struggles for separate schools (Hostetler 1974; Hostetler and Huntington 1971:54–67) are based on reactions to the content of public school classroom sociocultural conditioning. The Amish are very much aware of the sociocultural implications of the power to define criteria for teacher selection and the adoption of classroom materials. Local school battles over curricula often are struggles over the legitimacy of particular bodies of knowledge and subject areas. The emergence of required subject areas and bodies of knowledge in school classrooms in effect implies their legitimacy. Conflicts over local control of public schools involve who is to have the power to select textbooks and teachers, competing claims for observance of local ethnic traditions and celebrations in classrooms, and struggles to define what norms and values (sociocultural orientations) are to be exhibited and transmitted in the school. Not every local school system exhibits the same high degree of national integration witnessed at West Haven. I have walked into elementary schools in East Los Angeles, for example, and seen student-produced wall murals of Zapata rather than mass-produced posters of Santa Claus. Some public school systems are more locally oriented than others.

　　A formal curriculum of instruction is not a characteristic of every educational system. Standardized curricula are associated with bodies of knowledge formally separated ‚out from other aspects of life, and are associated with the formal distribution and stratification of knowledge in ranked and state-level societies. In prestate societies, however, the particularization of knowledge into a segmented curriculum is rare. Village and hunting/gathering societies are small enough to pass on their core traditions informally. The curriculum is life itself, and the subject areas to be taught and learned occur situationally. Knowledge is not abstracted from day-to-day life, as it is at West Haven. Within cultures such as the Tiwi or the Hopi, the process of sociocultural transmission seeks to incorporate children into local groups. A child learns what he or she has to know to become an Inuit or a Hopi. But if a state-run school is placed in these cultures and children are forced to attend, the level at which knowledge and skill areas seek to integrate children becomes supralocal (Collier 1973; Wax, Wax, and Dumont 1964). The mandated curriculum both directly and indirectly prepares children to become Invit-Americans or Hopi-Americans. At West Haven, the introduction of a formal curriculum in kindergarten similarly functions further to incorporate children into supralocal state and national sociocultural networks.

The presence of a formal curriculum helps render the social organization of kindergarten different from that of preschool. Kindergarten children are expected to attend school all day, and the period of adjustment to the social and cultural system of the classroom all too quickly comes to a close. Kindergarten sessions usually contain 100 more minutes of classroom time than does preschool, and the classroom process of sociocultural conditioning is as much physical as it is mental and social. It is physically demanding to sit in a small wooden chair for hours on end. The degree of self-control (3/3) public school children very early are expected to exhibit is impressive, but Americans, it is said, prize endurance (Arensburg and Niehoff 1964; Hsu 1972).

Can one expect school classrooms to be like this all the time? Are there periodic changes in the classroom event and activity pattern at West Haven?

The major classroom event patterns we witness are stable. The times at which particular classroom events occur, the spaces in which they occur, and the sequencing of their occurrence do not vary. In the morning, aides are required to be in the room before the teacher arrives, and teachers are required to be in the room before the children arrive. A master school schedule staggers recess and lunch periods by grade level. An observer returning to West Haven tomorrow would find the pattern of the elementary school classroom event streams similar to those described here. Major event and activity patterns are part of the classroom culture and society and exist independently of teacher whim. Becoming a teacher (Eddy 1969; Spindler 1955) often means being selected because of personality and attitude congruency with ongoing classroom norms and values. But within this stable event structure, the patterns of specific classroom activities do vary. We expect day-to-day variation in the behaviors of individual students; the same toys, for example, are not played with by the same students every day. One may not witness tantrums every day. Films are not shown every day. The classroom observations presented here were recorded during the middle part of the school year, and a narrative emphasis on holidays was not apparent during classroom observations made during other parts of the school year. For instance, in the spring considerable classroom time is spent on the placement testing of first and fourth grade students. Specific classroom activities at West Haven are not the same all the time.

By the end of the early grades, important core social and cultural characteristics of the classroom way of life have been either directly or indirectly presented to the children. The early grades form age groups of children, emphasize the separation aspects of schooling as a rite of passage, and initiate and prepare children to be students. Before the passage into schooling proper, children at West Haven are conditioned to the culture and society of the classroom world.

4
The Lower Grades
This Is the Way We Go to School

Then the pilgrims desired with trembling to go forward; only they prayed their guide to strike a light, that they might go the rest of their way by the help of the light of a lantern. So he struck a light, and they went by the help of that through the rest of this way, though the darkness was very great.

John Bunyan,
The Pilgrim's Progress

FIRST GRADE: THE WORK ROUTINE

First grade is divided into two groups of students and three classrooms, primarily on the basis of recommendations from previous teachers. There are two groups of low students, and the grade level continues the spatial stratification of the student cohort.

First grade rooms exhibit a similar physical organization, although there is some room-to-room variation in furniture shape and arrangement. Toys, puzzles, games, and other materials are jammed into every bookcase in each room, and papers, books, and other materials are piled everywhere. Though crowded, these rooms actually contain fewer materials than either the preschool or kindergarten classrooms. The walls of the kindergarten rooms are beige; the floor is green tile, and the ceiling gray acoustic tile. These colors and textures enhance the warm atmosphere of the classrooms. In each room, posters and student-produced visual displays cover virtually every door and wall. An alphabet of small and capital letters is above each blackboard. Scenes of American life, cut from popular magazines, are taped to the closet doors. The rooms are tactile, sensate, and primarily reinforce literacy activities. National celebrations continue to be displayed visually, and both rooms exhibit commercially and student-produced Thanksgiving and Christmas scenes. One room displays a large papier-mâché and cardboard turkey suspended from the ceiling on a string. Occasionally during the class day,

93

children reach up and twirl the turkey with their pencils. "Happy" is printed on one side of the turkey; "Thanksgiving" on the other. The other first grade classroom is decorated with student-produced displays of various holiday-related food stuffs: turkey, corn on the cob, peas, and the like.

First grade classrooms are dense in comparison with previous rooms, and classroom spaces are defined by more separate pieces of furniture. The greater amount of furniture decreases the amount of open, unfilled space and renders the classroom environment less encouraging of random movements by the children (see Figure 5). The teacher's desk (A_1) continues to be separated spatially from student desks and physically is situated to facilitate the monitoring of student areas. Classroom social status and role distinctions between teachers and students continue to be reinforced spatially. Classroom furniture shapes and physical arrangements, then, reinforce student mobility patterns controlled by the teacher; students are permitted to move from table to table and from place to place in accordance with differing classroom activities. Further, furniture defines classroom areas of more specialized function. There is, for example, a decrease in interaction-reinforcing round tables; round activity tables (A_3) are retained for group reading activities. The classroom rug is comparatively small and not prominently placed. Interaction-reinforcing pieces of round furniture spatially are overshadowed by task-oriented, distance-reinforcing pieces of rectangular shaped furniture. Tables and chairs fill the room, and the dispersed furniture placement pattern complements the classroom emphasis on an individualized student curriculum. First grade classrooms segment student activities more than those in previous grades. There are more classroom places for specialized first grade activity to occur, and this spatial pattern corresponds to the specialized curricular activity common to this grade: individualized reading instruction, reinforcement by the teacher of self-learning, and small group student activities. The teacher routinely assigns students, or small groups of students, to work on specialized activities at one of several tables (A_3) in the room. The spatial proximity of individual student tables (A_4) reinforces close student interchanges, coaction, and cooperation. Individual student tasks are carried out in specialized, single-purpose work areas. The classroom communalism witnessed in previous grades is decreasing; the first grade classrooms physically and spatially reinforce individualized behaviors. Classroom

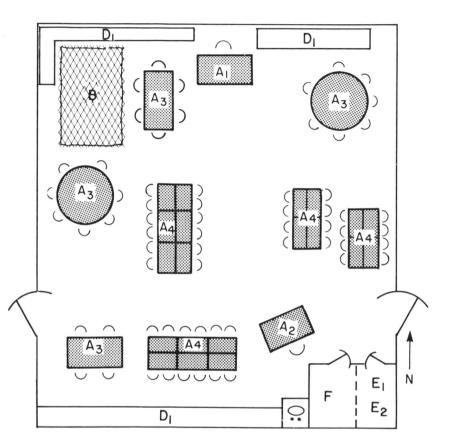

Figure 5. A First Grade Classroom

Legend
  A_1 = teacher's desk   B = floor rug
  A_2 = teacher aide's desk   C = chair
  A_3 = classroom activity desk D_1 = bookcases/storage areas
  A_4 = student desk E_1 = teacher's closet
                               E_2 = students' closet
                               F = lavatory

furniture shape and furniture placement are used, at the teacher's discretion, both to keep students apart and to permit them to work together.

The teacher of the low sessions described here is a tense white female in her early thirties, who has taught at West Haven for four years. Her aide is a heavy-set black female in her mid-thirties. Students in the high sessions are taught by a black female in her early fifties, who has taught for four years. Her assigned aide is an energetic black female in her early twenties. There were twenty-four students in the high group present on the days of observation: five white males, eight white females, six black males, and five black females. There are nineteen students in the low group sessions: eight black males, four black females, three white males, and four white females. As in all the classes, these ratios vary from day to day because of absences caused by illness, travel, truancy, and so on. First grade students are from six to seven years of age.

A Low Classroom Session

8:45 A.M. The teacher and the aide arrive before the students. They straighten up the room and set out several piles of materials for the day's activities.

Adult structuring of learning experiences. Continued coactive behaviors among the children. Adherence to neatness/order classroom norm.

Students come in small clumps and clusters from the buses. They take off their coats, without being told, and put them in the closet. The teacher and aide assist in the removal of their outerwear.

The noise level is high, and many students are shouting. Some are running around the room. The teacher sarcastically tells them to be quiet. Her voice has a whimsical, singsong quality. Her attitude is one of forced composure, and she does not yell or shout. As the voice and background noise levels drop, she sarcastically says, "Thank you," implying that she really does not mean it. Characteristically, she uses her voice to convey a double meaning.

Internal division of the student peer group. Some students comply with norms more than do others.
Use of sarcasm for the control of students. Distancing behaviors.
Public ridicule of children; a classroom background for mutual aggression/hostility.

Several students take turns using the toi-

Toilet procedures em-

phasizing autonomy, regimentation, and privacy are internalized.

Patriotism and deference to national authority.

Literacy training.

Emphasis on the production of material products. Demonstration/proof of knowledge.

Autonomy and individualism. Differential praise.

Emphasis on products. Private property.
Demonstration/proof. Reinforcement-seeking behaviors.

let. They do not ask the teacher's permission to do so; they voluntarily form lines while waiting. Everyone uses the light switch and closes the door.

9:00 A.M. The teacher tells the students to stand and face the American flag in the upper front corner of the room. In unison, they recite the Pledge of Allegiance.

The teacher and aide have put together some illustrations and drawings made by the students into small "books." As students leave their desks to gather around, the teacher and aide hold up a finished copy for all to see. The drawings have been photocopied, folded, and stapled down the center. The cover of the booklet says, "I Wish. . . ." Inside, students have drawn pictures completing this thought. As the teacher turns the pages to show them the drawings and completed sentences, students almost climb on each other in order to see. As she says the name of the boy or girl who drew each picture, the students look about until they see that person, smile, and then clap for him or her. When a name is read, others reach over to pat or rub that student's shoulder. They seem to derive great pleasure in identifying with the wish and the drawing of each particular person. Some of the completed sentences include: "I wish I had a house and my mother was living with me. I would run away and my shoes would always be raggedy. I wish for a house with nice furniture in it and a sun over the top of it. I wish for a house with a dog in it eating food up and a Mama fixing greens. I wish for a tree, a house, and candy for Christmas." The teacher passes out a copy of the completed book to each student. A frenzy of excitement ensues, and students run to one another to show off their drawings and to look at the pictures of others, and many run to show the observer their work. The teacher does not tell them to quiet down but allows their energy to dissipate. When it is fairly quiet, the teacher tells them to take their seats.

Order as a prelude to further classroom activity.

Event Transition 1

9:15 A.M. The teacher tells the class to gather in a circle on the rug. She sits down in a chair. Near her is a portable chart listing homonyms. As the teacher points to them, students sound out letters that rhyme. She admonishes students frequently and stridently to pay attention and to repeat each word precisely as she says it. If there is the slightest hesitation on their part, the teacher again tells them to look carefully, to listen, and to pay attention. The tone of her voice implies a threat.

Different height = authority position. Maintenance of spatial separation. Literacy training. Obedience training. Rote. Right/wrong mastery. Emphasis on task orientation and concentration.

9:20 A.M. The exercise completed, students are told to take their seats. As the teacher prepares the next activity, a girl runs up to her whining that a boy has taken something from her desk. The teacher blithely smiles, tries to humor the girl, but does not reprimand the boy or otherwise indicate that she took seriously what the girl said. She asks the girl to go back to her seat and take out her workbook.

Readiness position. Rapid succession of activity. Knowledge treated as a segmented, rather than a holistic, experience.

Tattling is an expression of peer competition for teacher rewards (Goetz 1976:40; Henry 1957).

Dispute over property.

9:35 A.M. The teacher draws three widely spaced parallel lines on the blackboard with an implement shaped like a lawn rake. Within these lines she writes:

Teacher reinforcement of an implied expectation of individual self-reliance.

Dan can see the fire.
Will you put the dime in the box?
Mike's Dad has a flat tire.

Economic reference.
Automotive/technology reference.

That wine is not Jim's.
Can a big dog jump that wire?

Obedience training. Emphasis on sequence and procedure. No self-generated spontaneity.

She tells students to take out their workbooks and work on these sentences. "Do your writing first and your coloring second," she says. They copy the sentences on the board and then color a mimeographed connect-a-dot drawing of several illustrative scenes.

Control by recourse to sarcasm and ridicule. Pleasing the teacher reinforces guilt and expected self-discipline.

The noise level is fairly high. When the teacher criticizes students for making noise, her sarcastic voice implies that they are disappointing her. Several times she is heard to say sarcastically, "I don't like that" in response to a loud voice or noise.

These interruptions condition the children to learn task orientation and concentration amid distractions. The hegemony of the administrative sector is illustrated by its continuing right of access to classrooms.

A continuing series of interruptions occurs all morning. The aide leaves and returns frequently. The door does not have a vacuum return and loudly slams shut. An older female student delivers a set of filmstrips to the teacher. An office worker enters the room to request several ditto masters (for typing mimeographed material) from the teacher. Students apparently ignore these sudden noises and interruptions. The teacher, though, is visibly upset at the frequent interruptions. Angered, she gets up to lock the door. Locking the door does not stop the interruptions; it only momentarily delays them.

Differential grouping and the spatial separation of ranked "ability" groups.

Autonomy.

Literacy training.

9:50 A.M. While most of the students work on group assignments, the aide and the teacher take small groups of students to opposite corners of the room where they sit at tables visually isolated by movable room dividers. Both groups work on activities using plastic flash cards on which are printed single words. The teacher is working on set contrasts. She briefly flashes the students words

such as "top/bottom" and "larger/smaller."
The teacher's tone of voice often implies the
answer to her question. More frequently than
not, students simply nod their heads in agree-
ment or disagreement.

Compliance/obedience.

10:00 A.M. The teacher calls two more
students to her group and tells them to work
on the letter *B*. After starting them on their
exercises, she does not intervene. The noise
level within the group copying exercises from
the board is high, and the teacher frequently
stops to tell them sternly but sarcastically, "If
you cannot talk quietly, you cannot talk at all."
After she leaves, the noise level drops somewhat, though it is never absolutely quiet in
this class. Students seem to be permitted to
talk, even loudly, while they are doing their assignments. The teacher intervenes only when
they begin shouting at each other.

Recurring segmenta-
tion of classroom activities.

Expected self-mainte-
nance.

The pattern is for low
sessions to spend more time
on behavior modification
and to exhibit less compliance with established classroom norms and values
than high sessions.

10:05 A.M. The aide calls out the names
of four students, who take books from their
desks and go to her table. The students in the
main writing group finish their assignments.
As they do, they get up and go to the aide's
desk to put their half-folded papers in a wire
basket. They go straight back to their seats to
begin coloring their pictures. For the most
part, these students do their own work,
though they frequently talk with their neighbors.

Public display of differ-
ential ranking and prestige.
Responsibility for personal/
private property.

Production of prod-
ucts. Demonstration/proof.
Submission to external standards of evaluation.
Expected autonomy.
Individual responsibility for
work.

A black male and a black female sit at
desks spatially removed from the main group.
The aide tells the observer that they are isolated because they habitually disturb others
and prevent them from doing their work.

Differential grouping
and status expressed spa-
tially.
Primacy of work and
autonomous task orienta-
tions.

Students in the small activity groups tend
to shout out the answers to the teacher and
the aide. They are told not to do this because
other students are not able to concentrate on

Continuing regulation
of spontaneity. Emphasis on
work. Autonomous task orientation. Competence must
be demonstrated.

Emphasis on procedure and the management of emotions.

their work and will not have a chance to answer. Despite this warning, students continue to leap to answer or to shout out a response before raising their hands.

The teacher looks at the work turned in by the wandering students, frowns, and appears disappointed. She shows the observer some of the work. She points out the paper done by a giggling black female, which contains only two words. Again oblique and sarcastic in her remarks, the teacher shrugs as if to say, "What can you expect."

Public display and ridicule. Hostile/belittling behavior.

Literacy training.

Many students in the writing group have finished their work and are coloring their drawings. Several students sit with their hands in their mouths, staring into space or at the others in the room. The teacher tells them to get a book or to work on another drawing.

Primacy of work.

11:05 A.M. The teacher and the aide each call four new students to their groups. Four black males wander around the room, yet the teacher does not intervene. Most white students sit at their desks, apparently doing their work. One black male, characterized by the teacher as a "problem," watches as a white female goes into the bathroom. After she closes the door, he waits for a few seconds, gets up, then runs to open it. The girl loudly shouts, "Get out of here!" Grinning broadly, he shuts the door. The aide turns to tell him to sit down. Seeing others wandering around the room, she tells them to sit down and to find something to do.

Continuing differences in classroom behavior by sex and by color. Some students, differing by color and by sex, exhibit more compliance with classroom norms and values than others. This behavior will serve as a basis for "labeling" (Rosenthal and Jacobson 1968).

Continuing emphasis on spatial confinement and order.

Event Transition 2

Order. Readiness position.

Rhetorical—they are going to do so anyway.

11:25 A.M. The teacher and aide dismiss their groups, and the students return to their seats. Presently, the aide asks if they would like to put their things away and everyone shouts,

"Yeeeess!" The aide then asks, "When your things are put away, what are you supposed to do?" "Put our heads down!" they shout. Several students are slow to follow this procedure and start to giggle. The teacher sarcastically stares at them saying, "You *know* how I expect you to act!"

Reinforcement of procedure. Deference position. Differential compliance.
Emphasis on behavior modification. Expected self-discipline at this grade level/age.

11:30 A.M. The teacher and aide prepare for the noon meal. A student, a black female, is designated to be the leader. The name of each student in the class is tacked, in a circle, to a freestanding bulletin board near the aide's table. Inside the circle are paper arrows pointing to several names; the arrows are labeled straws, messenger, milk, trash, spoons, paper, and napkins. Students talk among themselves while waiting for the hot lunch cart to arrive. A white female asks the teacher if she saw "A Charlie Brown Christmas" on television last night. The teacher had not seen this special, but other students had, and soon everyone is talking about the program.

Adult handling of food.
Rotating housekeeping tasks = responsibility training.
Paraphernalia culturally required in the ritual handling of food. They are mass-manufactured commercial items reinforcing consumerism (Henry 1963).

Reference to mass media. National celebration (Christmas).

11:40 A.M. The hot lunch cart arrives, and the aide wheels it inside; the teacher calls the students, by table, to line up. There is considerable shoving as students make a fierce dash to be first in line. As punishment for shoving, the teacher makes two black males go to the rear of the line. The teacher and aide dish up each plate; students take them and return to their seats.

Regimentation, competition, and ranking. Assignment of low rank and spatial position; low ranking as punishment.

Once the students are served and seated, the teacher says, "Let's say our prayer." Students clasp their hands and bow their heads. Following the teacher's lead, they say grace.

Order and regimentation.
Religious ritual in association with formalized consumption of prepared food.

Each student gets up when finished to deposit waste in the large metal container in the corner of the room. The aide collects the metal forks. The teacher calls each student, by

Neatness and cleanliness. Expected self-maintenance.

High spatial rank as reward for compliance. Expected self-maintenance.

name and quietest students first, to get coats for recess. They line up by the door when dressed. Neither the teacher nor aide checks their clothing. The aide puts on her coat and leads them to the playground.

Event Transition 3

12:00 P.M. Recess.

Increasing segmentation of educational activities. Increased spatial mobility. Autonomy. Individualization.

12:30 P.M. The students burst into the room. Hurriedly, the teacher tells them not to take off their coats because they are going to music class. The aide hands each student a name tag so that the music teacher can identify them. Students still exhibit the energy and activity stimulated by the playground. To

Control by threat of exercise of power of cessation of activity. Adult monitoring.

quiet them, the teacher threatens that they might not go to music. They quiet down. When all the name tags are distributed, the aide leads them to the music room.

Event Transition 4

12:35 P.M. Music class.

Neatness and order. Self-maintenance. Attention-positioning.
Adult distribution and handling of materials.

1:05 P.M. The students return from music class, take off their coats, and hang them in the closet. The teacher tells them to take their seats. When seated, the teacher passes out several sheets of the wide-lined paper. During this session, students write down and respond to the incomplete math problems previously written on the board. Several times the teacher tells them, "Do your own work. Don't let anybody tell you anything, OK."

Emphasis on finishing. Peer support and coaction are discouraged. Emphasis on autonomy.

In comparison with the high session, students exhibit more passive-aggressive behaviors and less adherence to established classroom norms.

The students are still restless from their excursions to the playground and music room, and there is a persistent background noise of murmuring, low talking, shuffling of feet, rattling of papers and books, coughing, scraping of chairs, and wiggling of bodies on the hard chairs.

Continuing differential

Students, especially black males, are not

working consistently. They tend to concentrate on their assignments for several minutes, talk for several minutes, then return to their assignments, and so on.

behaviors by black males and more compliance by whites with behaviors valued in the classroom.

Event Transition 5

1:50 P.M. The teacher dismisses her small group, then wanders around the room looking at the math work of the students.

Monitoring and evaluation.

2:00 P.M. The aide dismisses her group. The teacher tells the class to get ready for afternoon recess. They put their things away and lay their heads on their desks. A black male throws a pencil across the room. The teacher glares at him. He holds her gaze. Quietly, she tells him never to do that again because he might hurt someone. He casts his eyes down but smiles to himself. The teacher turns away. By tables, the teacher tells students to get their coats and line up by the door. The aide puts on her coat and, when all are in line, leads them to the playground. The lines are noisy but orderly.

Expected self-maintenance (Goetz 1976:40).

Rest. Care of the body. Conscious violation of classroom norms. Nonverbal threat gesture.

In loco parentis concern with safety. Passive aggression.

Differential ranking and reward.

Order. Adult monitoring.

Event Transition 6

2:30 P.M. Students return from the playground and go directly to their seats. Breathless and still excited, they sit and talk loudly among themselves. By tables, the teacher tells them to hang up their coats in the closet. On the way back to their seats, they take a book from the rack by the door. Students are talking very loudly. There are several clusters of students around the room, each engaged in various activities.

Readiness positioning. Waiting.

Monitoring of expected behavior.

Literacy training.

Behaviors counter to and not compliant with classroom norms and values.

Event Transition 7

2:45 P.M. The teacher and aide set up a filmstrip projector. The teacher goes to the

Adult manipulation of

valued machine technology.
Expected responsibility
for personal materials.
Responsibility training.

National celebrations
and origin legends are visually reinforced. Stereotypic
reinforcement of national
folklore. These images are
commercially produced and
serve to transmit national
culture through local school
systems.

Self-selected student
grouping by color and sex.

Ritualized association
of particular foods with particular activities.
Physical violence is a
conscious violation of classroom rules. Tacit acceptance
by teacher.
Peer monitoring indi-
cates different norms and
values held by the student
peer group.

Value of technology.

front of the room to pull down a viewing
screen while telling the class to put away their
books. Students scurry to put away their materials.

Two filmstrips are shown. The first is entitled *Thanksgiving* and the second *Grandfather's Boyhood Thanksgiving*. The initial filmstrip presents a version of the story of the first
Thanksgiving. It depicts Pilgrims in colonial
dress around a food-laden table in a forest
with Native Americans in traditional dress
and the children of both groups gathered
around the table. Everyone is smiling. The
narrator says that Thanksgiving is a time of
peace and fellowship. Pilgrims gave thanks for
surviving in the new land, and Indians were
invited to share in their bounty and good for-
tune.

In the front row, save for one black female, all the students are white. They sit in a
single row about a meter from the screen. The
black students cluster to the sides and the rear
of the room. Everyone silently watches the
filmstrip. Occasional comments are made
about the illustrations or in response to a nar-
rated remark.

At the end of the filmstrip, students clap
and jokingly ask for popcorn. While the filmstrip is being changed, several black males begin roughhousing on the floor. One looks in
the teacher's direction before hitting another
boy on the shoulder. The teacher does not respond. There is some giggling and shoving
toward the front of the room. The teacher sarcastically frowns, and students begin to
"Shhhhh" one another. Two white females sitting next to the teacher put their hands over
the projector's exhaust fan and giggle. The
teacher gruffly says, "That's an expensive

piece of equipment!" The teacher continues to stare disapprovingly at them until they stop. They did not actually touch the projector.

Adult handling of valued materials.

The characters in the second filmstrip are decidedly Anglo-American. All the houses depicted are mansard-roofed cottages with white picket fences. There are horse-drawn sleighs and tables overflowing with food. The women, in aprons, gather around the stove, while the men sit in overstuffed armchairs smoking thick cigars with their thumbs hooked in their vest pockets. Children make snowmen in front of a large red barn. At the end of the day, the father tucks them in bed under thick patchwork quilts. Smoke wafts softly up the chimney of the house.

Stereotypic association of national legends with Anglo-American subgroup. Neolocal housing pattern is deemed normative. Autonomy. Material abundance. Sex-role stereotyping.

Age-role stereotyping. Nuclear family as normative.

Event Transition 8

3:20 P.M. When the second filmstrip ends, students again loudly clap and begin talking among themselves. The teacher tells them to get ready to leave.

Expected self-maintenance.

When they are in their seats and fairly quiet, she tells them to put on their outerwear. "People with *red* on, go get your coats. . . . Now, people with *blue* on, go get your coats. OK, now everyone else may go!" Students lunge toward the closet. There is little shoving but quite a bit of banging around in the closet, upsetting of hangers, and slamming of doors. As they return to their seats the teacher hands out some of their past work, ostensibly to show to their parents.

Ranking and differential grouping of the students.
Behavioral departures from classroom order and procedure norms.

Emphasis on products. Evaluation.

The teacher tells them to put their chairs upside down on top of their desks and to line up by the door. They are extremely noisy and quick in doing so. Chairs are tossed or half-thrown up on the tables, but the teacher does

Recurring housekeeping tasks as ritualized prelude to separation.
Behavioral departures from customary classroom separation norms. The

norms are made explicit through their violation.

Tacit teacher acceptance of unruly behavior. Lack of ritualized separation gestures between teacher and students.

not intervene. Before the teacher is ready, the aide begins to take students to the bus. Some students are not yet dressed to go. Others are noisy and disorderly in line. Many students run to catch up while others have not yet put their chairs on their desks. The teacher has a pained, frustrated look on her face. Still, she does not intervene. Instead, she continues passing out corrected papers as students run to catch up with the aide. Many students do not keep within the yellow line while running down the hall. Closing the door, the teacher runs to see them to the bus. Both the teacher and the aide return to straighten up desks and to pick up myriad pieces of paper from the floor.

Recurring ritualized entry procedures.
Comparatively more emphasis on order than in the low session.
Expected self-maintenance. Responsibility training.
Personalization of space. Order.
Neatness and order norms.

Comparatively more emphasis on ritualized greetings and teacher-student contact than in the low session. Sex-specific (female) nurturing behaviors.
Males require discipline by spatial confinement.

A High Classroom Session

8:45 A.M. The teacher and aide prepare for the arrival of the students. After students get off the bus, they line up outside the classroom door, and the aide goes outside to stand with them. The aide lets the students in the room, four at a time. Fairly quietly, students hang up their coats and do not receive assistance in removing their outerwear. In the closet, each student's name is printed above the space and hanger on which the coats are placed. Boots are stacked near the door.

Most students say hello to the teacher and to the aide. Both say hello to the students. The teacher is amicably chatting with students, her voice pleasant. She asks a black female if her face feels better today. She asks another about her homework. Several black males are wandering around the room, and the teacher immediately tells them to sit down. They do. The teacher tells a black male to pull in his chair as he sits down. He quietly does so.

Ready compliance.

Without being told, students take out books and materials from the storage areas under their desk tops. The noise level increases. The teacher calls out the names of individual students, then pauses. They quiet down. She also calls on several sections. She says "Section 1" or "Section 2," then pauses. They quiet down.

Self-regulation and internalization of procedure. Responsibility for private property.
Control by appeal to self-discipline.
Depersonalization. Ordering by replication of essentially similar units. Regimentation.

By section, the teacher asks students who have brought lunch money to give it to the aide. Any notes from home are to be given to the aide. Without knocking, a secretary from the office comes in. She walks across the room, gives a note to the aide, then turns to leave. The aide hands the note to the teacher. Few students look up.

Increasing amount of administrative tasks. Continuing office interruptions of, and hegemony over, the classroom.

When the aide has finished collecting money, the teacher tells the students to stand quietly for the Pledge of Allegiance. A leader is chosen. In a loud and reverent voice, the class begins singing in unison. Their right hands are placed over their hearts as they face the American flag hanging in the upper front corner of the room.

Event Transition 1

9:00 A.M. Standing in the front of the room, the teacher tells students to take calendars from their desks and asks questions about dates. After asking the name of the day and receiving a correct response, the teacher asks a white female to put the date on the larger calendar hanging from one of the room dividers. Passing in front of the observer, she quietly says, "Excuse me." She writes the date on the handmade calendar that has squares and the name of the month but no numbers.

Authority position.

Time as linear and sequential. Basic sociocultural orientation to, and perception of, reality.

Propriety norm. Etiquette.

Authority position.

Indirect command. Pleasing the teacher associated with self-discipline. Compliance/obedience.

Students are compliant with classroom norms. No passive aggression. Conformity. Modeling.

Continuing images of/references to national legends/celebrations. Ritualized association of particular stereotypic activities with particular events. Mathematics training.

Literacy training.

Adherence to norms. Modeling.

Differential grouping and ranking. Procedure and self-regulation norms are internalized.

Responsibility for property. Spatial separation.

Autonomy. Self-regulation. Finishing and mastery norms.

9:15 A.M. In beginning a new activity, the teacher goes to the front of the room while asking a black female to pass out wide-lined sheets of paper. The noise level rises as the paper is passed out. The teacher says, "I'm getting a lot of noise that I do not like!" The noise level drops to a low murmur, then falls to zero. The teacher begins writing on the board. She takes a rakelike implement, with three pieces of chalk in the fingers, and draws even lines on the board. Periodically, she turns around to glance at the students. While her back is turned, the noise level does not rise. Watching her write, students begin writing on their papers. On the left side of the board, the teacher writes: "Thanksgiving Day. Over the river and through the woods, to Grandfather's house we go, the horse knows the way to carry the sleigh through the white and drifting snow." Addition and subtraction problems are written on the right side of the board:

$$5 + 2 = \qquad 7 + 5 =$$
$$4 + 3 = \qquad 7 - 4 =$$
$$9 + 6 = \qquad 7 - 3 =$$

and so on. In the middle of the board the following words are written:

Cannot	Schoolhouse
Into	Treetop
Fireman	

It is very quiet in the room as students copy what the teacher has written on the board.

9:40 A.M. The teacher calls four students, by name, to a table in the rear of the room. Automatically, they put up their board work, take workbooks from their desks, and go to the table. The aide calls the names of three students who go to a table in the opposite corner of the room. Students doing board work do not look up. Students do their own work without supervision.

The aide asks her group questions about a previous reading assignment. She says to a white female who interrupted another student, "Shawn, will you give her a chance to speak!" A black male gets up from his seat to show the aide the letters he has copied. He is beaming. The aide merely looks at it, acknowledges it as correct, and turns away. The boy sags a bit and goes back to his seat. By contrast, the teacher playfully flicks the nose of a white female student and smiles. The teacher and the girl break into giggles. The aide is saying to her group, "I want you to read what Tony [a character in their book] said *just the way Tony said it!*" The aide keeps an eye on the larger group still copying from the board and periodically turns to glance at them.

Individual accountability for demonstration of knowledge.
Autonomy.
Boys consistently receive less nurturing, solicitude, and attention than do girls.

Two black males, special education students, are seated at desks apart from the others. They persistently interfere with other students to the extent that they are not able to do their work. Isolated, they sit by each other and are prevented from interacting with other students. One starts inching his way toward the group. The aide glares at him. She yells, "Stop it!" He stops. She glares at him for several seconds.

Conformity and obedience.
Task divisions of labor.
Monitoring the continuing lack of student privacy.

Differential grouping and labeling. Status and prestige spatially reinforced. Primacy of work.
Spatial confinement associated with different students receiving different classroom experiences. Space consciously used to maintain boundaries between ranked subgroups.

10:00 A.M. The teacher looks up, slightly raises her head, and arches her eyebrows. The aide nods her head. The teacher dismisses her group. She then calls four new students, who stop their board work, take several books from their desks, and go to the teacher's table. The same occurs at the aide's table.

Nonverbal signaling; shared social and cultural expectations.
Expected self-direction.
Maintenance of personal property. More complex scheduling.

Event Transition 2

Rest period. Care of the body.

Student self-discipline. Adherence to food norms. Food rituals. Newness reinforced.

Regularly occurring and rotating housekeeping tasks.

Event Transition 3

Attention-seeking. Demonstration of skill.

Denial of spontaneity. Primacy of work and a task orientation. Nurturant disciplining. Compliance.

Public ridicule. Separation of work/play.

Finishing. Task orientation. Monitoring and evaluation. Autonomy.

Differential praise and reward associated with pleasing the teacher. Right/wrong mastery.

Manipulation of emotions as motivation technique.

Permitted mobility is training for responsibility and self-discipline.

Expected self-maintenance.

Internalization of classroom norms.

10:05 A.M. Before starting her second group, the aide prepares and then passes out paper cups full of orange juice. The students do not touch or drink the juice that is put before them. A leader is chosen to say grace, and the students drink only when the aide has given everyone a cup. They lunge at the juice and gulp it down. A white female collects the cups and throws them away.

10:10 A.M. The teacher and aide begin their second group's activities. A black male gets up to show the teacher a book he is reading. The teacher stops her work, turns to face him, puts her hands gently on his shoulders, draws him to her, and quietly tells him never to interrupt a reading class while it is working. He is told to go back to his seat. He goes back to his seat. The aide shouts, "I'm glad that you have time to play. That's why you never get any work done."

10:20 A.M. The teacher dismisses her group. Several students go back to copying board work. The teacher walks between and among the students still doing exercises on the board, praising their work and correcting when necessary. Her praise is conveyed in voice and posture, and she smiles and draws out her sounds while frequently touching their shoulders. When displeased, her shoulders sag and droop, and she frowns, but does not speak.

During this period students get up from their seats, without permission, to go to the board, to get a fresh sheet of paper from the teacher's desk, or to go to the bathroom. Completing their objective, they immediately return to their seats.

A white female, crying that something is in her eye, runs up to the aide. She comforts the girl by embracing her. Her voice is soft as she puts her arms around her. The aide holds her for a few seconds, then the girl quietly returns to her seat.

> High degree of nurturing and student/teacher contact as compared with the low section. The nurturing of females.

10:35 A.M. A black female, a volunteer student aide from one of the upper grades, enters the room. Without any direction or acknowledgment, she tells the special education students to accompany her to a small table, isolated by room dividers, in the back of the room.

> Unscheduled interruptions as training for student task orientation and concentration. Responsibility training.
> Differential student grouping expressed spatially.

10:40 A.M. The teacher goes to her table after checking the progress of the students but calls out the names of three people. When they look around, she merely tells them to get to work. The noise level remains very low: bodies moving, chairs scraping, and paper rustling.

> Idea of linear progress.
>
> Control by appeal to self-discipline. Emphasis on task orientation.
> Adherence to classroom work norms and values.

10:45 A.M. The aide calls five new students to her table.

A white male is giggling with a neighbor rather than copying his exercises. Very slowly the teacher says, "I'm afraid John is not going to get his work done." The boy stops talking and goes back to his work. To a white male who was leaning toward his neighbor she says, "Timmy, will you just do your work and let James do his!" The teacher glares at him for a few seconds so as to reinforce her message. They go back to work.

> Spontaneous coaction. Indirect reprimand reinforces expected self-discipline. Primacy of work/task orientation. Compliance/obedience.
> Spontaneous coaction. Emphasis on autonomy. Individual responsibility for work. Nonverbal threat gesture. Compliance.

10:55 A.M. The aide dismisses her group.

11:05 A.M. The teacher dismisses her group and walks among the students who are still working. The aide goes to the teacher's desk to get an eraser for a student. The observer asks why the pencils do not have erasers. The aide replies that it is to make students

> Monitoring and supervision.
>
> Emphasis on right answers. Compliance. Particulate notion of time.

become more conscious about doing their work right the first time.

Event Transition 4

Authority positioning. Play as reward for finishing work. Competition. Differential rewards. Division of the student peer group against itself.

11:15 A.M. The teacher stands in the middle of the room and announces that the people who have finished their math work get to hear a story. Several students whoop with joy and almost run to the rug area. Those students who have not finished silently go back to their tasks.

Unpermitted mobility = violation of classroom work norms.

Indirect reprimand instills guilt. Appeal to self-control.

Obedience and compliance.

Paul, one of the special students, has left his seat again and is wandering around the room. He is interfering with the work of several students at the math table. The teacher says, "Paul, we have been kind to you this morning. You will have to be kind to us." He looks at her sourly, then returns to his table.

Peer coaction permitted during play but not work. Continuing use of space as an expression of status.

Orientation toward national celebrations.

Students gather on the rug in a tight semicircle. The teacher sits in a chair at the front of the circle and holds up the book so students can see the illustrations. The story tells of a family's Thanksgiving adventures. With their outstretched fingers, the students follow the lines read by the teacher. Students loudly clap and shout at the end of the story.

Event Transition 5

The work period in the high session is longer than in the low session (see Figure B-3, Appendix B). Recurring food rituals. Regimentaiton. No food sharing. Autonomy.

11:25 A.M. The teacher tells students to get into line to wash their hands. The aide is preparing the noon meal. When finished, students quietly return to their seats. When they are seated, the teacher tells them to be very quiet. The aide brings a hot lunch cart to the door, and by section, the teacher tells students to line up by their tables. One by one, students are called up to get their plates. They

Waiting.
Peer competition.

take the plates back to their seats and wait for the others. As the teacher calls another section, each student runs to the corner of the table to try to be first in line. A few students say, "Thank you," when they receive their trays. Whenever a student says, "Thank you," the teacher says, "You're welcome." While waiting in line, students invariably fold their arms over their chests. A leader is chosen to bless the food. As the hot lunches are being served the teacher says, "OK, cold lunch people, you may start." Students look at one another while eating and occasionally speak. When finished serving, the teacher and aide take their plates and eat in a partitioned alcove near the outside windows. Considerable attention is paid to the manner in which the students eat. The teacher says loudly, "Raquel, you are putting too much food in your mouth." Later, the aide says to a student, "Let's not be a pig!" She says sharply to another student, "Are you going to eat your meat or wave it in the air?" Several students, both black and white, are out of their seats talking with their neighbors. The teacher says, "We don't have anybody that is ready to go out, do we?" The students quickly sit down.

Frequently, students tattle on each other. Twice during mealtime students run up to the teacher and loudly tell her that another student is talking or otherwise doing something forbidden. From the tone of the students' voices it seems they want the teacher to intervene—and punish the offending students. The teacher smiles and tells them not to worry about it. A white female runs up to the aide to tell her something that another student is doing. There is a whining tone to her voice. The aide simply tells her to go back to her seat. A black male runs up to the aide loudly whining that a neighbor ate her cookies before she ate

Ranking expressed spatially (first/last). Lineality. Propriety and etiquette norms. Waiting posture.

Food distribution pattern is a basis for ranking. Some students cannot afford to bring cold lunches from home.

Socioeconomic differences are exhibited.

Again, the spatial expression of age/status/role distinctions.

Food norms emphasize the value of moderation and restraint, the denial of spontaneity, and the control of emotions.

A rhetorical question reinforcing expected self-discipline. Control by threat of cessation of activity. Compliance.

Tattling is an expression of intragroup competition for teacher rewards and illustrates that the peer group is not mutually supportive. There is more tattling in the high session than in the low session, more acceptance of classroom norms and values by students in the high session, and more competition for those rewards.

Teacher emphasis on self-reliance and responsibility.

her vegetables. The aide frowns and tells him not to worry about it.

Event Transition 6

There is enormous amount of waste here. Conditioning for newness and consumption. Waiting.

High spatial rank (first) as reward for adherence to classroom norms and values. Regimentation. *In loco parentis* care of the body. Safety.

Expectation of more self-maintenance in the high session and more instances of rotating responsibility training. Adult monitoring.

11:55 A.M. The meal finished, students go to the wastebasket to dispose of their plates, cups, napkins, straws, and forks. They return to their seats and sit quietly until everyone is finished. When the teacher and aide finish, students are told, quietest sections first, to get their coats and line up by the door for recess. "Let's get in line with our arms folded," says the teacher. "It is cold out there so be sure that you button up." "Be careful with the coat hanger," she is saying to a student, "so you won't hurt anybody." The teacher and aide assist only when students are not properly dressed. A black male is designated as leader. This means he has to hold the door open for the others. The aide takes the students to the playground.

Event Transition 7

Recurring ritualized entry emphasis on order and neatness.

Authority positioning. Emphasis on finishing and completing. Compliance/obedience. Following a model.

Required proof/demonstration. Right/wrong mastery. Emphasis on self-reliance.

Handraising is a form of competition as well as a gesture of deference to authority. Classroom success depends on the opportunity to demonstrate/prove com-

12:00 P.M. Recess.

12:45 P.M. Students return from the playground. Clothing is hung in the closet. The teacher tells students to take their seats.

Standing in front of the room, the teacher tells the students to take out the work they started that morning, and she begins to correct their papers. Writing on the blackboard, the teacher uses a wooden pointer to illustrate specific examples. She asks students to volunteer to respond to each example. Students mark their own papers as correct or incorrect. Students energetically raise their hands, waving them in the air in small circles to attract the attention of the teacher. As she looks around the room deciding on whom to call, hands follow her. In trying to attract her attention, students leap from their seats; they do not speak, but there are strained expressions on their faces as if they want to burst and scream to attract her attention. The enthusiasm is contagious, and occasionally the teacher has to tell individual students to quiet down.

Alvin, a special student, is out of his seat again. While commenting on a problem, the teacher goes over to him, touches his shoulder, and tells him to go back to his seat. She says that he is not to bother Janet because she wants to do her work. Alvin goes back to his seat and sits there looking at the rest of the class.

The words earlier written on the board by the teacher are now explained as compound words: cannot, into, fireman, schoolhouse, and treetop. The class has to separate each word into its component parts. When called upon by the teacher, students take turns going to the board to indicate each word of the compound. When a student pauses or hesitates, many hands shoot up and shouts of "I know . . . I know!" come from the group. The teacher ignores this effort and waits for the student to answer. In response she usually says, "That's very good thinking." In criticizing a response she might say, "I don't think I like that one very much," or "If I were you I would pay more attention." When this happens, other students raise their hands and shout for the teacher's attention. Once the teacher snaps, "When you children yell like that, the other children cannot think!" The students stop. After a minute they again stand up in their chairs and bounce up and down, gritting their teeth, with their hands nervously flapping at their sides. "Stop all this mouthing

petence. Rewards are differentially distributed.

Management of emotions. Self-control.

Comparatively high degree of physical contact. Control by spatial confinement. Value of work. Task orientation. Compliance. Special students are not made to work.

Literacy training.
Individual responsibility for demonstrating competence.

Peer competition to demonstrate right answer. Individual accountability.
Emphasis on problem-solving. Pleasing the teacher as reward.

Indirect reprimand reinforcing self-discipline. Peer competition.
Defense of child against peers. Competition expressed nonverbally.
The noise level is the loudest it has been all day. The high students comparatively are more orderly than the low students. Initial attempt to control by appeal to self-discipline, then by

exercise of power to suspend activity and force a submissive posture.

Control by changing activity. Personal responsibility for property.
Rhetorical exchange appealing to self-discipline.

Compliance. Self-control.

Monitoring and evaluation.
Authority positioning. Task division of labor.
Emphasis on procedure and following directions.

Forced compliance to norm by threat of cessation of play.
Nonverbal, spatial behaviors are important messages about authority.
Peer monitoring of adherence to classroom norms. Required deference to teacher.

Monitoring and evaluation of right/wrong responses reinforces mastery. Standardized evaluations.
Emphasis on order and

and mouthing!" The voice level drops, but the nonverbal noise remains the same. The teacher issues a stern, direct command for them to put their heads down on their desks. She stops the correction work and waits for them to put their heads down. When it is quiet, the teacher puts down her pointer and says, "OK. Let's open our spelling books." There is a bustle of activity as workbooks are dug from desks and other materials are put away. Rhetorically, the teacher says to the aide, "Miss Gold, did I say open mouths?" Dramatically, the aide pauses, looks around, and then says, "No . . . no, you didn't." The class looks from the teacher, who is on one side of the room, to the aide, who is on the other, and the talking ceases.

1:25 P.M. While the teacher wanders around the room looking at student work, the aide goes to the front of the room to begin the spelling lesson. The aide takes quite a bit of time explaining how she wants the worksheets filled out. At the end of each segment of instruction she asks, "Do you understand?" Invariably, students answer, "Yeeeesssss." During this activity the noise level increases. The aide simply says, "I didn't ask for any talking. Settle down or we won't have recess." She stops what she is doing, stands at the front of the room with her arms folded, and glares at them until they are quiet to her satisfaction. While waiting, a black female looks at a black male who is fidgeting and very indignantly says, "She's waiting!" The aide circulates among students, looking at what they are writing on their worksheets. If the response is correct, she stamps it with a rubber stamp. If it is incorrect, she says so and moves on. Several students run up to the aide with their work. Again, the aide either ignores them or pointedly tells them to wait their turn.

Both the teacher and the aide emphasize that students should do only what they are told to do when they are told to do it. A white male is reprimanded for drawing a picture on the back of his paper. A black male is using crayons for writing when he is supposed to use a pencil. The teacher and aide take considerable time telling, indicating, and explaining to the class exactly what they want it to do, how they want it done, and in what order.

procedure. Denial of spontaneity. Examples of obedience training and adherence to a priori procedures.

2:00 P.M. The teacher asks students whether they want an afternoon recess; they raise their hands to indicate their preference. They vote to remain indoors, and sporadic clapping and whooping are heard. They say, "We won . . . we won," but others are quick to retort, "but we won yesterday!"

Rhetorical because the aide has suggested there might be too much snow outside. An orientation toward giving these students responsibility. Continuing peer competition.

The teacher tells the students that, if they wish, they can play with the toys for a while. She leaves the choice of toy up to them. Most of the students go to the toy area, but several students remain at their desks doing their board work. The noise level increases. The teacher says, "Let's use our inside voices." A black female says, "Shhhhhhh" by placing an index finger to her lips.

Self-reliance and decision making. Students who continue working are held in high regard by the teacher.

Work/play distinction. Peer monitoring of classroom norms.

The teacher is chatting amicably with the observer and several students. A white female raises her hand. Without the slightest malice she says, "Aren't we wasting our time?" The teacher pauses, looks at her, then begins to laugh. She says, "I was enjoying our talk. Maybe we should move on."

Peer minitoring. Students have internalized several classroom norms and values. Notice the equality implied in the teacher's acceptance of the girl's admonition.

Event Transition 8

2:45 P.M. The aide says that it is time for a story, and the toys should be put away. The

Time/activity and place/activity coordination.

Emphasis on procedure and the denial of spontaneity.

aide and the observer are talking when a white female comes up with a question. The aide very quickly tells her never to interrupt while others are talking. The student silently returns to her seat.

Personal/private property shows adherence to literacy norm. Space linked to status.

References to transportation and mobility/industrial technology.

The aide reads a story from a book a black male brought to class. She sits on a chair, and the students gather around her on the rug. The story is about railroads, cars, and other forms of transportation. Every eye is fixed on the book's illustrations, and several students climb up on their knees to see the illustrations better. The aide holds the book higher. Watching the illustrations, their mouths remain slightly open in wonderment. A few students have their hands or thumbs in their mouths. There is no noise. At the end of the story the students clap and shout with pleasure. The aide smiles.

Event Transition 9

Expected self-maintenance. Monitoring and evaluation.

Public display of differential praise and reward. Peer competition is reinforced. Emphasis on products. Finishing/completing. Play as reward for work. Public ridicule.

3:00 P.M. The teacher tells the students to return to their seats and put away their work. While they do so, she goes to look at the work of several students. She holds up one paper and says, "See how good it is to keep busy. This is a good paper." Others are warned that they must finish their work by tomorrow morning if they want to see a film in the afternoon. One black male mumbles that "we sure better 'cause they will kick us out if we don't." In spite of themselves, the teacher and aide glance at each other and laugh. The teacher says, "We will *not* kick you out, you know. Let's not be so crude. . . . Let's try to say that we might just not get to see the movie." The aide is still trying not to laugh. As the teacher continues to walk around, students become extremely aggressive in trying to show off

Fear and anxiety are not acknowledged in this classroom.

Approval-seeking of teacher rewards. Competition. Demonstration and proof.

their work. They pull, shout, and try to get the teacher's attention: "I don't like the way all of you are talking at once!" she says.

Emphasis on order and procedure.

Event Transition 10

3:15 P.M. The teacher tells students to get ready to go home. In a flurry of activity, students put away their work and materials, then sit quietly at their desks. They are dismissed, quietest tables first, to put on their outerwear. A black male's shoe is untied, and he goes to the teacher to ask her to tie it. "We can't have six-year-olds who can't tie their shoes, can we?" she says. A black female asks the aide to tie her shoelace, and the aide tells her that she knows how to tie her own shoe. The student ties her shoelace.

Expected self-responsibility for personal materials. Readiness position/waiting.
Reinforcement of norms through ranking.

Expected self-reliance and maintenance through guilt. Different levels of expectation accorded each age group.

After putting on their outerwear, students return to their seats. Notes requesting parents to send lunch money are pinned to their coats. Next, they are told to put their chairs upside down on top of their desks. They silently stand where their chairs were.

Waiting. Regimentation.
Recurring administrative and housekeeping (nonacademic) tasks (Goetz 1976:40). Waiting. Regimentation.

The teacher tells them to line up by the door by groups, quietest groups first. Her voice rises when she tells them not to run. When they are in line, students automatically fold their arms over their chests.

Ranking. Regimentation. Sequencing. Lineality. Order.
Waiting. At-attention positioning.

The aide leads the line of students to the front doors. Everyone walks inside the yellow line on the hall floor. The teacher puts on her coat and brings up the end of the line. Students smile and say good-bye to the teacher and aide, who return the farewell.

Regimentation. Lineality. Adult monitoring.
Ritualized separation gestures expressing recognition/contact.

A primary theme expressed in the first grade narratives is the classroom emphasis on work, and considerable attention in one fashion or another is given to getting students to adhere to the work routine of the classroom society. Work is associated with a series of related classroom features: student autonomy/individualism (1/12), procedure/sequence (8/5), and student self-maintenance (2/3).* For instance, the incidence of student adherence to classroom norms and values is high (13/13) for both sessions. Student familiarity with the classroom way of life at this point is assumed by the teacher, and student self-maintenance (2/3) and self-control (24/1) are expected. In comparison with the earlier grades, there is a significant decrease in incidents of classroom violence: (66) in the low session and none at all in the high session on the days of observation. Work is ranked (6) in the high session and (25) in the low. The emerging work pattern in these classrooms is analogous to work patterns prominent in the wider society (LeCompte 1978; Rodgers 1978; Sieber 1979). Learning to work in each instance means learning to function appropriately in densely populated, visually stimulating, perpetually noisy environments often without privacy and subject to continual interruptions. Children are conditioned to a complex set of work-related rules. They are expected to accept orders from a manager (6/4), follow bureaucratic routines (8/5), concentrate on tasks at hand amid distractions (10/16), produce tangible products (15/65) on demand that are evaluated (20/20) by the manager (12/29), compete (27/7) for scarce rewards, and learn to tolerate working alone (1/12). Like Prufrock in T. S. Eliot's "The Love Song of J. Alfred Prufrock," the culture of the classroom is obsessed with time. Students increasingly must either be doing something or be preparing to do something. The phrase "Get back to work!" is heard as often in the classroom as it is heard in the factory or the office.

Compared with the kindergarten sessions, first graders spend more time on work and work-related activities: a 19 percent increase for the low group and a 23 percent increase for the high group (see Figure B-3, Appendix B). Furthermore, the amount of classroom time devoted to stories on the days observed decreased from 23 to 4 percent. Stories and work each reinforce different features of classroom life. Story time is associated with group coaction (26/27), sharing, and spontaneity. Work invariably is associated with autonomy (1/12), independence, and task orientation (10/16) (see Figure C-3, Appendix C). In channeling more time into work, students in the high session better develop behavior and habits that soon become very important to success in the classroom

---

*These paired numbers refer to features of low/high sessions summarized in Figure C-3, Appendix C.

society. There is no formal rest period (characteristic of the earlier grades) in either first grade session; potential rest time is channeled into work (25/6) and reinforces task orientation (10/16), expected self-maintenance (2/3), and self-control (24/1). Rest time occurs, if at all, during the lunch period and, if approved by the teacher, during recess. Neither first grade session exhibits a formal play period, and longer periods of classroom time are devoted to work. Increasingly, classroom life is marked by ceaseless activity rather than periodic inactivity.

There are additional differences between low and high first grade classroom sessions. In the high session there is more activity occurring, and a greater number of core classroom characteristics are expressed more consistently. High session students are more compliant (2) than low session (28) students. Behavior modification ranks (40) in the low session but did not occur in the high session on the days of observation. High session students are hardworking (6), task-oriented (16), and reinforced to complete and finish (47/25) their classroom work properly. The teachers in both sessions use public ridicule as a control mechanism, but its use is more pronounced in the low session (9/49). The relationship between the teacher and the students in the low session is as emotionally distant and adversarial as the relationship between the teacher and the students in the high session is accepting and close emotionally. The emotionally distant relationship between teachers and low students helps keep the children from fully embracing the classroom culture and society. Low group students are not concerned with pleasing a teacher (58/36) who does not accept them. Accommodation of students is in rapid decline, and the occurrence of early grade *in loco parentis* behavior is low in both sessions (48/54). The teacher says the low students will have to "catch up" to meet the challenges of the second grade. Her assumption is that everyone in the second grade is "in the same bucket." This is not necessarily so. Differentiated grouping and the spatial stratification of students assures that there always will be two or more unequal "buckets." Consequently, it is unlikely that low students will catch up to high students. Differentiated classroom grouping is entrenched firmly in the middle grades, and there is little pretense that low students will catch up.

Finally, the myriad films shown in the earlier grades, mostly in the low sessions, are important vehicles for the political socialization of students. The films emphasize holidays, and holidays for the most part transmit national sociocultural myths, legends, and themes. The

West Haven classroom orientation toward national values is exhibited through the often taken-for-granted association of holidays with particular stereotypic images and symbols: rabbits with Easter, eagles with national power and authority, pine trees with Christmas, and turkeys with Thanksgiving. These symbolic associations are prominent in the wider culture, and typical Thanksgiving classroom scenes encapsulate and make visible the legitimizing myths chartering the national society as a whole. By state law all public school children in the United States are required to be taught the paraphernalia associated with national myths, legends, and themes roughly at the same time and in the same manner. On the days films about Thanksgiving were shown in West Haven classrooms, we would not be surprised to find similar films being shown in other public elementary schools. West Haven is required to observe Christmas, Easter, Father's Day, Halloween, Independence Day, Labor Day, Lincoln's Birthday, Memorial Day, Mother's Day, St. Valentine's Day, Thanksgiving, and Washington's Birthday. These required observances are woven into the classroom lessons (14/33). Students and teachers spend a great deal of time making Halloween and Thanksgiving paraphernalia. West Haven's multiethnic township observes important holidays and celebrations of its own, but the paraphernalia and symbols associated with local sociocultural orientations are not represented in the material artifacts found in the elementary school classrooms. West Haven school people talk about schooling being organized around holidays. The school year begins around Labor Day two-thirds of the way through the calendar year, has its middle around Christmas at the end of the calendar year, and ends around Memorial Day in the middle of the next calendar year. If students do not know anything else, they know the holidays, mostly by virtue of the pervasive political association of national holidays with the organization of the school year.

Are all public elementary schools alike? Do all of them place classroom emphasis on the same kinds of political and economic conditioning or on the same temporal and spatial orientation?

Public schools are more alike than different and have to be so because they are an institution universal to national society as a whole rather than one unique to particular local community settings (Cohen 1975; Dreeben 1968; Parsons 1951:182–300). Public schools vary in the amount of influence their local sociocultural contexts carry (Wax 1971). There are, for instance, urban elementary schools serving student populations ethnically and socioeconomically more homogeneous than that at West Haven. The observed classroom event and activity pattern of these schools might emphasize social control, vertical teacher/student conflict, or high rates of student "pushouts" (Eddy 1965; McDermott 1974; Ogbu 1974, 1978). Then, too, there are public elementary schools serving the children of local groups more economically advantaged than those at West Haven. Descriptions of classroom observations made in these schools might reveal emphasis on social and cultural similarities between teachers and students, more attention given to individual students, or more material resources in the classrooms (Henry 1955, 1963; Leacock 1969). Public schools differ, but their differences are like musical variations on a single recognizable theme.

SECOND GRADE: COMPETITION

There are two classrooms in second grade: a group of all-day high students occupies one room, and two groups (morning sessions and afternoon sessions) of low students occupy the other. Student scores on state-mandated assessment tests given at the end of the first grade, and the recommendations of previous teachers ostensibly determine the composition of high and low student groups.

There is less visual and physical material in second grade classrooms than in previous rooms. A few student paintings are hung on a string strung across the front of the windows. Alphabets, without anthropomorphic figures, are still above the blackboard, but there is a noticeable lack of animals and objects associated with the marking of time. Most of the objects in each classroom are labeled; block-printed student- and teacher-produced signs are taped to each item, which have letters missing from the word designating it. For example, a sign stuck to the wall clock in one room reads "——ock." Shelves are labeled depending on their contents: "——uzzles," for example. The other room exhibits the same items but more of them. The classroom environment nonverbally continues to reinforce literacy training. Classroom walls are painted green, the floor is green tile, and the ceiling gray acoustic tile. Both second grade classrooms exhibit commercially produced and student-made displays pertaining to national holidays. Commercially produced posters are taped to the sides of each teacher's gray metal file cabinet, depicting Thanksgiving scenes similar to those in previous grades. One poster depicts an Anglo-American family in a living room watching television with a dining-room table, laden with food, prominent in the background. Students continue to be visually saturated with the images and symbols of the national culture.

Although the furniture arrangement varies slightly, each room exhibits the same basic floor plan (see Figure 6). The classrooms are packed densely with furniture. Students sit one to a desk (A_4). The shape of the classroom furniture and the pattern of furniture arrangement reinforce private rather than public spaces and an individual rather than a group work orientation. There is increasing physical distance between students while they are working, and the pattern of furniture placement inhibits student coaction. This classroom physical environment discourages random student movement. Students' desks (A_4) form three spatially distant clusters, and every student is associated with, and at most times is supposed to be in, a particular space at a particular time. Classroom spaces physically express status distinctions because students of similar reading ability are usually required to sit together. Access to the teacher's desk (A_1) is limited, and its spatial placement enhances the teacher's surveillance of the student area while physically manifesting status/age distinctions normative in the classroom society. Individual, work-oriented classroom furniture arrangements dominate the more collective, group-oriented furniture arrangements of the early grades. More second-grade student classroom time is spent at the A_4 than the A_3 tables. There is only one round interaction-enhancing activity table (A_3) in the classroom. Common-seating rectangular tables (A_3) are grouped together and spatially are distinct from individual-seating tables (A_4). The classroom spatial emphasis is on student independence rather than interdependence and physically reinforces the curriculum emphasis on competition rather than student coaction. The coactive-enhancing, group-oriented rug area common to previous classrooms is not present. Work begins verbally to dominate West Haven's curriculum, and second grade classroom environments nonverbally also emphasize work rather than play.

The low group of students is taught by an intense black female in her mid-twenties, who has taught at West Haven for four years. A graduate of the West Haven secondary school, she is one of several people in the school system who returned to the village to live and work. Her aide is a quiet, matronly white female in her mid-fifties. The high group of students is taught by a black female in her early fifties, exuding dignity and confidence, who has taught at West Haven for fourteen years. Her aide is a white female in her early fifties. Students are from six

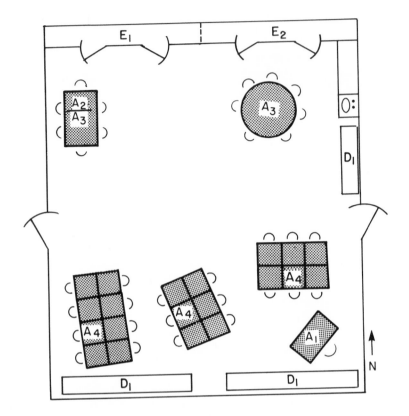

Figure 6. A Second Grade Classroom

Legend

A$_1$ = teacher's desk   C = chair
A$_2$ = teacher aide's desk   D$_1$ = bookcases/storage areas
A$_3$ = classroom activity desk   E$_1$ = teacher's closet
A$_4$ = student desk   E$_2$ = students' closet
                        ⊡ = sink

to eight years of age. The low group is composed of thirty-two students: six black males, four black females, two white males, and four white females in the morning group and four black males, nine black females, two white males, and one white female in the afternoon group. In the high group, there are twenty students: four white males, three white females, nine black females, and four black males.

A Low Classroom Session

Recurring adult supervision of entry procedures. Though primarily inhabited by children, schools are situations defined by adults.

Internal division of peer group: some work and some play. Different degrees of internalization of classroom social norms.

8:45 A.M. The aide is in the room straightening desks and arranging material for the day's activities.

As students enter the classroom, the aide oversees the removal of their outerwear. After removing their coats and boots, students take books from the shelves near the closet door. A group of students forms a small circle at one end of the room to play a game of jacks. Both males and females and blacks and whites are in the group.

Event Transition 1

Nonverbal control signal. Stimulus/response conditioning. National orientation.

Linear, sequential, and particulate conception of time. Right/wrong mastery. Individual accountability. Analogous reasoning.

Right/wrong mastery. Peer competition. Evaluation.

Requirement of proof/demonstration.

9:00 A.M. The teacher arrives, and when all the students have removed their coats, she claps her hands several times and tells them to take their seats. The class stands to recite the Pledge of Allegiance. When the students are seated, the teacher begins an activity using the large calendar on the wall. She asks a black male to go to the calendar to tell the class what letter is next to today's date. He gives her the correct letter. Then the teacher asks a white female, whose first name begins with the letter previously mentioned, to go to the calendar and ask another student to tell her what month it is, what day, what day it was yesterday, and what day it will be tomorrow. As he responds, she indicates to the teacher whether the chosen student is correct.

Satisfied with their responses, the teacher

randomly calls on students, asking other questions about the telling of time. Students leap out of their chairs, wave their hands at the teacher, and shout: "I know. . . I know!" Laughing, the teacher says if they keep jumping up like that they will go right through the ceiling! Her tone of voice, though, says they really should not behave that way. For several seconds students sheepishly look at the floor, but when a question is asked, they proceed as before.

Emphasis on self-restraint and control versus competition for the scarce reward of recognition and the permission to display knowledge.

The teacher comments on yesterday's work. She is pleased with the papers and praises the class as a whole before singling out, by name, the work of individual students with which she is especially pleased. She turns to a white female, half smiles, and says she is able to do such good work because "a certain boy" did not "bother" her that day. She smiles a knowing, coy grin. Both the teacher and the girl briefly cast their eyes down for a second and smile.

Evaluation on the basis of subjective rather than objective criteria. Pleasing the teacher. Emphasis on products. Differential public praise and reward reinforcing peer competition.

Sexuality approached indirectly and with discretion. Sex-role socialization.

9:20 A.M. The teacher begins a writing exercise involving the entire class. She asks a black female to go to the storage area, take out writing paper, and pass out several sheets to each student. While this is being done, a white female is asked to go to another room for a tape recorder. The student nods her head and leaves the room. In the back of the room, the aide previously has set out neat rows of pencils and crayons on a table. Without being told, students go and get a set. When they are seated, the teacher carefully stresses and enunciates directions for the assignment. The teacher then asks several students to tell her what she has just said. If they hesitate, she admonishes them to listen more carefully. Satisfied with their responses, she tells them not to

Literacy training.

Regularly-rotating administrative tasks = responsibility training. The precise distribution of scarce, valued materials. Significant status and responsibility attached to permitted mobility outside the classroom.

These low session students have fewer personal/private possessions than do the high students. Following orders and procedure. Demonstration/proof.

These comments rein-

force the denial of spontaneity. Obedience/compliance with procedure.
Obedience training. Modeling.
Emphasis on procedure and conformity.

Expected self-direction.

Recurring internal differentiation of the classroom peer group.
Responsibility for personal/private property.

These low session students retain emphasis on sharing and cooperation, thereby preserving the unity of the classroom peer group. Less internalization of several established classroom norms and values than in the high group.
Control by appeal to expected self-discipline.

We will continue to witness the pattern, across grade levels, of low sessions spending comparatively more time on behavior modification and adherence to established classroom values and norms.
Neatness. Emphasis on adherence to norms. Notice there is less accommodation here than in earlier classroom sessions. Mastery is expected.
Threat of physical violence and sanction of outside higher authority.

hurry, to write slowly, to take pride in their work, and to think before they write.

Before class the aide had written several sentences on the board for students to copy. The teacher tells them to place two fingers between their letters, for proper spacing, because they are not being careful enough with their spacing. She then says they can start work. The white female returns with the tape recorder.

9:35 A.M. The teacher and aide go to tables in the back of the room, and each calls out the names of specific students. These students take workbooks from their desks and go to the tables.

The noise level rises as individual group work begins. Students copying sentences from the board chat with one another. Clusters form at one edge of the class as students work together. The activity level rises. Mobility increases. There is a sudden cacophony of scuffling chairs, coughing, rustling of papers, and low mumbling. The teacher says it is too noisy and draws out her words as if implying a threat. The voice level drops, but the background and activity noise remain.

Before she starts her small group's lesson, the teacher turns to tell a white female to get to work. Glancing about the room, she quickly tells another white female, who is rapidly scribbling with her head on the paper, to work carefully and not to rush through her work. The startled student looks up. The teacher tells her, and the class as a whole, as her voice rises, that she will not accept any more sloppy work. If it is sloppy, it will have to be done over again. The white female does not respond quickly enough, and the teacher turns to face her, saying she had a long talk with the girl's father and that she has permission to use a paddle if she does not behave. The teacher loudly praises several students who are quietly sitting alone and doing their work, then casts a pouting glance around the room before turning back to her group.

Differential public praise. Autonomy.

The small groups work on word sounds. The teacher tells students to put their hands to their throats to learn how the sounds feel. A white male runs up to the teacher and tells her that a white female is bothering him while he is trying to work. The teacher pauses, pouts to convey her anger, then calls the offending female over to her table. The child is hesitant and stops about two meters from the teacher, her face cast down and her shoulders slumped. The teacher, conveying anger, evenly and calmly tells her to come closer. She repeats this request several times until the female is within half a meter of her. Directly in front of the student, almost face to face, the teacher tells the girl to look at her. The student tries but cannot, mumbles softly, and keeps her head bowed and eyes cast down. The teacher tells her to leave the student alone because he, stressing "he," is trying to do his work. Other students stop their work to watch the unfolding event. The teacher glares at the female. Neither says anything. Presently, the teacher angrily says, "Do you understand!" The girl nods her head, and the teacher tells her to return to her seat. The girl looks as if she is going to cry but goes back to her seat and sits motionless for several minutes. Then she goes back to copying work from the board.

Literacy training.

A core classroom norm is the primacy of individual task orientations. Public displays reinforce the importance of this classroom norm.
Nonverbal, spatial pattern of dominance/submission.

Submissive posture.

Nonverbal threat gesture.

Requires further submission.
Spatial confinement.
Autonomy and self-reliance. No peer support.
Composure under stress.

10:45 A.M. The main group of students increases its activity and noise levels. Students are talking loudly and getting up from their seats frequently. The teacher glares at them. A

Knowledge not its own reward. Lack of adherence to classroom norms and values.

Tattling dissuaded.
Emphasis on propriety
norm and following proce-
dure.
Indirect reprimand ap-
pealing to self-discipline.
Demonstration/proof.

Identification of self
with product. Guilt. Lack of
nurturing.
Public display rein-
forces adherence to norms.
No nurturing. Right/wrong
mastery.

Overt physical violence
is rare in the later grades; it
is supplanted by more latent
expressions of anger.

Tattling = peer compe-
tition for teacher approval
and rewards.
Lack of nurturing and
accommodation seen in earlier classrooms. Teacher emphasis on moral norm. Au-
tonomy and self-reliance.

white female comes up to the teacher and tells
her something another white female is doing
to her. Turning angrily on the girl, the teacher
says, "I'm talking to Beverly!" and to a black
male she says, "Terence, I can still hear your
mouth!" When a black female comes up to
show her work, the teacher sarcastically says,
"Karen, are you proud of this paper!" With
downcast eyes, Karen returns to her desk.

With disgust, the aide comments on the
sloppy work turned in by a white male. She
sarcastically corrects the shape, or nonshape,
of his letters. He is told to get another sheet
of paper and do it over.

Two white females have been arguing all
morning. One girl was rehanging her coat
when the other one systematically began
throwing coat hangers at her. Visibly angry,
the teacher goes to the closet and yells at the
offender to stop. The girl silently stands there
pouting while the other girl nonchalantly goes
back to her seat. Then the attacking girl quietly crawls into the closet and begins crying.
The teacher returns to her goup. A black male
runs up to her and points out the girl crying
in the closet. The teacher looks at him and
says, sarcastically, "That is all right, she should
be crying about what she has done." The boy
goes back to his seat. For several minutes, the
girl, Anna, cries in the closet. Few students
show the slightest interest in her plight. The
nonchalance is eerie. The student is still sob-
bing. Suddenly, the teacher, without turning
around, shouts that that is enough and that
Anna should get out of the closet and come
over to her desk. Drying her eyes, Anna
slowly walks over to the teacher. Anna's head
is downcast, and she does not say a word. Few
students look up as she crosses the room. She

stops three feet from the teacher. The teacher tells her to come closer. Rhetorically, the teacher asks her what the problem is. She says that she has been bothering her sister all morning. As she talks to Anna, the teacher's voice grows softer and softer. She lowers her head and tries to look at the girl. The students silently watch. The room is silent. The teacher asks Anna how she would like it if she were treated the way she treats her sister. Anna begins to sob silently but painfully. The teacher pauses and says that she *should* feel bad about her behavior and that she should apologize to her sister and then go to the bathroom to wash her face. The teacher speaks gently now and half embraces Anna. She pushes back Anna's long hair to see her face. She asks, "OK?" Anna nods her head, turns, and approaches her sister. Standing three feet away, Anna passionately says she is sorry. The pleading, distraught tone in her voice says she is apologizing for other things as well. Her sister acts as though she is not there, slowly gets up, and walks past her to the pencil sharpener. Anna breaks into hysterical sobs and runs from the room. No one looks at her, as her sister nonchalantly returns to her seat. Sometime later, Anna returns to the room. She is composed, as if nothing has happened. Anna sits down in her seat, next to her sister, and goes back to work. Students turn away and go back to their work. Neither Anna nor her sister speaks to the other for the rest of the day.

Recurring dominance/submission pattern important to the reestablishment of teacher authority and customary classroom norms and values. The exchange is made public as a lesson to others. There is no privacy in the classroom, and intimate matters are made public. Moral instruction (empathy/solicitude for others). Manipulation of guilt. Required suffering as necessary for rectifying moral transgressions.

Required submission. Cleanliness and neatness.

Giving and withdrawal of affection as mechanisms for reinforcement of classroom norms and values.

Students must internalize autonomy, self-reliance, self-control of emotions, and composure under stress.

11:00 A.M. The teacher dismisses her small group and tells the class to get ready for lunch. The aide dismisses her group. There is a burst of energy and a flurry of activity. Stu-

Event Transition 2

Expected self-maintenance.

Products. Proof/demonstration. Evaluation.

Waiting. At-attention posture is a sign of self-control and discipline. Adult monitoring and evaluation. Passing inspection. Cleanliness. Regimentation.

Reinforcement of literacy. Ranking and differential rewards.

Public ridicule. Lack of accommodation. Spontaneous peer support or aid is not sanctioned. Emphasis on autonomy and individual accountability. Sexual segregation. Waiting. Signaling self-control. Continuing regimentation.

Increasing instances of segregation. Internal classroom divisions by sex. Spatial segregation and ritual avoidance. Waiting. Ranking. Competition. Sexual segregation. Adult monitoring. Order. Regimentation.

dents put their work in a wire basket labeled "morning" on the aide's desk, return to their seats, sit quietly with their heads resting on their folded arms, and watch others in the room. When they are all seated, the teacher stands at the side of the room briefly scanning them. Satisfied with their behavior and quietness, she tells them to line up to wash their hands. She calls out letters, emphasizing the sound of each. Students whose first names begin with the letter she calls out wash their hands first, if they recognize the sound of the letter. A black female briefly rises from her chair, appears confused, looks at the teacher, who does not say anything, then sits back down. She seesaws like this several times until the aide and teacher begin laughing at her movements. A neighboring black male tries to whisper to her, and the teacher loudly tells him not to help her if she does not even know the sound of her own name. Everyone finally is in line; the males are toward the rear of the line, and the females are toward the front. Students fold their arms over their chests while waiting in line. They go to the hall door and form another line after washing their hands. Again, they fold their arms over their chests. Several students bring lunches from home, and at this point they freely get them from the closet. The closet is divided by sex; females have their belongings on the left side, males on the right. When everyone is standing by the door, the aide draws two numbers from a cup full of paper to determine which group will leave first. The females draw the higher number, and they whoop and cheer. The aide leads the students to the lunchroom. They march single file inside the yellow line on the floor.

11:15 A.M. Lunch period. Recess.

11:45 A.M. Returning from the lunch-room in an energetic line, students burst into the room and go to the closet to put on their coats. They are going to recess, then to another teacher's room in the afternoon. The teacher does not get up, and students put their clothing on by themselves.

12:05 P.M. The afternoon class comes into the room. They were in another second grade classroom this morning and are breathless with energy and excitement after recess. The activity, mobility, and noise levels are high. The teacher goes to the front of the room and tells them to settle down. She tells them to begin their afternoon assignments, and everyone begins working without further direction. Presently, the aide asks four students to take workbooks from their desks and go to her small table. A white male runs up to the teacher and says very loudly and excitedly that he saw several big boys smoking while he was in the bathroom. He beams, as if expecting a reward. The teacher frowns and glances at the aide, who, giving an "I know" glance back, gets up and leaves the room. Shortly, the aide returns saying she found two male teachers to go into the bathroom, where they found two students from the high school smoking.

The activity and voice levels are high. The teacher says that if they cannot be quiet, they will have to put their heads down. Knowing they are not quiet enough, the students put their heads down. When they quiet down, the teacher says they can lift up their heads. The class immediately obeys.

Event Transition 3

Permitted mobility within the school building and more complex sequential scheduling.

Increase in expected self-direction and internalization of procedures.

Event Transition 4

Differential student grouping and ranking expressed in time and through space.

Authority positioning reinforcing right to control.

Fragmented, sequential experiences. Self-maintenance.

Private property. Responsibility training. Tattling.

Schools are organized around age grades kept apart spatially. Spatial rites of passage ("progress") associated with age as well as ability.

Sex segregation expressed in classroom toilet norms.

Control by threat of cessation of activity. Required submission posture. A message is that the teacher still has control over their bodies. Obedience/compliance.

Personalization of property.
No nurturing. Emphasis on self-reliance and expected self-maintenance at this grade/age level.

Problem-solving.

Primacy of work. Task orientation.

The aide tells a black female not to take an eraser from the teacher's desk. Students frequently ask either the teacher or the aide how to spell a word, and they are told they should already know how to spell that particular word.

1:10 P.M. The teacher and the aide are working with their small groups. The teacher writes several words on the board that students have to put into sentences. The voice and activity levels in the main group increase. Increasing mobility seems to be tolerated, and the teacher intervenes only when students are not doing their work.

Event Transition 5

Readiness, a transitional stage between major events.
Sex-role accoutrements.
Regimentation. Adult monitoring.

1:45 P.M. The teacher dismisses her group and tells the class to get ready for art. The aide dismisses her group. She tells several females to leave their purses in their desks because they cannot take them to art class. The students line up by the door, and the aide takes them to art class.

Event Transition 6

Adherence to/internalization of established classroom norms and values.

Products requiring evaluation. Differential grouping.

Mastery is required. Lack of toleration of mistakes. It is assumed, at this point, that children ought to have internalized classroom procedures.

2:45 P.M. The students are very orderly and quiet in returning from art class. They file into the room, immediately go to their seats, take out materials, and begin working on their assignments. Voice and activity levels are low. As they finish their work, students get up to put the papers in a wire basket on the aide's desk labeled "afternoon."

The teacher and aide are checking student work. A white female has worked page two of her workbook instead of page three, the assigned page. Visibly angry, the teacher calls the girl over to her and sternly tells her that she did not listen to the directions and did not pay attention when the assignments and workbook page numbers were written on the board. She tells the girl to erase all of page two and to sit down and do page three. Sarcastically and angrily, she dismisses her by saying she did the page wrong anyway!

Right/wrong mastery. Emphasis on finishing/completing. Ridicule. No tolerance.

Most of the students have finished their work and are wandering around the room looking at some of the posters and other materials. A few sit quietly at their desks watching others. A few form small groups and talk in low voices. The mobility and low voice levels seem permitted; the teacher intervenes only when a student interrupts the work of another or talks too loudly. When they finish their work, students are expected to wait until the others finish. This continues for about forty-five minutes.

It is work that is important. Children are permitted more spontaneity before and after work; a form of play rewarding finishing/mastering work.

Waiting. Self-control. More time is spent waiting than in the high sessions.

Event Transition 7

3:30 P.M. The teacher tells the students to finish putting away their work. When the teacher and aide dismiss their small groups, there is a general flurry of activity as the students clear their desks, then sit down to wait until others finish. They hurry to see who can straighten up first. By name, quietest students first, the teacher calls them to put their crayons on the rear table, get their coats, and put their chairs on the desk. Finally, they go to line up by the hall door. The teacher emphatically tells them in a loud voice again to be sure their crayons are on the desk. In front of the students the teacher tells the aide to check their pockets and watch them closely. She tells the observer that they pick out the best crayons and take them home.

Expected self-maintenance.

Order and neatness. Waiting. Self-control. Competition. Ranking.

Ranking. Differential reward to reinforce adherence to classroom norms. Order. Regimentation.

Public ridicule. Personal search as a violation of private space/personal integrity. Demonstration of authority and power.

A white male balks at the teacher's procedures and arrogantly says he has something to

Stress on higher status; teacher expects deference.

Autonomy. Deference by others indicates high status. Attempt to activate ranking norm.
Compliance/obedience.

do after school, that his mother is coming to pick him up, and that he does not want to wait in line. The teacher tells him pointedly that he has to do what everybody else who rode the bus to school has to do. He gets back in line.

No messages are pinned to students' coats. Responsibility is expected/assumed at this age/grade level.

The aide gives several students notes to take home, then the teacher takes them down the hall and sees them to the bus. They walk single file inside the yellow line on the hallway floor. The aide remains in the room arranging stray desks and putting away instructional materials.

A High Classroom Session

Recurring adult monitoring. High degree of self-maintenance and internalization of procedure. These student behaviors show adherence to/internalization of established classroom norms and values.

8:45 A.M. The teacher's aide prepares for the day's activities. Students arrive in small clumps and clusters. Coats are hung up, and boots are stacked in the closet. Near the hall door, several large piles of well-worn magazines and readers are stacked on a long table. As they come in, most of the females take a book from this table without being told to do so. In the left front corner of the room there is a small table holding a phonograph and other equipment. Several males, both black and white, begin using these materials. Other males form cross-color conversational groups. All the females are seated and reading. The students are comparatively quiet and orderly. The aide has yet to issue any directions to the class.

Differential student grouping and activities by sex. Girls consistently show more adherence to classroom norms and values than boys. Male manipulation of machine technology (sex-role stereotyping).

Self-selected student spatial segregation by sex and color. Increasing internal division of the student peer group.
Spatial clustering and isolation of black males.

Student seating is patterned by sex and by color. There are two clusters of males: one in the front of the room near the audio equipment, the other in the rear rows of the classroom. Females are in the rest of the room. The three black males who earlier clustered in the front of the room have been placed in each corner of the room. An older-appearing black male sits at an isolated desk, apart from the other students, and is the only student in class to put his feet up on the desk. He is not doing any work but only watching the others. He appears restless and frequently stands up by his chair and makes furtive efforts to walk around the room or to go over to the main group. The aide frequently tells him to sit down. There are three pairs of black and white females sitting next to one another engaging in a high degree of verbal and nonverbal interaction, interaction not seen among the males. When white and black males sit together, there is always more space between them than among the females.

This pattern is repeated in other classrooms.

Sign of defiance indicating nonadherence to order norm, showing control over his own body. Containment.

Attempt to exercise control over body/movements.

Differences in interaction patterns by color and by sex are signs of internal subgrouping. Male autonomy and consistently less interaction than among females.

Event Transition 1

Authority positioning.

9:00 A.M. The teacher goes to the front of the room to call the class to attention, and students move automatically to put up their reading materials. Students stand for the Pledge of Allegiance. When everyone is seated, the teacher asks students, individually and by name, to relate what they did over the weekend. A black female shyly talks about her weekend trip to Midville. Her voice and eyes light up as she begins to describe an incident when her cousins got into a fight and started throwing bricks at each other. The teacher and aide quickly break in, say that was nice, and move on. A white male talks about his experiences at a cub scout meeting. One black male excitedly tells of his trip to Midville to see the film *The Trial of Billy Jack*. He wants to tell about the karate, kung fu, and fighting and starts to rise out of his seat in excitement as he

Self-maintenance. Ritual of national allegiance.

Show-and-tell illustrates lack of student privacy. Public display of personal incidents.

Lack of emphasis on overt physical violence, but latent violence and aggression are normative.

Students are mentioning towns near West Haven; status of mobility outside West Haven. The mass media as a socialization influence.

mimics the movements and yells from the movie. Again, the teacher gently stops him.

Students are speaking in extremely low and hesitant voices, and the teacher frequently interrupts to tell them to speak up. After a while, in desperation, the teacher asks them to stand up so others might hear better. Standing up has the opposite effect, and most students seem to become even more shy and hesitant.

9:15 A.M. The teacher begins a new activity. On the board the aide has written a series of declarative sentences, each with a word omitted. To the right of each sentence are written three substitute words from which the class is to pick the one that best completes the sentence. When they finish the board work they have to write a short story about anything they did over the weekend. Several students ask the aide if they can go to the bathroom (see Figure 2). They leave the room one at a time. Each returning student calls the next one to go. Students leave their seats without permission to sharpen their pencils, wash their hands, get second sheets of paper, or take crayons from the center table. In most cases, they are quiet and immediately return to their seats.

9:20 A.M. A small, screened-off table is placed near the front of the room. Presently, the teacher calls out four students by name who take out workbooks and troop to the table. The teacher tells them to work on sounds and syllables.

10:00 A.M. The aide calls four boys to a screened-off area in the opposite corner of the room. She asks them questions about the illustrations in their reader. The noise, activity, and voice levels are very low; there is a persis-

---

Marginal notes:

Public performance subjected to peer competition as well as to teacher evaluation. No clear rewards.

Problem-solving.

Literacy training. Emphasis on creativity and imagination but always secondary.
Permission requesting = deference to authority. Permitted mobility outside the classroom. Expected self-control. Responsibility training. Behaviors illustrating student adherence to established classroom norms.

Recurring spatial subdivision/isolation of the peer group.
Personal responsibility for private property.
Literacy training.

Required demonstration/proof of knowledge. Public classroom display. This "noise" (Henry

tent background noise of rustling papers and bodies, occasional coughs, and the scraping of chairs. Students push their chairs in place under their desks every time they get up. There is a very low level of talking among the students as they practice saying words to themselves.

Several students complete their board work. As they finish they get up, fold their papers in half, and neatly place them in a pile on the teacher's desk. Two white males drift over to the teacher's small group, lean over the divider, and watch. The teacher tells them to go back to work. They do.

The teacher drills her group on word sounds and the recognition of syllables. As students respond, she verbally and nonverbally praises them. She does not praise merely for responding but only when a correct answer is given. To engender acceptable responses, the teacher scolds and pressures the students. In correcting student responses, she leans close to them and looks at them directly, demanding an answer. The students fidget and move away from her by leaning back in their chairs. While the teacher is seeking answers from certain students, others pressure her to let them answer. If she calls on a student and he or she hesitates in the slightest, a clump of hands appears from nowhere and twitches in the air for the teacher's attention. Unless the teacher calls on a specific student or otherwise demands a specific answer from someone, the class tends to shout out the answer in unison. The teacher admonishes them to "do their own work."

10:30 A.M. The majority of the students are drawing pictures to accompany their stories. The teacher gives little direction to the

1963) is information about the norm of task orientation.

The pattern is for high sessions to comply better with norms such as neatness, order, and quiet than do low groups.

Internalization of classroom procedure norm. Products.

Task orientation is reinforced. Ready compliance.

Literacy training.

Differential, public teacher approval reinforcing mastery and "rightness."

This incident illustrates conditioning for composure under stress. Value of control over body and emotions. Individual accountability.

Peer competition and aggression are formalized. Only one person can be acknowledged. "Right" knowledge has to be demonstrated.

Emphasis on autonomy and individual responsibility.

Self-maintenance and

control. Responsibility training.

Adherence to classroom norms.

Right responses mastery. Hint of withdrawal of teacher approval and affection as motivation.

Obedience/compliance.

Finishing and mastery. Expected self-discipline. Responsibility training. Products. Proof.

Administrative interruptions without deferential permission requesting shows more inclusive authority. Student exposure to concepts of ranking and hierarchy.
Waiting. Self-control.

various activities taking place, and the class is left on its own. The teacher and aide attend to their small groups. The room is orderly and quiet.

The teacher tells several members of her group that they will have to go over their previous work to correct mistakes. She berates them to listen to her directions. Then she helps them find the specific mistakes they made. Without objection or balking, students do as they are told.

11:05 A.M. The teacher dismisses her group, telling them to finish the correction work on their own. Turning to the class as a whole, she tells them to put away their materials and to turn in their assignments.

At this point and without knocking, a secretary from the principal's office walks into the room. She walks up to the teacher, hands her a note, smiles, then walks out. This sudden interruption has no effect on the students. No one turns around or appears startled. Students sit quietly in their seats, their heads resting on their folded arms, waiting for the teacher while she reads the notice and chats with the aide. The room is extremely quiet.

Event Transition 2

Cleanliness. Regimentation. Waiting. Self-control.

Regimentation. Adult monitoring.

11:10 A.M. The teacher calls out for students to wash their hands for lunch. She dismisses them by rows and from front to back to get in line by the counter. With arms folded across their chests, they quietly stand in line. After washing and drying their hands, students get in line by the hall door, and the aide leads them down the hall to the lunchroom (see Figure 2).

Event Transition 3

11:15 A.M. Lunch period recess.

11:35 A.M. In a ragged line students straggle in from the lunchroom, go to the closets and put on their outerwear, then get in a line by the door in preparation for recess. The line is quiet and orderly. When the aide comes in, she puts on her coat and takes them to the playground.

Self-maintenance.
Student adherence to classroom norms and procedures. Self-regimentation. Waiting.
Play spatially separate from classroom work.

Event Transition 4

12:00 P.M. Students straggle in from the playground. They toss their coats into the closet, and the teacher tells them several times to hang them properly. They do. A white female runs up to the teacher telling her something that happened on the playground. Rather ruefully, the teacher says that the matter should not concern her and should be resolved by the people involved. Her snappish manner conveys her annoyance at the girl's behavior.

Neatness and order classroom norms are reinforced. Compliance/obedience.
Another instance of tattling = approval seeking and peer competition.
Emphasis on self-reliance and autonomy. The teacher does not understand the classroom function of tattling.

Event Transition 5

Many students stand in the middle of the room watching the others come in. The teacher snaps her fingers, and they all scurry to their seats. Without further comment or direction, students take work from their desks. Many work on assignments previously begun. Once their morning work is finished, they are free to pursue activities of their own choosing.

Control by nonverbal signal. Compliance/obedience. Self-direction. Finishing and mastery.
Play as a reward for finishing work.

12:05 P.M. The teacher and aide leave the room on an errand. As the teacher and aide leave, the door is left slightly ajar. Older students from high school are passing down the hall to the lunchroom, and they are noisy. None of the students seem distracted. Those finished with their work begin playing with the few toys and games in the room. Most are actually learning games of one sort or another.

Here, for the first time, we see instances of students not monitored by adults. Trust and responsibility are implied. Compliance with established norms mostly occur in the high sessions.
Increasing environmental emphasis on work. Problem-solving games.

Spatial separation of work and play. Right/wrong mastery.

Emphasis on age/grade-related performance expectations. Lack of nurturing and accommodation seen in early classroom sessions.
Right/wrong mastery.

Puzzles are prominent. The teacher refers to these as "quiet" toys. All these materials and related activities are confined to one corner of the room.

12:10 P.M. The teacher and aide return. Several students come up to ask for comments about their work. One black female is dismissed sharply. The teacher says, "You ought to be able to count your syllables by now!" The teacher checks the morning work and hands back papers with mistakes to be corrected.

Event Transition 6

Compliance/obedience. Mathematics training.
Autonomy. Individual accountability. Adherence to classroom norms and values.

Right/wrong mastery. Emphasis on rote procedure. Following orders. No explanation given.
Rotating responsibility and leadership training. Problem-solving.
Demonstration/proof. Following model. Rote teaching and learning. Conformity to procedure.

12:35 P.M. The teacher tells students to put up the puzzles and games and to take their seats. They immediately do so. They are told to take out their math workbooks and to put their names on the worksheets. The class is very quiet and orderly. The teacher works with the group as a whole, and she stresses that they should be careful to put down the correct mathematical sign and not put a division sign where they would want to add. She adds that "all these little things are important." After these preliminaries a student is chosen to read one of the problems in the workbooks. The teacher asks what kind of problem is involved: multiplication or division. Satisfied with their response, the teacher proceeds to work the problem on the board while students follow along in their books. Sometimes the teacher pauses to ask a procedural question, and the class responds in unison. She asks the students, again, if they know what they are supposed to do. They do. Satisfied that they understand the procedure, the teacher tells them to work the remaining problems themselves. As they begin working,

Self-maintenance. Responsibility training.

the teacher and aide walk between the desks, peering at student worksheets. Corrections are made immediately. The teacher stresses the proper sequence for working the problems, for example, not putting the minus or plus sign before writing the number. When students make mistakes, the teacher tells them to be more careful and follow directions. A white male is told to read his problems more carefully, not to rush, and to read with the punctuation. Others are told to do their own work and not to worry about what someone else is doing.

Right/wrong mastery. Conformity to procedure.

Obedience training.

Autonomy. Individual responsibility for work.

The teacher pauses occasionally to look at a student's work in order to illustrate a point to the whole class. She might ask if anyone knows how to do a particularly troublesome problem. Hands shoot up. If a student is called upon and hesitates in the slightest, the others wiggle their hands to get the teacher's attention. The teacher encourages students to work through the problems, and she ignores the wiggling hands.

Public exposure of individual mistakes. Reinforcement of peer competition. Right/wrong mastery.
Competition to display knowledge. Procedure.
Autonomy and individual accountability. Mastery.

Students are berated and loudly scolded for not following directions, especially if the teacher provided an example of how to solve a particular problem. The teacher often asks them to make sure to keep their numbers *under* each other. They must write slowly and carefully as well as do their own work.

Internalization of procedure is expected. Adherence to norms. Right/wrong mastery.
Following procedure. Order. Autonomy.

1:15 P.M. The teacher tells the students to put away their math work and to take out their spelling books. In so doing she says, "Let's see if we can be good spellers today." When the students are ready, the teacher gives them two words to write in their workbooks. She says a word, pauses, says it again, pauses, uses it in a sentence, pauses, then tells them to write it down.

Expected self-maintenance. Pleasing the teacher.

Literacy training. Problem-solving.

Right/wrong mastery.

Spontaneous coaction. Emphasis on autonomy. Obedience/compliance. Authority positioning. Responsibility training.

Monitoring and evaluation. Right/wrong mastery. Differential praise. Public evaluation as motivation. Peer competition.

Event Transition 7

Required observance of national celebrations reinforced by the sharing of food.

Bias toward females. Responsibility training. Permitted mobility outside the classroom is status enhancing. Peer competition by sex. Public ridicule of the males. Further division of peer group by sex and color.

Control by power of spatial confinement. Obedience.

Place/activity coordination.

Continuing association of particular foods with ritualized events.

Self-selected internal division of the student peer group by sex.

Stereotypic sex-role socialization.

After giving them the words, the teacher walks around the room looking at their responses. She notices a black male looking at a neighbor's paper and sharply tells him to turn around and do his own work. He does. She returns to the front of the room and tells them to correct their work. They correct their own papers, and the teacher spells out the answers. While so doing, she walks between the desks looking at their papers. If she notices students with several mistakes, she loudly berates them for not paying attention. The teacher loudly praises those students who do well.

1:35 P.M. Students put away their papers. The class is planning a pre-Thanksgiving meal to be eaten later this week, and it is time to prepare some of the food. The teacher scans the room and picks out four female students to go to the lunchroom to get utensils. Several boys vocalize their displeasure at not being selected. The teacher tells a black male that he and his "buddy" cannot be trusted together *in* class. There are snickers and laughs. While the girls are getting the utensils, the aide says they should wash their hands before handling the food. The noise and mobility levels increase. As they become boisterous, the aide tells them to sit down and be quiet. They do.

The teacher and aide walk to the long activity table in the rear of the room from which they take out several bags of large apples. Students divide themselves into groups that will work on food preparation and those that will not. Those who will handle the food again wash their hands. A group of males, both black and white, begin playing among themselves. The students, primarily female, clustered around the table at the rear of the room are given knives with which to peel the apples. At this point, the teacher and some of the students ask the observer if he would like to join them. Other than the observer, there are no males at the table. Throughout this activity, no boys volunteer to help with the food preparation or are called upon to do so. The teacher, aide, and observer spend considerable time demonstrating how to peel an apple to slice off the skin rather than cut chunks from it. This proves to be a difficult task, and the large dish is quickly filled with the gouged remains of their work. The aide puts the apples on a hot plate, brought from the lunchroom, and shows the girls how to boil them. "Stir constantly," she says, "and don't let the food get too hot." The girls say very little and are attentive in doing everything they are told.

Segregation by sex. Primary female manipulation of food. Activity/skill basis for sex-role stereotyping. Differential distribution of knowledge by sex.

Acceptance of trial-and-error mistakes marks the activity as play.

Routine task orientation and compliance. Following a model.

Event Transition 8

2:00 P.M. The teacher tells the students to get ready for recess. They take their seats. The aide tells the girls they must wash their hands after handling food. Forming a line, they do so. When everyone is seated, the teacher dismisses them, by tables, to get their coats, line up by the door, and follow the aide to the playground.

Expected self-maintenance. At-attention positioning. Cleanliness. Procedure. Regimentation. Ranking. Regimentation and linearity. Adult monitoring.

2:10 P.M. Recess.

Event Transition 9

2:40 P.M. The students return from recess. Several black females tussle as they take off their coats, and one runs up to the teacher and tells her that another female is bothering her. The girl in question quickly retorts that she did not do anything. The teacher sighs, droops her shoulders, and tells all of them that they have to look after their *own* behavior and

Spatial separation of work and play.

Tattling = peer competition.

Reinforcement of norm of expected self-reliance and individual accountability.

Order as prerequisite to other classroom activity. Compliance/obedience.

not blame others. She then tells them to take their seats because they have to be quiet before they can do anything else. They take their seats.

Event Transition 10

Status distinctions spatially expressed.
Self-selected spatial segregation by sex.
Spatial isolation of different status groups. Differential learning events.

Continual orientation to national legends and mythology.
This student violates the basic rule of not interrupting work.

Spatial confinement/isolation from the group as punishment. Compliance. Nonverbal threat gesture.

Continuing classroom emphasis on time.
Continuing lack of nurturing and accommodation. Age/grade expectations.

Females are permitted mobility. Differential grouping by sex.
Cleanliness.

2:45 P.M. While the aide looks after the boiling apples, the teacher prepares to read the students a story. She tells them to sit on the floor in front of her chair. All the males sit together at the sides and back of the semicircle, while the females clump together in the front. The black male isolated from the class sits at his desk working a puzzle.

The story is about the Pilgrims and Thanksgiving. Students sit at the teacher's feet, mouths open, staring up at the illustrations. Now, several students turn around to watch the isolated black male, who is being noisy. The teacher stops the story, turns around, and sharply tells the boy to put away the puzzle and take his regular seat. He pouts but obeys her. She glares at him until he is seated. The teacher again starts to read. At the end of the story, the students smile and clap their hands.

In response to a question from a student, the teacher reviews material on how to tell time. She says, "I'm not going to have any of this big hand and little hand talk. Tell me what time it is!"

The aide is tending the apples, and several white females get up and go over to the counter area. They ask to help with the stirring. The aide shows them how to stir and how to hold the pan and admonishes them not to get hair in the food. The teacher asks the class if anyone can bring in several potatoes tomorrow. There are several volunteers.

At this point, several black males become boisterous. They are playing and rolling around the floor. The teacher tells them to go to their seats and to put their heads down on their desks. They do so.

Differential behaviors by black males as a subgroup. Control by spatial confinement and isolation.
Deference and submission.

Event Transition 11

3:20 P.M. The teacher stands up and tells the students to get their coats and take them to their seats. There is a flurry of activity without any running, shouting, or shoving. When they are dressed and seated, the teacher stands in front of the room and calls students, quietest first, to line up by the door. They put their chairs upside down on top of their desks before leaving. On the way out the door, students say good-bye and wave to the aide, who smiles and says good-bye.

Authority positioning.

Adherence to classroom norms. Self-control. At-attention positioning. Regimentation. Waiting. Ranking.

Separation gestures illustrating emotional closeness are more common in high than in low sessions.

3:25 P.M. The teacher stands by the door waiting for the lower grades to pass. When it is their turn, she takes the students to the bus and everyone walks single file inside the yellow line on the hall floor. At the building door, students wave good-bye and smile at the teacher, and the teacher smiles and waves back at them. The aide remains in the classroom arranging chairs and picking up scraps of paper from the floor.

Waiting. Ranked, hierarchical organization. Regimentation. Separation gestures.
Recurring task ranking and divisions of labor. Housekeeping tasks emphasizing neatness and order.

The classroom sociocultural system of the lower grades is more intricate and more diverse than that of preschool and kindergarten; students are faced with greater demands from the teacher. Accommodation, leisure, nurturing, and other *in loco parentis* behaviors are deemphasized; there are increased teacher expectations for student peer competition (1/7) and self-maintenance (4/5).*

The second grade sessions continue the work orientation and activi-

*These paired numbers refer to features of low/high sessions summarized in Figure C-4, Appendix C.

ties emerging in the first grade sessions. The following associated features frequently occur: student compliance with and obedience (14/1) to the teacher's directions, expected student mastery (2/3) of literacy tasks, incessant teacher evaluation (16/24) of student written materials (24/19), and increasing student competition for the teacher's attention. There is a simultaneous demise, on the other hand, of previously frequently occurring features such as time socialization (72/81), permitted spontaneity (70/79), and the emphasis on toilet rituals (73/–). By the second grade, the teacher assumes the internalization of these basic classroom norms and values (9/2). Students, perceiving the reward structure of the classroom culture, behave in a way that indicates their realization that little is to be gained through continued sharing (67/78) and cooperation (56/–), but everything is to be gained through peer competition (1/7).

The high and low sessions are similar in a number of respects. Art and story time, for example, rotate among groups of second grade students. Both sessions spend approximately the same amount of time on work-related activities. Comparing low sessions for the first grade (Figure C-3, Appendix C) and the second grade (Figure C-4, Appendix C) shows increasing classroom emphasis on the following: peer competition (27/1), expected student mastery of tasks (61/2), student compliance with and obedience to (28/14) teacher directives, and student self-denial of spontaneity (44/18).

An important work-related development occurs in both high and low sessions during the second grade. A sociocultural distinction between work and play (Arensburg and Niehoff 1964; Benedict 1938; Jackson 1968:31–33) is evident. In the early grades, play occurs inside the school and is confined to specific (rug) areas in the classrooms. Progressively, these inside play areas are deemphasized spatially until they gradually disappear. Toys are replaced by learning games, and play moves outside the building to the playground. From this point on, play is not supposed to take place inside the classroom. The classroom becomes the exclusive work segment of the education complex, and there is a specific time and place for the pattern of activity termed play. By way of analogy, in any given office building there are specific spaces in which one is expected to work, and one is dismissed from these places at designated times in order to relax in other spaces. Conditioning to the classroom distinction between work and play also is conditioning to an analogous pattern common in the wider society and culture outside the

school. The classroom culture indirectly teaches students that education/
work is not to be overly enjoyed. If education/work is enjoyed too much,
it becomes play. The rampant spontaneity and careless enjoyment witnessed on public school playgrounds rarely are seen in public school
classrooms. In the classroom, work coalesces around activities students
are required to perform for the teacher; their bodies, labor, and time are
under the direction of another person. Education/work is autocratic and
goal-directed. Play, on the other hand, involves activities students generate and do for themselves. Play and leisure time, personal time, often are
one of the predictable rewards for dutiful work both in the classroom
and in the wider society.

Most of the work-related classroom behaviors, ideas, and physical
features emerging at this grade level are associated with literacy training (24/19), even though the narratives show the occurrence of other
methods of expression such as nonverbal gestures and oral discourse.
Literacy is associated with the historical development of the state (Fried
1967:238–39), and the classroom emphasis on literacy training is yet
another indication of West Haven's high level of participation in national networks. Although many of their parents remain functionally
illiterate, elementary school children at West Haven must learn to read
and write. Literacy training through required public schooling is an
important vehicle through which national culture (Cohen 1970:71) is
disseminated to children. Literacy regulates the flow of production in
the classroom and serves as a frame of reference for a considerable
amount of student activity. There are economic aspects to the classroom
as a small society, and classrooms can be compared with respect to their
mode of production, distribution, and consumption of goods and services. The way of life of the lower grades is concerned especially with
the organization of student labor for making specific products. Productive resources are under the control of, and usually distributed by, the
teacher. Classroom tools and technologies, the means of production, are
provided through state funds.

Marshall McLuhan (1964:155–62) finds significant sociocultural
orientations associated with literacy. Reading and writing the printed
word condition for a lineal, sequential orientation toward the world.
Children at West Haven, by way of analogy, learn to read and write while
seated alone at separate desks. Like the segmented letters that form the
segmented words that form the segmented sentences that form the segmented paragraphs that form the individual stories on which the stu-

dents work, reading and writing are autonomous acts. The portability of the book and the pen make it possible for a child to read and write in isolation. Literacy alters time and space and permits participation in realms not immediately accessible otherwise. Literacy reinforces individualism (Mead 1971:68–70) and makes it possible to experience the world indirectly. Literacy conditions people for a particular orientation toward themselves as well as toward the world and plays upon parts of the body different from those stressed by nonliterate modes of expression and communication. Literacy training reinforces order, control, and physical coordination and conditions for an emphasis on the eye over other sense organs. The narratives show that learning to write "correctly" involves the precise rote copying of a model without spontaneity or interpretation. Precise hand-eye coordination and muscle control are required. Edmund Carpenter (Carpenter, Varley, and Flaherty 1959) tells us that because their primary methods of communication and expression are oral and aural, the ear is the sense organ emphasized in traditional Inuit culture. The ear, says McLuhan (1964:81–90), is associated with dance, music, and oral modes of communication primarily relied on for sociocultural conditioning by preliterate people.

School constitutents believe, correctly I think, that literacy is one of the primary weapons students must possess to secure later access to and effective participation in the national society and culture. At West Haven the acquisition and demonstration of literacy skills quickly become the basis on which student competence, rank, and prestige are defined. The narratives show, though, that the organization of customary classroom life sometimes impedes the equitable transmission to and acquisition of literacy skills among students (McDermott 1974; Ogbu 1979). Differences in the amount of time devoted to literacy training, for instance, continue to distinguish low and high sessions.

The social and cultural way of life of the lower grades centers on reinforcement of the rules and routines associated with the specialized, nearly full-time occupation of being a student. Being a student at West Haven Elementary School invariably is associated with work, literacy, and growing to adopt the classroom culture and society as one's own.

5
The Middle
and Upper
Grades
Differential Student
Experiences

*There must be in society hewers
of wood and drawers of water.
If all are good penmen, where
are those who will contentedly
live through a life of toil?*

Thomas Ruggles,
History of the Poor

THIRD GRADE: SORTING AND GROUPING

Third grade is organized around nine-week subject periods. Each
student takes physical education three times a week and art twice a week,
and music alternates between these marking periods. Students doing
remedial work, from either the high or low group, attend the mathematics laboratory located in the main building, while the others have math
sessions in their regular classrooms. Thus the spatial placement of the
math lab (see Figure 2) helps stigmatize it as a place for slow learners.
Low group students do not take music or physical education; instead,
the math lab is substituted, and they go to art only once a week. West
Haven increasingly is presenting different categories of knowledge and
sorts of information to different groups of children in different physical
spaces.

Third and fourth grade class sessions are held in converted mobile
homes (see Figure 2). These rooms are intended to be functional and
give the impression of a basement workshop; they lack the toys, decorations, and other visual materials prominent in early grade classrooms.
Middle grade classroom environments are oriented toward efficiency and
reflect the curricular focus on work. Students are not here for their own
pleasure or to be entertained. Rooms are paneled with wood, and the
ceilings are covered with gray acoustic tile. A row of casement windows
is set between the hall doors. Lavatories are partitioned off inside each

room. In the first room that was observed, tie-dyed curtains, made by the teacher, cover the lower half of the windows. In the second (high) classroom, roll-down window shades have file cards taped to them indicating "Magic Words": "I'm Sorry," "Please," "Good Morning," "I Love You," "Excuse Me," and "Thank You." In each room, there are two blackboards on the shorter side walls; above each is the familiar upper- and lowercase alphabet series. A display entitled *Third Grade Observer* is posted on a bulletin board in the high group classroom. The display assembles clippings, brought from home by students, under such headings as "Daily Life," "West Haven News," "State News," and "Sports"; these are the first specific visual references to local life observed in the elementary school classrooms. A large commercially produced poster of a smiling bumblebee taped to the blackboard says, "Let the reading bug bite *you!*" An elaborate teacher-made chart listing the names of students (and ranking them) who read required books as well as the number of pages read per week is tacked to the rear wall of this classroom. Each classroom has a set of the *World Book Encyclopedia* and a metal world globe.

In the low classroom, Christmas themes abound. A small though heavily decorated pine tree is in the front corner of the room. Several pictures of Santa Claus are cut from crepe paper and are taped to the blackboards. The pictures show a large, smiling white male of indeterminate age. A white beard flows down the front of his furry red suit, and a bulging red cloth sack is tossed across his back. Neither picture has a caption, suggesting that students have internalized the symbolic reference. A papier mâché and crepe paper sled, drawn by a team of reindeer, is displayed above a rear blackboard. No captions accompany these scenes. Several bookcases crammed with textbooks and other reading materials line the side walls. A small plastic Nativity scene sits on top of a bookcase. In the second room, a picture from a magazine of a manger scene is taped to the rear wall. An elaborate, commercially produced display spelling out "Christmas is . . ." is taped to a blackboard. The phrase is completed with a series of words such as "Santa Claus," "ornaments," "cookies," "wreaths," "baby Jesus," "families," and "presents." Commercial production is reflected here as few of these displays are constructed by the students or by the teacher. The classroom environment is less and less the student's and more a reflection of the influence of the mass-marketing economic sector of the wider society.

There is a dramatic increase in the amount of furniture in mid-

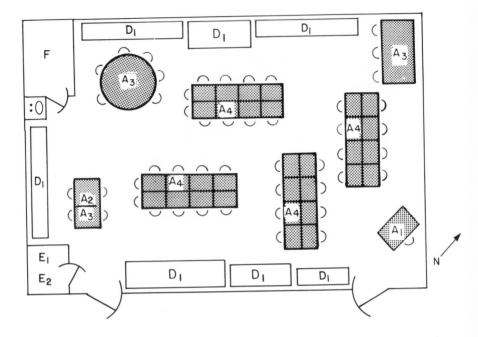

Figure 7. A Third Grade Classroom

Legend
  A_1 = teacher's desk   C = chair
  A_2 = teacher aide's desk D_1 = bookcases/storage areas
  A_3 = classroom activity desk E_1 = teacher's closet
  A_4 = student desk E_2 = students' closet
                                      F = lavatory

dle grade classrooms, compared with previous classrooms. Third grade rooms are smaller than previous rooms, and there are fewer open spaces permitting and encouraging student movement. Classroom space is defined by furniture filling most of the room (see Figure 7). The number of pushed-together tables (A_4), each seating one student, increases. Each student is associated with, and oriented around, a specific unit of classroom space. Unpermitted, random student mobility is not sanctioned by the teacher, and students are expected to be in their places when roll (required attendance record-keeping) is taken. A distinction between public (interaction-oriented) and private (interaction-inhibiting) classroom spaces is reinforced physically. The only public spaces in the room are by the teacher's desk (A_1) and by the activity tables (A_3), relegated to distant corners of the room. The interaction-oriented activity tables (A_3), spatially deemphasized, are used for the construction of class projects, for small group reading lessons, and for other collective and coactive student activities. The spatial placement of the teacher's desk permits her to monitor the room. There are two doors on the front wall of the classroom, one at each end. Teachers tend to block off one door not only to increase the amount of usable classroom floor space but also to permit better control over student movements. Furniture shapes and the pattern of furniture arrangement spatially reinforce individual task orientations, inhibit student coaction and collective work efforts, and reinforce student separateness and autonomy. A physical orientation toward student interaction in this room is retained only in that individual student desks are grouped into four clusters of eight. Most of third grade classroom time is spent with students working at their individual desks; correspondingly, the grading system reinforces individual responsibility for one's own work as well as increasing peer competition for grades. The classroom physical and spatial conditioning encourages student independence rather than interdependence.

The teacher of the low students, a quick-moving white female in her mid-twenties, has taught at West Haven for five years. The high group is taught by a vibrant black female in her mid-fifties, who has taught at West Haven for twelve years. Students are seven to nine years of age. The low group had fifteen students present on the days of observation: four black females, five black males, three white females, and three white males. In the high group, there are twenty-three students: nine black females, two black males, six white females, and six white males. In the high groups there is a noticeable absence of black males, while in the low groups the number of white females declines.

A Low Classroom Session

8:45 A.M. The teacher's aide is in the room setting up materials for the day's activities. The teacher arrives as the students come in from the buses. Students hang their outerwear on hooks on the rear wall. They then go directly to their seats.

Recurrent adult structuring of educational experiences. Time/place coordination. Adherence to norms.
Waiting. At-attention positioning.

Event Transition 1

9:00 A.M. The teacher calls the class to order. Everyone says the Pledge of Allegiance. Standing in the middle of the room, the teacher says that a number of students have colds and are absent today and suggests that the class write get-well cards to them. First, though, they have to finish their assignments. The aide is taking roll and collecting lunch money from several students.

Order. Authority position. Required attendance. Solicitude. Health and well-being.
Play as a reward for work. Finishing.
Required attendance monitoring and administrative tasks.

Event Transition 2

9:15 A.M. The teacher turns to the board to write out the day's assignments. Students can have some free time if they finish before recess. Finished writing, she turns to ask if there are any questions. Several students begin talking without raising their hands. Angered, the teacher sternly tells them, "Raise your hands rather than just shouting out your questions!" Presently, students raise their hands to get the teacher's attention. A black male asks a question about how they are to go about doing their work. Somewhat distractedly, the teacher retorts, "You can do it any way you want to, I don't care. Just so long as you get it done!" The boy still has a puzzled look on his face but does not pursue his question.

Expected self-maintenance. Play as reward for work.

Spontaneity followed by emphasis on procedure and deference to authority. Obedience/compliance.

Expected self-reliance. No accommodation. Finishing. Obedience/compliance.

Norm violation followed by behavior modification; emphasis on deference and order. Monitoring and evaluation.

Recurring differential grouping and ranking spatially expressed. Isolation of ranked groups.
Responsibility for private property.

References to national myths. Peer ridicule illustrating split in peer group internalization of classroom norms and values.

Defense of children adhering to classroom work norm.
Passive defiance/threat gesture.
Peer competition is a constant feature of classroom life.

Accommodation to environmental noise. Concentration.
Administrative hegemony over classroom territory.

Differential grouping and ranking.
Separation gesture.
Classroom procedure norm is internalized. Self-maintenance.

Products. Required evaluation.

Students again are talking without raising their hands. The teacher says, "I want hands, not mouths!" The teacher wanders between the students looking at their work.

9:30 A.M. The teacher calls three students to a small table in the front of the room. Soon the aide goes to a table at the rear of the room and calls out the names of four other students, who take several books from their desks and go to the table.

A black female argues with a white female about whether Santa Claus is dead. Sarcastically, two neighboring black males claim that there *is* no Santa Claus! Sticking out her tongue and wagging her head, the girl gives them both a "you-are-crazy" look. One of the boys guffaws loudly, and the teacher glares at them, then says that they had better be quiet because the other groups are reading and students are trying to do their work. Sullenly, one of the boys looks at her, then turns back to his work. The girl quickly turns around and smiles at their misfortune.

10:00 A.M. A buzzer near the teacher's desk sounds. Startled, the observer flinches but the students show no reaction. The buzzer, the observer is told by a neighboring student, is part of the communication system linking the converted mobile homes to the main building and signals that it is time for the several special education students in the room to go to their class. As they leave, other students say good-bye and wave their hands. This event transpires without the teacher's intervention.

Several students complete the assignments the teacher outlined on the board. As they do, they get up quietly to put their papers on one side of the teacher's desk. The teacher gets up from her small group to give each of these students a Christmas card she has purchased, depicting traditional Christmas scenes. The teacher wants the class to write a short story about each scene, and the cards can be taken home by the students to give to someone in their family.

Orientation toward national celebrations.

Emphasis on imagination/creativity follows work, that is, has lower academic value.

There is an ever-present classroom background noise of coughing, chairs scraping the floor, materials being moved around on desks, and the rustling of paper. Several students continually mumble over their work. When talking occurs, it is confined to the same set of students: a group of two black males and two black females, sitting somewhat apart. The teacher continually reprimands them. Presently, she yells at the two girls for not doing their own work. "Cool it," she says. "Let's get on the stick!" The two girls had been rearing back on their chairs, watching the other students and making faces at each other. The teacher says these activities should be saved for free time.

Work noise is information about the nature of the classroom setting; reinforcement of task orientation. Autonomy.

Lack of adherence to classroom norms by black student subgroup. Spatial separation of black and white students.

Aggressive/distancing behaviors signaling nonparticipation (Jackson 1968: 83–111).

10:45 A.M. The class is interrupted by loud knocking on the door. Frowning, the teacher gets up to answer it.

A parent, a middle-aged black woman, brings her son into the room. Apparently the student had done something requiring her to come to school. At the teacher's invitation, they step into the classroom, and all the students stop their work and turn to watch.

Authority hierarchy.

Appeal to higher parental status as punishment and control mechanism.

Loudly, the woman berates her son for being lazy and causing problems in school. Coolly, the teacher holds up her hands while saying that she does not give him work that she knows he cannot do. Shaking her head, the woman says she does not know what to do. She is wearing a rumpled coat and a worn

A further example of the lack of privacy in classrooms. Private matters are routinely put on public display, serving as examples for other students. Control mechanism.

scarf that barely covers her head. She is not wearing gloves. Her hands are knotted into prominent veins. Over and over, she rubs and twists her hands together. Her face is lined, tight, and haggard. As she turns to leave, she says that whatever the teacher wants to do about her son is all right with her. Standing to one side, the boy silently looks at the floor.

After the boy's mother leaves, the teacher takes the student to her desk and sits down with him. The class still watches silently. She puts her arms on his shoulders and quietly asks if the problem is all over now. Slowly, the student nods his head. The teacher then asks if he wants his mother to come to school every day. Slowly, he shakes his head no. The teacher says, "OK," gently rubs his shoulder, and takes him to his seat. With their eyes, the other students quietly follow.

Soon after this incident, the class becomes restless. Students complain about their work. The whining increases, and the teacher sarcastically says, "One often has to do things that one does not want to do." Then she gives them a disgusted glance. Many students, especially the clump of black students, are just going through the motions of doing their work.

As most members of the class work on their Christmas cards, distractions increase, and students look around the room, stare at the floor, or interact with their neighbors. No student leaves his or her seat. Loudly the aide shouts at several students in her group, "Do your own work!"

Across the room, the teacher yells at several people, "Don't rush! Don't rush it! That's how people mess up. You've got to learn to take your time."

11:05 A.M. The aide dismisses her group

Deference to teacher authority. Example of teacher functioning *in loco parentis*. Subordinate status and rank of the child in this dialogue.

Public display and ridicule.
Discipline by manipulation of emotions. Finishing.
Control by instilling guilt and fear.
Teacher affection as reward. Compliance.
Public display of intimate student matters is a routine feature of classroom life.

Sarcasm and ridicule. Implied lack of self-control. Withdrawal of affection.
Containment. Differential student adherence to classroom norms and values.

Behaviors indicating lack of involvement and participation in the classroom. Passive resistance. Autonomy.

Procedure. The pattern is for more classroom time to be spent on student behavior modification and control in the low than in the high sessions. Finishing/mastery.
Task divisions of labor

and tells them to plan on finishing tomorrow. The aide works in the lunchroom, so she has to leave ahead of the noon hour to help prepare meals.

(by sex and age) in classrooms are similar to those in the wider society.

The teacher finishes with her small group and assigns work to take home. A black male says that he does not want to take any work home. At first, the teacher is angered at his belligerence, but gradually her voice softens as she asks him why. He drops his head, and his face tightens. He says that his father gives him trouble when he brings work home. Seeing his pain, the teacher says, "OK. Maybe we can work something out." The other students silently sit watching and listening.

Taking work home is age/grade-related and implies responsibility and self-direction. *In loco parentis* functions in the classroom are also the basis for further differentiation and ranking of the peer group. The continual public displays of personal, private matters.

The teacher asks a black male to respond to a word she is holding up to the class. He fidgets and looks at his desk. Seeing his hesitation, other students throw their hands into the air trying to capture the teacher's attention. Ignoring them, she continues to stare at the boy. A neighboring white female whispers something to the student, and the teacher explodes, "Is your name Otis? I want an answer from Otis!" She turns to face the offending female and thrusts her face forward. The girl moves back in her seat. The teacher continues to glare at her. Turning to the boy, she gently but sternly tells him that he should not pout because he cannot do the work. The boy does not respond. The teacher turns away and tells the group that if they did not finish the morning work they must take it home and finish it there. The teacher dismisses her small group.

Literacy training. Peer competition.

Emphasis on individual accountability. Finishing. If they have not already done so, children must learn to function autonomously.

Control by violation of personal space. Nonverbal threat gesture.

"Don't-give-up" norm. Emphasis on work.

Products. Finishing. Expected self-direction. Play as reward for work.

Event Transition 3

11:30 A.M. The teacher tells the group to get ready for lunch. Several students are talking loudly. Sternly, the teacher says she will

Expected self-direction. Control by implied

threat and appeal to self-discipline.

Order. Personal responsibility for materials. Deferential positioning.
Compliance/obedience as precondition to classroom order.

High rank as reward.

Classroom propriety norm requires student autonomy/isolation. Physical violence.

Self-maintenance. Tattling = peer competition for teacher rewards.
Emphasis on student autonomy and self-responsibility/self-maintenance.

Peer aggression.
In loco parentis appeal to care of the body/safety.
Personal property theft.
Individual student self-maintenance.
Horizontal aggression. Defends peers only against certain forms of attack. Passive resistance.

Regimentation. Order. Compliance/obedience. Order. Regimentation.
Continual adult monitoring.

count to ten. The implication is that they must be quiet before she reaches ten or something bad will happen to them. Students quickly put away their materials and quietly put their heads down on their arms folded atop their desks. The teacher begins counting but only reaches four when the room is quiet enough to satisfy her.

Quietest tables first, the teacher calls students to put on their coats and outerwear. While they are dressing, the teacher excuses herself to go into the bathroom. A white female looks up and softly punches another white female on the shoulder. Two black males feign boxing with each other. Other students continue putting on their coats and boots. When the teacher returns, a black female quickly runs up to tell her loudly that two males were fighting while she was in the bathroom. Frowning, the teacher tells her not to worry about it.

As students try to get their boots from the pile on the floor near the door, there is some pushing and shoving. The teacher angrily tells them to stop because someone might get hurt. A black male takes someone else's gloves, and the teacher scolds him, saying that he should not take things that do not belong to him. A black male calls another black male a "black chump." Angrily turning on him, the teacher spits out to him, "Shut your mouth!" Viciously, she stares at him. The male sulks, pouts, but does not return the stare.

The teacher tells the students to line up by the door. Putting on their clothing, they do so. Then on a signal from her, they leave the classroom in a single file. The teacher follows them to the lunchroom where other teachers on "monitor duty" take charge. The teacher and the observer eat in the teachers' lounge.

Spatial separation reinforces status differences.

11:40 A.M. Lunch period. Recess.

Event Transition 4

12:30 P.M. The teacher leaves the lounge early to meet students returning from lunch and recess. Standing at the door, she scans them as they come into the room. Presently, she singles out a black male who went outside in tennis shoes. She tells him *never* again to go outside without wearing boots. The male sheepishly looks up at her. She glares at him and says that he had better not do that tomorrow. She tells other students to hang up their coats.

Monitoring/supervision.
In loco parentis concern with safety/care of the body.

Neatness. Order.

Event Transition 5

12:45 P.M. The teacher tells students to take their seats. Voice levels are moderate as students follow her directions.

When seated, the students work on their morning assignments, if they have not finished them. Most have not. Several students whine and are told if they do not finish the work in class, they will have to take it home. A white female complains that she cannot find one of her books. The teacher angrily tells her, "If you can't be responsible for your materials, I guess we are just going to have to send a note home to your mother or give her a call." The female stops whining.

The teacher is at her desk doing paperwork. The students are restless. The teacher periodically glances up from her work to scan the room, and this movement usually is enough to contain the students' restlessness.

Several students raise their hands to ask

Order as prelude to further classroom activity. Compliance/obedience.

Finishing/completing.

Control by appeal to self-discipline.
Emphasis on self-maintenance and accountability for personal property. Compliance forced by threat of appeal to a higher authority (mother, not father). Compliance/obedience.

Maintenance of control over their physical movements. Compliance/obedience.

Permission requesting = deference to authority.

Propriety and etiquette classroom norms.

Expected student self-maintenance and self-reliance are reinforced.

Emphasis on responsibility for personal materials; the lack of private property serves as a basis for differences in classroom ranking and status organization. Property dispute.

Territoriality and subtle fights over space occur more frequently than is seen in these narratives.

We will see other instances of territorial/property conflicts between teachers and black males (McDermott 1974, 1977).

Again, we see more violations of established norms in low than in high sections and more emphasis on behavior modification

to go to the bathroom. The teacher insists that they say "please" and "thank you." Students come up to the teacher's desk and ask her how to spell a word. The teacher appears annoyed and generally tries to get them to work out the answer themselves.

1:00 P.M. Throughout the day there has been a steady interaction between several older black males and females in the room. During the morning, they argued about a can of crayons. None of these students have crayons though all the other students do. One of them would take the crayon can, so the others could not get it. Then another would do the same. The crayon can moves back and forth all morning, accompanied by grimaces, frowning, angry stares, and threatening mumblings. One male is the most possessive. One of the black females is afraid to go to his desk to get the crayons. She complains to her somewhat larger friend, who gets up to snatch the can from the boy's desk. Then, whether he needs them or not, the boy gets up to go over to the smaller girl's desk to take the can. When the girl whines that she needs the crayons, the teacher looks up from her work and angrily tells all of them that she does not want to be bothered any more about those crayons; they have been passing around those crayons so much today that she does not know *whose* are whose. "Anyway," she shouts, "they are the *class's* crayons!" One of the boys pouts and mumbles under his breath. But he does not say anything to the teacher. The girls smile.

1:10 P.M. Again, the students are becoming restless. More students are getting up from their seats to sharpen their pencils or go to the washroom. The voice level is moderate, but the background and mobility noise increases. As a counter the teacher gets up and begins walking around the room, ostensibly to look at their work. She pauses and singles out several students who, she feels, have made expecially good Christmas stories and drawings. She asks these students to hold their work up for the class to see. Reticently they do so. Praising them, the teacher says that they ought to put their names on their work. The students are embarrassed at this special attention. The other students merely look at them.

and monitoring as a control mechanism. Differential praise (Goetz 1976:40).

Public display.

Peer competition is reinforced. The teacher divides the peer group against itself by rewarding students who adhere to classroom norms.

Event Transition 6

1:40 P.M. The teacher tells the students to get ready for their Monday activities. Class periods are short on Monday; students have an art class, a music class, and a math lab session. The students put up their materials. Now, the teacher tells them they can finish their work tomorrow; they do not have to take it home with them. The students smile and shout with glee.

Increasing fragmentation/complexity of the educational experience. The linear sequencing of experiences. Time/activity coordination. Finishing/completing.

While putting up some materials, a black female comes up to the observer and shyly asks, "Were we good?" Bending down to her, the observer smilingly tells her not to worry. He is here just to watch and learn about what goes on all day. He is not going to grade them and does not care whether they are "good" or "bad." He is sitting and watching what they do, that is all. This answer seems acceptable to her; she smiles and returns to her seat.

Anxiety, fear, and approval-seeking. Classrooms are competitive, anxiety-inducing environments. There is continual evaluation in one form or another (Henry 1966; Lippitt and Gold 1959; Smith and Geoffrey 1968).

1:50 P.M. The teacher designates a black female to clean off the blackboards and asks a black female to unplug the Christmas tree lights. She asks a white female to pass out the art folders. When their assigned tasks are completed, they retake their seats.

Rotating housekeeping tasks and administrative tasks (female bias) = responsibility training.

At-attention positioning.

Ranking as reward.

Expected self-maintenance. Housekeeping tasks. Regimentation. Waiting. Physical violence.

Violation of self-responsibility classroom norm.
Deference as punishment.
Passive aggression occurs with more frequency among females than males on all the days of observation. Compliance/obedience.

Regimentation. Order.

Continual adult monitoring.
Spatial segregation by status and role.

Recurring adult structuring of the educational experience. Time/place coordination.
Student self-direction and maintenance. Adherence to classroom norms.

Ritual of national allegiance. The ceremony is required by the school administration and the state, although not all teachers adhere to the rule.

2:00 P.M. Quietest students first, the teacher dismisses the class, and they put on their coats and boots. Then she tells them to put their chairs on top of their desks. They then line up in front of the blackboard. While the teacher is getting some of her materials together, an argument involving some of the black students occurs. Someone pushed someone else. There is a lot of loud recrimination, denial, and shifting of blame. The teacher intervenes and tells a black female, as her punishment, to hold the door open for the students. The girl begins to pout. She half stomps around in anger, whines at the teacher, but does not challenge her. At this point, the teacher yells at her to do as she is told. Still pouting and mumbling, the girl holds the door open as the students leave.

In a straight line, the students are led to the art room (Figure 2). They will be dismissed for the day by the art teacher. When the art teacher takes charge of the students, the teacher and observer go to the teachers' lounge.

A High Classroom Session

8:45 A.M. The teacher and aide set up materials in preparation for the day's activities. Students arrive from the buses and, upon entering, hang up their overcoats and stack their boots neatly in the alcove. As the students take their seats of their own accord, the teacher reintroduces the observer, then tells them to stand for the Pledge of Allegiance. Facing the faded flag in the front corner of the room, students place their right hands over their hearts, and the teacher leads them in the pledge. When finished, she asks if they would like to sing Christmas carols. While clapping their hands, students bob up and down in their seats with glee. As the teacher leads them, students sing "Silent Night" and "Rudolph the Red-Nosed Reindeer."

Recognition of national observances required by the school administration and the state.

Event Transition 1

9:00 A.M. The teacher passes out the morning assignments. Students work on correcting previous work. The teacher and aide go to small tables in opposite corners of the room and call several students to each table.

Expected self-direction. Right/wrong mastery.
Recurring differential student grouping pattern.

The aide carefully explains the directions for the assignment. After correcting previous work, they will work on word substitution exercises. To make certain they understand her directions, the aide goes over a trial example with the students. Both the teacher and the aide ask if there are any questions. Students who understand begin working; those who do not are approached by the teacher and aide, who explain directions individually. As the students begin working, the teacher says, "Let's make sure everything is very neat and we will not have to rip up the papers." And to a white female who is slow in getting started, "Let's be quiet. Let's not disturb others."

Recurring emphasis on procedure. Following orders. Obedience training. Literacy training.
Following a model. Rote. Obedience training.

Self-direction is expected.

Neatness. Lack of nurturing and tolerance of mistakes.
Quietness.
Primacy of work.

As the papers are passed back, some students smile and shout "Yeaaaa," while others, seeing their grades, slump, pout, and remain silent. Few look to see their neighbors' grades. Students are expected to correct the mistakes and pass the papers back for the teacher to check.

Ranking and evaluation by universalistic criteria (grades).
Peer competition for scarce rewards (grades); ranking. Expected self-direction. Right/wrong mastery. Demonstration. Evaluation.

Several students have many errors on their papers. The aide goes to one of the smaller tables at the rear of the room and works with students individually.

The spatial expression of differential grouping and ranking is a basis for labeling (low/high).

Differential grouping = different groups of students have different educational experiences. This play activity is a reward for students mastering work.
Differential grouping in association with color differences.

The teacher starts a small group of students working on a play involving a puppet theater designed and constructed by a group of the students. Quite a bit of noise comes from this area. From time to time, students in the main group pause in their work to watch. With the exception of one black male, the students in the play group are white.

Students work on their assignments in an orderly manner without supervision. There is no nervous fidgeting, aimless wandering, or nonverbal interaction. Students are permitted to get materials or supplies and to go to the various work areas of the room.

Permitted mobility in this high session assumes self-direction. Responsibility training.

The reinforcement is for task orientation and self-control amid various stimuli.

Many of the students stop to watch the others work on the play. There is some background noise of low giggling coming from the back of the room. The teacher looks up to tell them not to pay this group any mind but to continue with their work and ignore the distraction.

Differential grouping, ranking, and labeling. Self-maintenance. Demonstration. Proof.
Right/wrong mastery.

9:45 A.M. The aide calls "Group B" to her reading table. Students take workbooks from their desks and file to the rear of the room. Each student reads short passages from the workbook while the aide carefully listens and corrects if necessary.

9:50 A.M. The teacher asks the observer to help her by taking several students to one side of the room and listening to them read. The teacher keeps a file card for each student noting his/her grade reading level and the number of pages read each day. Most students read ten pages or so a day. That is the limit the observer sets while working with his group. Using the teacher's desk, the observer takes several file cards and calls students to read. The students are not hesitant in reading to the

Literacy training.

Autonomy. Individual responsibility for work. Ranking. Progress; an important theme in American national culture.

Demonstration/proof.

observer, a stranger, and do not shy away from him. As each student finishes, the observer writes down the date and the number of pages read.

10:00 A.M. A black female student aide comes in to help the teacher. Without being told, she takes several cards to another desk and proceeds to call up students. In turn, students read to her. No one takes notice of this interruption.

Students are exposed to other age grades. Responsibility training for the older students.
Task orientation and concentration.

The students seem intensely involved in reading, and everyone looks forward to being called. Those working with the observer read until asked to stop.

10:30 A.M. The student aide leaves for the day. The observer listens to those students who still have not read.

Event Transition 2

At this point, the teacher suddenly looks up and says, "All right!" All the students stop working. In the morning, they have a daily five-minute break. Several students run to be first in line at the pencil sharpener while others line up to go to the washroom. A few sit in their seats talking together. Several males punch each other on the shoulder. Most of the students run straight to the aquarium, where a small crowd gathers to watch the fish. Other students watch the gerbils running on the treadmill inside their cage.

Expected self-maintenance.
Regimented work/rest periods. Peer competition. Regimentation.

Physical violence.
Permitted spontaneous play as a reward for work.

Event Transition 3

10:35 A.M. The teacher keeps a small ship's bell on her desk. She picks it up and rings it several times. Students scamper back to their seats and begin working. The teacher dismisses those students who worked on the play. She goes to a small table toward the rear

Factorylike control/order by nonverbal signal.
Stimulus/response conditioning. Self-maintenance.

of the room, sits down, and calls four students to join her. The noise level increases, and the teacher says that they should not be so noisy. The voice level drops. When the teacher or aide reprimands behavior, the tendency is to shout out the student's name, wait until he or she turns around, then stare at him/her.

11:00 A.M. The aide calls another group of students to her table. As students finish correcting their work, they place it on the teacher's desk.

Students are disciplined for preventing others from doing their work. For example, they are allowed to stand up while they work but are not permitted to go to other people's desks. The teacher catches a white female out of her seat and at another student's desk and takes all her credits away. Hearing this, a white female sitting next to the observer says, "Wow! *Six* credits!" In the classroom reward system, each student is given several tickets, strips of paper, that are used as credits. When the student's behavior prompts the teacher to intervene, the student loses a credit. The more credits a student loses, the more work that student has to perform around the classroom, such as cleaning the blackboard. When a student has no credits remaining, recess privileges are suspended.

Event Transition 4

11:25 A.M. The teacher rings her bell and tells students to put away their work, and they neatly place books and materials in the storage area. They are concerned that everything is neatly stacked in its own place. As the aide leaves to work in the lunchroom the students smile, wave, and say good-bye to her. She says good-bye, then they quietly put their heads

---

Control by appeal to student self-discipline. Compliance. Nonverbal threat gesture. Appeal to self-control.

Recurring differential student grouping. Finishing/completing. Play as reward for work.

Norm of autonomy. Primacy of work and task orientation. Autonomy. Ban on coaction. The public display of punishment instills fear and anxiety while presumably reinforcing compliance with classroom norms and values.

Public display and ridicule by peers as controlling factors. Spatial confinement as punishment.

Stimulus/response conditioning. Nonverbal signal. Neatness and order norms.

Predominance of separation gestures in the high sessions, indicating close-down on their folded arms. Without requesting permission, they file, one at a time, into the washroom. They always close the door after entering, and they always wash their hands after exiting.

ness between teacher and students. At-attention positioning. Permitted mobility.
Adherence to propriety and cleanliness norms.

The teacher is punching a hole in each student's lunch ticket. The observer questions a neighboring student. She says they have to bring money from home to pay for their lunches. Many of the students at West Haven are not eligible for the school's free lunch program because their parents make too much money. The teacher tells students who brought their lunches from home to get them and put on their outerwear. They are to go to lunch in the main building and then to recess. Putting on her coat, the teacher takes them to the lunchroom and shortly returns to have lunch in the classroom.

Increasing teacher administrative tasks.

Increasing manifestations of socioeconomic differences as potential basis for status and prestige ranking (high/low).
Differential grouping.
Increasing range of spatial mobility.
Adult monitoring. Spatial separation by status and role.

11:30 A.M. Lunch period. Recess.

Event Transition 5

12:30 P.M. When students return from the playground, there is a traffic jam near the door as they try to enter the room and remove their outerwear. The noise level is high, and students are laughing and loudly talking. As they struggle to get in the door, the teacher turns to them and says, "All right!" The voice and activity levels drop. Students quietly put up their clothes and take their seats.

Indirect reprimand appealing to expected self-control. Compliance. Adherence to classroom norms.

Event Transition 6

When the class is seated, the teacher reads them a Christmas story. Students bob up and down in their seats and clap their hands. The teacher goes to the front of the room to sit down. Students climb on their desks in order to get closer to her. The teacher periodically pauses to hold up the book so students can see

Required observation of national celebrations. Literacy training. Authority positioning. Note the permission for spontaneous behaviors during semiplay period.
Reference to national mythological figure.

Aural reinforcement of national celebrations. Emphasis on products.

Visual material reinforcement of national celebrations.

Reference to ceremonial songs accompanying national celebration.

Manipulation of spontaneity (Henry 1959).

Control by power of cessation of activity. Horizontal aggression and peer hostility are an indication of internalization of classroom norms and values.

Differential rewards, prestige, and ranking are reinforced. Compliance. Deference positioning.

Mathematics training.

Procedure norm is internalized. Obedience training. Personal responsibility for property.

Obedience training. Proof/demonstration.

Expected self-maintenance. Responsibility training. Adherence to classroom norms.

the illustrations, and they freely comment upon the story. The teacher says, "Doesn't Santa look happy?" and the class shouts, "YEEEEAAA." After the story, the teacher asks if the class would like to sing a Christmas song from their books. The students enthusiastically agree. These books are illustrated colored stories about Christmas. The teacher leads them in singing "Silent Night," but she stops singing when it gets too loud. Many students are carried away with the spirit of the songs and overdo what the teacher wants. The teacher is disturbed and tells them to put away their materials. There are loud groans of protest. Quickly, several students start to blame others they feel were singing too loudly. The teacher interrupts their bickering and quietly and sarcastically says that everyone should *not* try to be the leader in doing these activities because "that's why they only have one leader in bands." Students frown and are sullen but automatically put their heads down on their folded arms.

1:15 P.M. The teacher writes several addition, subtraction, multiplication, and division problems on the board as students silently watch her. She says they are going to work on their math for a while. Without being told, students take out paper, pencils, and workbooks. The teacher goes through several examples on the board, emphasizing that students should listen and follow directions. In working out the examples, she calls on several students for answers. Satisfied with their responses, she then tells them to work on the problems until she rings the bell. The classroom is quiet.

1:45 P.M. The teacher rings the bell, and students quietly put away their work, then put their heads down on their desks awaiting further instructions.

Today, the students have gym class. By tables, the teacher dismisses students to put on their coats and line up by the door. The process is orderly and quiet. The teacher does not take them to the gymnasium but holds the door open for them. Only when they are outside does the class break into a run and begin to use their "outside voices." The teacher remains in the classroom.

2:45 P.M. Panting and breathless, the students return from the gymnasium and congregate near the door. While talking with the observer, the teacher frowns to quiet them to her satisfaction, and without direction they go to their seats and continue working on the board assignment.

3:00 P.M. The students work in virtual silence. The teacher gets up from talking with the observer to ring the bell. Quietly, students put away their work, then place their heads down on their folded arms.

The teacher sets up a filmstrip projector and says they will watch a film on safety. The students perk up, bob up and down with excitement, and climb up on their desks to see better. The teacher says, "Let's react to each other and listen to each other. If you have something to say, the easiest way is to raise your hand." Students freely comment on the

Event Transition 7

Obedience training/nonverbal stimulus-response signal. Compliance. At-attention positioning.

Care of the body. More complex scheduling/differentiation of the curriculum. Adherence to norms and values.

Responsibility training given to students in the high sessions. Demonstrations of self-discipline and adherence to classroom norms.

Event Transition 8

Comparative lack of time spent on behavior modification. Children in high sessions are compliant, self-directed, and easily controlled. Finishing/completing.

Event Transition 9

Adherence to norms and values.

Authority positioning.

Stimulus-response conditioning. Deferential, at-attention waiting positioning. Waiting.

Adult handling of machine technology.

Emphasis on safety.

Mobility, spontaneous behaviors, coaction are permitted during/are indicative of play-oriented activities

Emphasis on propriety and procedure. Order and deference norms are reinforced. Permitted spontaneity. Proof/demonstration. Peer competition.

The value of trying and not giving up.
Peer competition for access to display of knowledge. Right/wrong mastery.

Conflict between latent and manifest norms. Students in the high sessions are permitted more spontaneity in association with their demonstration of adherence to established classroom norms and values.

film. The teacher periodically asks questions about the film, and many are eager to answer.

They continually have their hands up in the air. One black male is not called on so he leaves his hand in the air, propping it up with his other hand. If a student is called upon and hesitates, the others leap out of their seats and shout, "I know! I know!" The teacher reminds them that they should not interrupt and that they should listen to one another.

Toward the end of the filmstrip, many students have taken off their shoes, are lying on the tables, or are grouped around the teacher. At the end of the film, they clap and whistle.

Event Transition 10

At-attention waiting positioning. Expected self-maintenance.
Ranking on the basis of adherence to norms and values. Regimentation. Order. Adult monitoring. Adherence to norms. Order.

Customary separation gesture.
Spatial separation of constituents by status, age, and role.

3:20 P.M. The teacher puts away the filmstrip projector and tells the students to take their seats and get ready to leave. When ready, students put their heads down on their folded arms and become very quiet. The teacher calls them, quietest students first, to get their coats and line up by the door. Putting on her own coat, the teacher takes the students to the bus. The students still walk inside the yellow line on the right side of the hallway floor. They wave and smile good-bye to the teacher. The teacher waves and smiles good-bye. Shortly thereafter, the teacher and the observer go to the teachers' lounge before leaving the school complex about a half-hour later.

The behavioral and attitudinal gap between high and low group students widens during the third grade. The low session devotes time to behavior modification (33/–)*, the high session does not. Aspects of

*These paired numbers refer to features of low/high sessions summarized in Figure C-5, Appendix C.

classroom life in the low session are reminiscent of the strain toward order characteristic of the lower grades; teacher commands to "Raise your hands!" and "Do your own work!" signal a lack of adherence (23) to customary classroom norms and values in both instances. The third grade low session emphasizes the following: student deference (6/22) to the teacher; teacher monitoring (7/28) of student behavior; regimentation (17/39); order (3/14); waiting (44/70).

Subtle tension and strain predominate in the low session, as if volatile pressures are being suppressed. Students resist the authority of the teacher, not so much by open defiance as by indirection (nonverbal threat gestures) and passive aggression such as restless fidgeting (25/–). Student fear and anxiety ("Were we good?") (35/54) are high. The teacher, likewise, strains against the students. Public ridicule (16/64) occurs with greater frequency than in the high sessions, and fewer ritual separation gestures (65/41) indicate less contact, as well as emotional closeness, between the teacher and the low students. When students look at each other's papers or try to give each other "right" answers to a question they consciously violate classroom norms, and such violations do not occur in the high session (30/–). Resistance to the established classroom sociocultural system does not involve all the students. By tattling and by attempting to enforce classroom norms through peer pressure, however, some students communicate allegiance to the classroom value system more than others, who cluster together in opposition to this larger student group. The high session, by way of comparison, is characterized by student adherence to/internalization of customary classroom norms and values. Self-control (5) and self-direction (6) are emphasized. Both sessions spend approximately the same amount of classroom time on work (31/20). The character of the work routine, as well as the student behaviors and attitudes surrounding classroom work, is different in each session. The high session continues the classroom emphasis on literacy training (59/17) begun in the early grades. The attendant characteristics of student task orientation (69/26), expected mastery (–/19) of classroom material, and required demonstration and proof (–/8) of competence also are stressed. High students are permitted spontaneity (15/51) of movement, play (–/36), and mobility (–/12) as rewards for adhering to these desired classroom behaviors and attitudes.

There also are more subtle issues. At West Haven, a pervasive ideal is the belief in the perfectibility of each individual child. Although teachers and administrators recognize that children are not innately equal in ability, they also believe that each child ought to be presented with an equal opportunity to develop fully his or her inherent capabilities. This ideal parallels a national belief in democracy (Arensburg and Niehoff 1964; DuBois 1955). In both instances the belief is that, given enough time and attention, each child ought to be able to develop his or her maximum potential. In school classrooms, this attitude translates into focusing sustained attention on the perceived needs of each individual child. Indeed, this pattern is mostly the case in the early grades at West Haven. The reality of schooling, though, is mass education, what Philip Cusick (1973:208) terms the "batch processing" of students. Although recognizing the bureaucratic difficulty of meeting this ideal, West Haven teachers and administrators nonetheless hold firmly to it and become concerned when children do not develop to what is felt to be their maximum potential.

We often aptly apply an assembly-line metaphor in discussing the process of schooling. During the middle grades at West Haven, the assembly line begins to jam up. Things (students) do not move along as smoothly as they ought to. Middle grade teachers, continuing the production metaphor, say that many students are falling behind schedule. At the third grade level, the ideals of perfectibility and egalitarianism collide with the realities of mass education. What can be done? The line must be kept moving. A presumably defective item cannot be permitted to slow down the assembly process. Students have to move along as best they can to make room for others coming up the line, even if they fall behind their age group. Patch them up and send them on. The ideal at West Haven is for grouping on the basis of age to parallel emerging grouping on the basis of ability. The middle grade reality, though, is that student age and ability groupings are becoming further differentiated. Age similarities are no longer as important organizationally as they once were, and to some extent neither is ability grouping.

There is a more intricate factor at work, a subjective factor associated with the differentiated manner in which students cluster and are clustered in middle grade classrooms. What increasingly matters a great deal to middle grade teachers is the nature and quality of student emotions and attitudes toward the sociocultural system of the classroom.

Many students in the low sessions are not emotionally committed to the classroom as a way of life. The teacher forces them to participate and tries to wrest allegiance from them. Many students seem not to want to be here, and they do not identify with or enjoy most of the classroom tasks required of them. The teacher reacts to this lack of emotional/ affective commitment to the classroom as much as she reacts to low test scores. Students throwing books are quickly reprimanded, and they are chided for presenting sloppy work. Students not paying attention to the teacher or copying work incorrectly are met with derision and disgust. Looking around the room, dawdling, and other forms of passivity are student symptoms of emotional and affective withdrawal (Jackson 1968: 83–111). Required attendance mandates that students cannot leave the room, though emotionally they might want to. Whining represents student attitudes and emotions: "I do not want to do this work, but I am forced to. I will indirectly let you know that I do not want to do it." Low group students, for example, whine about not wanting to take work home. Work is not enjoyed, so the teacher uses it as a form of punishment: "If you do not finish this in class, you will have to finish it at home." Some students do not want to have much to do with classroom life while they are in it and certainly do not want to have anything to do with classroom life while away from it. These behaviors express attitudes and emotions, the teachers say, and not ignorance of classroom norms and values. Anyone introduced into a new culture at some point deliberates about whether that way of life suits him or her. Belonging to a society is more than merely being in it. The sociocultural system of the classroom wants new recruits, but it wants their hearts as well as their minds. West Haven elementary school wants emotional as well as intellectual commitment from students. In addition to stratification on the basis of test score ability, stratification occurs increasingly with respect to a student's emotional and affective orientation toward classroom social norms and cultural values. The affective and emotional level of a student's commitment to the classroom way of life, as implied through classroom behavior, invariably overlaps with whether that student is labeled by teachers and grouped as either high or low. School constituents, especially teachers, feel strongly about this issue. West Haven teachers are aware of the conflict between the ideals of student perfectibility and egalitarianism and the realities of mass education. What can they do?

Classroom teachers at West Haven have intricate rationalizations accounting for contradictions in the educational system. There are three prevalent positions taken by middle grade teachers: (1) arguments for student retention and a continued allegiance to an ideology of perfectibility and egalitarianism; (2) the grudging acceptance of some failure in the classroom, made palatable by blaming students; and (3) horizontally expressed aggression, viewing other teachers, primarily in the earlier grades, as the cause of "problem" student attitudes and behaviors.

Two middle grade teachers, voicing the first position, want to stop the conveyor belt, and they want the power to keep individual students at a particular grade level until they are performing (reading) at that grade level. These teachers want to take more time to help individual students and would also like the power to move students during the middle of the school year either ahead or behind when they complete a particular reading level. During an interview, one teacher angrily looked at me and asked why students are moved around only at the end of the school year. I said I did not know. Sometimes, she said, students complete a grade level during the middle of the year and have to sit around wasting time waiting for the other half of the year to end. "It doesn't make sense," she sighed. Bureaucratically, it is impossible for her, she says, to do what she feels ought to be done. The teacher of the low session says the only choice is to "throw away the book and concentrate on behavior." She feels powerless to do this, though, because she has to move students along. She agreed with several other teachers who say they feel "locked in." This phrase is heard repeatedly. Several teachers wanted to retain two students last year, but "the administration [the principal] made us move them on." The administration, they told me, feels that if a student is performing (reading) so poorly that he or she must be retained at a grade level, it is the teacher's fault for not working hard enough to bring the student up to "ability" to pass the tests. They say that the burden of proof for student performance always is on the teacher. Teachers are upset over their lack of power outside of the classroom to control the movements of students. Decisions filter down from the state Department of Education to the superintendent, then to the principals, then to individual classroom teachers. Much of the conflict between ability grouping and age grading is manifested in the parallel conflict between classroom teachers and the administrative bureaucracy. Teachers want more ability grouping, "taking students where they are," as they term it. The principal says he too would like each child to develop his or her maximum potential, but after a certain point ability grouping conflicts with the bureaucratic demand for age grading. Only factors such as excessive absences can bring about a case for a student's retention during the middle grades. School systems are age-graded, and the principal feels it is up to each classroom teacher to work with each child in a given age group. A ten-year-old student in the fourth grade "draws attention." He has, he told me, his own problems.

Teachers feel that parent attitudes also work against them. Most parents, teachers told me, are concerned more with their children "being in the grade they are supposed to be in" than with whether the children are maximizing their potential. Teachers question the utility of letter grades and are upset that both the administration and parents are concerned more with letter grades than with their personal assessments. Middle grade teachers write highly personal evaluations for each student's folder. Letter grades are standardized, universal, and permit comparability between schools. A formal grading system is a systematic procedure for identifying winners, losers, and runners-up (Turner 1961). Several teachers see letter grades as another instance of outside control over their classroom. Teachers holding the perfectibility viewpoint know that low placed and performing students will continue not to fare very well and that for the most part this is the result of structures and situations not of the students' own making. Middle grade teachers exhibiting these views are emotionally wrought and feel powerless to change the educational future of some of these children. They resign themselves to some student failure, acknowledge educational contradictions, but feel unable to do anything about them.

A second argument frequently heard among middle grade teachers is that the home life of some of the students (high group students in particular) better parallels the social and cultural way of life of the classroom than does the home life of other students (usually low group students):

> Middle class people have a high regard for education. They feel it is the indirect means to wealth, satisfaction and contributions to the world. The lower class child does not usually see his parents possessing such an attitude. Nor does he see them engaging in the intellectual activities the middle class child does. So the lower class child has a different attitude than the teacher. . . . Because of the attitude and the home pattern, the lower class child is not "in" if he enjoys school, makes good grades, and behaves. [(West Haven) *Paraprofessional Handbook.*]

These people associate socioeconomic class standing with classroom achievement, and low group students invariably are associated with low socioeconomic standing. Unmarried mothers, especially unmarried black mothers, frequently are singled out for condemnation. "These girls have children too young! They don't know how to care for these kids! They are not even interested in caring for them!" How, I interrupt, do you know this? "Oh, I know," a teacher says, still angry. "Young kids having babies. . . . Many times," she continues, "they ain't even married." Teachers, she says, wind up having to "babysit the kids": "We become babysitters. They send them off to school and expect us to raise and take care of them. We have to teach them how to act and behave, because they don't learn all that at home." She says that many of the low group students will fall further behind in school because parents let them watch too much television: "Television is ruining them! These kids have problems with sequences—days of the week, words, and so on. They have difficulty understanding verbal sequences and word order. They can't put words into meaningful sentences! People don't talk to them in the homes. It's crazy! *Everybody* is watching television! How are they supposed to learn how to function in school!" Teachers are certain of their judgments regardless of whether they have actually observed these children in their homes. They believe their opinions are valid as they explain a troublesome discrepancy between what is and what ought to be. "Parents do not read to their children," another teacher says, "so they don't learn to talk properly when they come to school." Still another teacher says she spends a great deal of classroom time reading to students because, for many of them, that is "the only time they are read to." Students watch television instead of doing their homework, and it is "a waste of time" for teachers to try to get them to take work home: "Usually, their parents don't help them with homework anyway." Two teachers say it is "not psychologically good" to keep students in classes when they are not "doing as well" as other students, and they argue for more homogeneous, ability-grouped classes. I point out that I have observed status differences between ability-grouped classes, but the teachers insist that some students ought to be in situations in which "they only have to do things they *can* do or are good at." But, I ask, shouldn't students be presented with things they *can't* do so they can learn how to do them? "Yes," they reply, "but we are more concerned with the self-image these children develop if they have to compete with the high kids." Another teacher says that "parents should be helping more to bring the kids up. Most parents around here think they can *buy* their kids an education. All they have to do is pay their taxes. Families want their kids to get ahead, but they turn the kids over to us to do it. They want their kids to succeed in school, but they want us to do all the work! They just expect too much, that's all, they just expect too much."

Finally, some middle grade teachers blame earlier grade teachers for the educational discrepancy between what is and what ought to be. The teacher of the low group mentions that her students came from this or that lower grade teacher, names that teacher, and blames her for problems she has inherited. She condemns teachers "who only see the job and not the child. They can't wait to get to the [teachers'] lounge or go home." These teachers, she says, "do not spend enough time with students." The teacher of the high session, on the other hand, praises the early grade teachers who previously had her students. She cautions, though, not to mistake "good work habits for good behavior." Even though her students have been taught to "work well," they still are not quite as "well behaved" as she would like.

Explanations of the reasons for student classroom success and failure polarize around the color of the teacher. Black teachers more than once told me that lower grade white teachers allow and encourage black students to "play too much." White teachers feel most students in general, and most black students in particular, do not have "much of a home life and the school ought to be a place they enjoy coming to where they can play and have free time." The black teachers do not blame students, their home environments, or the administration, but see the problem as "the permissive, 'creative' philosophies in the lower grades. There is too much play going on down there." "Have you observed lower grade classrooms?" I ask one teacher. "No," she responds, "teachers are too protective of their classrooms." They hear, though, that there is too much play going on. She feels she cannot do what she is supposed to do at this grade level if she has to spend time teaching basic student behavior and work skills: "That was supposed to happen in the lower grades." I point out that it *has* happened for students in the high sessions and for most of the students in the low sessions. "True," she says, "but it has not happened *enough* because there are some students who are not like that and they cause most of the problems." This black teacher has high group students but blames the performance and attitude of low group students on the fact that many of the lower grade teachers are white. She divides white teachers at West Haven into two categories: the missionaries and the martyrs. The missionaries, she says, feel that both black and poor white students exhibit bad school attitudes because of their home life

Their parents are not concerned about school, and consequently neither are the children. The only way to "save" these children is to teach them a different way of life. These teachers always talk about "changing" students. The martyrs, on the other hand, seem to be running away from their whiteness. They try to merge themselves with the students, romantically identifying themselves with their "plight." They talk about the sacrifices they make for students. The teacher with whom I was talking laughed. She says both types of white teachers are liberals, and she does not trust white liberals. She says that, deep down, most white teachers believe black students cannot learn anything "too complicated" and feel that it is best to give them more opportunities to "express themselves" than to expose them to intricate knowledge which they never will use. White teachers, on the other hand, said more than once that black teachers are too strict and too demanding, and they decry the constant pressure black teachers put on students. There is too much pressure to perform and to "get ahead," one said. They also blame the principal, a black male, saying that before he came there was not much classroom emphasis on reading. White teachers are quick to say that they are not against reading but that they do feel that students are being "pushed too hard." They fear that students will come to dislike school because too many demands are made of them and that eventually they will reject the school. "We ought to teach kids how to make a living," said a third grade white teacher, "but we should also teach them to be happy in whatever job they happen to get. Everyone can't have all the good jobs, and people should be satisfied with what they get."

Preoccupation with the characteristics of individual children and their homes signals adoption of core American beliefs in self-determination, free will, and the unimpeded responsibility of people for their own successes or failures (McGiffert 1963; Hsu 1972). This belief orientation inhibits attention to the historical, sociocultural, and environmental influences on differences in classroom experiences and outcomes. That an egocentric focus on individual children is of little utility in accounting for broad structural problems, such as differentiated student classroom experiences and outcomes, does not mean that individual differences do not influence classroom performance. The same level of classroom achievement is not to be expected from every child at West Haven Elementary School. As a group, though, children from subordinate subgroups, as John Ogbu (1978) terms them, do experience disproportionate school failure *despite individual ability* (Comitas 1973;

Dumont and Wax 1969; Paulson 1971). Inequality in society and in the school negates meritocracy of equal educational opportunity. The children from socioeconomically subordinate subgroups disproportionately exhibit low performance in school classrooms. These differences in classroom performance and school outcomes are related to stratified school and classroom experiences. Apart from any consideration of individual ability or intelligence, stratified societies in many ways limit the access of subordinate subgroups to resources such as adequate food and housing, as well as to the information and work necessary to secure them. In a stratified society inherent capabilities cannot predict the social role and status of individuals, and there is an inverse correlation between the numbers of available valued social roles and statuses and the numbers of competent individuals ascribed as capable of filling them (Fried 1967: 185–226). It is not so much a matter of children from subordinate subgroups disproportionately failing school as it is a matter of the way public schools manage disproportionately to fail the children from subordinate subgroups (Becker 1961; Leacock 1969; Illich 1973). Education is only one arena for the playing out of the human consequences of stratification and inequality.

　　Stratification in the educational subsystem of society assumes that different knowledge, information, and skills will be transmitted in different schools and will be differently distributed to children from various superordinate and subordinate subgroups within classrooms (McDermott 1974, 1977; McDermott and Gospodinoff 1976; Rosenbaum 1975). Cross-cutting customary color and sex boundaries, the stratified nature of schools and classroom life affects the development of each child's personal competence. The development of competence, as Ward Goodenough (1976) explains, requires (1) mental comprehensive ability; (2) a perception of self and personal goals making the development of competency appear appropriate and desirable; (3) freedom from emotional blocks in relation to the skills and knowledge in question; and (4) access to situations that provide opportunities to rehearse acquired skills as well as to receive guidance until proficiency is achieved. Ability is only one aspect involved in the development of competence (Freire 1973:3–58; Gladwin 1970:214–32; Ogbu 1979). The performance of competent behaviors is not synonymous with the ability to perform competently or with the possession of the information and skills necessary for competent performance. The West Haven classroom narratives show subtle ways in which some children, but not others, are encouraged to practice competent behaviors. To what extent are some children but not others made more emotionally comfortable in the classrooms? Do teachers equally attend to the development of healthy self-perceptions of all children? Do all of the children feel that success in the classroom culture and society is a reasonable goal? We assume that the children are free from mental deficiencies inhibiting the educational process of teaching and learning (Baratz and Baratz 1970; Ogbu 1982) and conclude that, if one wanted a mechanism for sorting new generations of citizens into the potentially advantaged and the potentially disadvantaged, one could do no better than to invent the stratified culture and society of ordinary public school classrooms.

FOURTH GRADE: THE DIE IS CAST

In the fourth grade, one section of high students and two groups of low students rotate between teachers. Reading, mathematics, social studies, handwriting, spelling, science, and the language arts are taught.

Beige paneling lines the walls of each classroom, and green carpet covers the floors. In one room a bulletin board exhibits a commercially produced wall display of a clown's face smiling at the following phrases: "May Day—1," "Memorial Day—30," and "Mother's Day—11." The display nonverbally reinforces the time/activity coordination of national holidays and the days of the month. Taped to the rear blackboard is a commercially produced poster of a smiling squirrel; it says: "Don't be a nut—READ!"

Storage shelves are crammed with textbooks, in contrast to an earlier classroom emphasis on story books. Information increasingly is presented to students via standardized texts. Each classroom contains a set of the *World Book Encyclopedia* and a world globe. Above each teacher's desk are several pull-down maps of various states and countries. The classroom visual emphasis includes an orientation to the world outside the student's local village area.

In the classroom occupied by the high students, a small, teacher-made poster saying, "Hit a Home Run—Score High in Spelling," a commercially produced calendar, and several student-produced examples of fraction problems are taped to the wall between the windows. Taped above the front blackboard is a sign: "What You Don't Know, You Can Always Learn." Above this sign is a commercially produced alphabet, in small and capital letters. The other blackboard exhibits a teacher-made poster display on Africa. Pictures of the pyramids, several dark-skinned "natives" with spears and leopard-skin clothing, and several white "explorers" in canoes are portrayed. Taped to the bathroom door is a rambling display of musical notes: "Tune up for Better Reading," it says. A display of papier mâché flowers, made by the teacher and the students, is taped to the rear blackboard. "Blossom in Spring," "Smiles," "Good Reading," "Good Manners," "Obedience," and "Neatness" are written in the center of the flowers. These visual displays nonverbally reinforce student adherence to the norms and values of the classroom culture and society.

Furniture shape and arrangement parallel the rectangular shape of the classroom, and the resultant classroom spaces are uniform (see Figure 8). Rectangular student desks, inhibiting interaction, spatially displace round, group-oriented activity tables. Student spaces are individualized and, compared with previous patterns of classroom furniture arrangement, the organization of fourth grade desks into two parallel rows lends a mechanistic quality to the workplace. The fourth grade curriculum stresses individual work; students are, for example, severely criticized for helping each other. Spending a year in this environment, students become conditioned to classroom behavioral norms of independence rather than interdependence, competition rather than coaction, and individual task rather than collective group efforts. The spatial separation of categories of school people is expressed more clearly at this grade level than at the earlier levels. The teacher's desk (A_1) is larger than and distinctly isolated from student desks (A_4). The increasing, conscious use of space and furniture arrangement to organize students and control their movements is manifested physically in the requirement that students ask permission from the teacher to move from their individual workplaces.

Fourth grade high students are taught by a black female in her early twenties, who has been at West Haven for four years. Her aide is a black female in her mid-thirties. In the morning, low students are taught by a white female in her late twenties, who has taught at West Haven for three years. In the afternoon, low students are taught by a black female in her mid-thirties, who has taught at West Haven for two years. Her aide is a black female in her mid-thirties. Students are nine and ten years of age. In the high session, eighteen students are present: two white males, four white females, seven black males, and five black females. In the low morning session, there are sixteen students: five black males, five

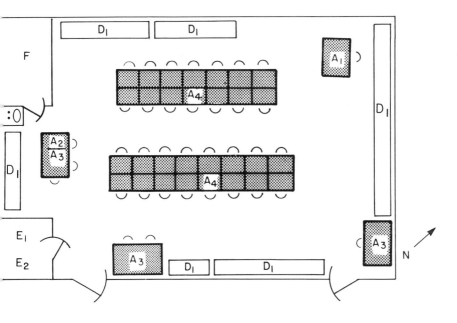

Figure 8. A Fourth Grade Classroom

Legend

A_1 = teacher's desk   C = chair
A_2 = teacher aide's desk D_1 = bookcases/storage areas
A_3 = classroom activity desk E_1 = teacher's closet
A_4 = student desk E_2 = students' closet
                                  F = lavatory

black females, four white males, and two white females. In the low afternoon session, there are fourteen students: two white males, two white females, six black males, and four black females.

A Low Classroom Session

8:45 A.M. The teacher and aide are in the room speaking with the observer. Both are waiting for the students to arrive.

Recurrent adult monitoring. Time/space coordination.

Suddenly, there is a loud noise on the stairs and the students open the door and pile into the room. They stomp their feet to shake the snow off their boots, take off their coats, and throw their boots in the corner. Few hang up their coats. Students gather around the teacher's desk, congregate in the alcove near the door, clump together with their friends, or stand around the room talking.

Lack of student adherence to established classroom norms.
No automatic assumption of at-attention, or deferential, positioning.

Event Transition 1

9:00 A.M. When everyone has arrived, the teacher goes to the front of the room, holds up her hands, and shouts, "All right! All right!"

Assumption of authority position reinforcing right of control. Appeal to self-control and self-maintenance.

Students slowly take their seats. They are still talking, and the teacher tries to talk over their voices. She stands in the middle of the room, her hands on her hips, angrily pouting. She looks at the observer with a grimace that says "What can you do?"

Maintenance of authority positioning forcing student compliance to classroom norms.
Public ridicule and belittling.

Over the noise, the teacher says there will be a spelling test today to determine if some children are ready to move from one reading group to another. Many students are out of their seats, loudly talking back and forth. The teacher yells, "All right! All right!" but to no avail. The aide sits and watches.

Lack of adherence to norms. Literacy training. Evaluation.
Standardized evaluation for differential student grouping/ranking.
Indirect appeal to classroom norm of self-control.
Adversarial, nonsupportive relationships.

The teacher stops yelling, almost in midsentence. Her shoulders sag perceptibly. She heaves a long, deep sigh. She has a

Nonverbal appeal to please the teacher. Deference positioning.

pained, dazed look on her face. The aide looks out the window. Presently, several students say, "Shhhhhhhh" to the loudest offenders. One black male loudly retorts, "Your Momma" and "Shhhhhh yourself!" Eventually, though, the noise level drops, and the teacher composes herself and continues the class.

Peer monitoring of classroom norms illustrates internal differentiation of students.

Event Transition 2

These students are not given administrative/responsibility training tasks. Belittling/ridiculing.

Student hostility is directed vertically (against the teacher) rather than horizontally (against each other.)

In comparison with high sessions, a high degree of peer solidarity and mutual support against the teacher is occurring.

Nonphysical violence. Adversarial relationship.

Control by depersonalization. Belittling and ridicule by comparison with lower-ranked age groups. Control by required deference positioning. Passive aggression.

Lack of compliance to classroom norms.

Differential grouping and ranking.

Self-reliance and self-maintenance are reinforced.

Different students are being exposed to different information. Different educational experiences are occurring in the same classroom.

9:10 A.M. The teacher and aide pass out the test, and students make joking remarks about the spelling words and improvise on the sentences. The teacher is flustered. She stumbles over her words, repeats herself, and contradicts previous statements. Students watch and wait for her errors, and when she makes a mistake or contradicts herself, some students, mainly a group of black males, loudly point out her error. The impression is that a trap is sprung. Dazed, the teacher looks up and tries to remember what she said. Many students smile at their antics.

The noise level is high. The teacher shouts, "OK, kindergarteners," stressing the latter word, "if we are going to act like kindergarteners, then we will have to lay our heads down until we can act like fourth graders." The voice level drops, though some murmuring continues. When she turns her back, the noise increases.

A white female, not taking the test, asks the observer about Greek mythology. The teacher had told her to ask the observer because she and the aide are busy. She wants to know what happened to Pandora after she opened the box. The observer is not certain. After some discussion, they decide to look in the encyclopedia. By this time several students, mostly black males, have gathered around to hear the observer talk about Greek mythology. Several students taunt the female, saying that "all that stuff" is not real. The female takes offense and blurts out that it is mythology and that it is not supposed to be real. The other students, particularly two black males, do not accept this explanation. They continue teasing her for her interest in the material. The boys are neither taking tests nor at their desks doing work. In fact, they have simply been lying on the floor with two other black males idly playing with their books and punching small holes in pieces of paper with their pencils. Amid their teasing, the observer shows the girl how to look up Greek mythology in the encyclopedia.

Adversarial relationship between students accepting established classroom norms and values and those rejecting them. Coherent, mutually coactive group of black males are the rejectors. Behavior contrary to norms not corrected by teacher.

Emphasis on task orientation and composure under stress.

Amid some scuffling and "playing around," one black male loudly calls another, "You black boy!" The second boy chases the first one around the room, follows him into the alcove, and punches him on the shoulder. The teacher loudly shouts, "All right!" and pulls them apart, then isolates the second boy in a corner seat. Both boys are laughing. The teacher frowns. Many students clap and whoop at the incident, and the teacher goes to the front of the room and says, "All right!" They quiet down for a few seconds, then the noise picks up as the teacher pauses to catch her breath. The teacher tells the observer that the black male who hit the other student is reading at the second grade level and that his present behavior is an improvement. In the past, he sometimes would get up and walk out the door, challenge the teacher physically, or use profanity in the classroom. She has been trying to get him to be more responsible for his actions and says he is better now. The

Dominance/submission ranking behavior.

Appeal to self-control. Control by spatial isolation.

Aggression directed toward the teacher.

Teacher is forced to assume authority position.

Ridicule. Explanation by recourse to ranked reading level and negative comparison with lower age grades.

Behaviors signaling rejection of established classroom norms and values.

Deference to teacher authority. The black males,

for the most part, are not compliant with classroom norms and values.

Differences in rank, status, and prestige expressed spatially. There are several classrooms here with different students having different experiences. Indirect appeal to classroom norm of self-control. Passive aggression.

Self-restraint and composure under stress are reinforced.

Competition between the teacher and the black males for control of the classroom. Competition over who will set classroom norms and values.

Responsibility training. Right/wrong mastery.

Self-initiated, non-sanctioned behaviors. Little adherence to established classroom norms and values. The tension in the classroom surrounding this pattern has to be experienced over time to be appreciated.

teacher selects a group of students sitting together at another table. She says these are the only students in class who are reading at the fourth grade level. She points to the long table in the middle of the room and says those seated there are all reading at the second semester third grade level and that those at the table in the back are reading at the first semester third grade level. Periodically, the teacher turns to face the class to shout, "All right!" The talking drops but picks up as soon as her back is turned.

Suddenly, she slams her book on her desk and yells, "That's enough. . . . That's it!" There is a slight pause as she tries to control her anger. The attention of the class is, for once, focused on her, and the room is deadly quiet. But she waits too long. In the back of the room, a black student says something under his breath, causing several neighboring students to giggle. Suddenly, the students turn from the teacher to the black males in the back of the room. Students start giggling and look toward the back of the room. The teacher continues talking with the observer.

10:00 A.M. When finished, students exchange papers to correct them. The teacher reads the answers. Constant comment, annotation, conversation, giggling, and unsuppressed whispers come from the students, but the teacher says nothing. Students do not raise their hands. They simply shout out comments, no matter who else is talking. The teacher tries to talk over them, but the drone continues.

After the papers are corrected, and while the teacher is preoccupied, students get up to go to neighboring desks, to poke one another, to drop books and other materials on their desks, to sharpen pencils, and to perform little jokes and antics in an effort to amuse their peers. Students are wandering about the classroom. The aide sits at her desk waiting for instructions. Presently, the teacher tries to regain control by pleading with the students. She says, in a soft voice, that she has had a trying day and that she wants them to calm down for her sake. Her plea momentarily is effective, and the noise and activity levels drop. Students return to their seats. While waiting for them to be quiet, the teacher stands in front of her desk with her arms folded across her chest. The teacher's face reflects suppressed rage, and she stands in the same spot, her hands clenched into fists, saying nothing. The class grows louder. Both her voice and face express strain, tension, and frustration. Suddenly, she tells a black male to remove his "Afro cap" in class and several others to go to the alcove to hang up their coats. The students do so amid groans and protests. Calmly, she threatens to cancel recess if they are not quiet. The students become quiet, and she tells them to work on their assignments while she conducts her reading groups.

10:20 A.M. The teacher and aide go to separate tables to work with specific reading groups. The teacher discusses the progress of each group, stressing the "good" work of the "top" students while explicitly castigating the "poor" work of the "low" students.

Several black males are teasing and taunting a white female who is trying to do her work. They poke and bully her, but she does not go to the teacher. One of the boys tires of this and for the amusement of his cohort leans back on his chair . . . way back . . . until . . .

Spontaneous self-generated behaviors are associated with the permitted activity in the lower grades.
Control by manipulation of emotions. Pleasing-the-teacher behaviors.

Compliance indicated by voluntary spatial confinement. Authority positioning used to legitimize control.
Norms of self-control, restraint, and composure under stress.

The Afro cap is a style of hat worn by some black males in West Haven.
Control by power of cessation of activity and confinement. Expected self-maintenance.

Recurring spatial expression of ranked grouping.
Differential public praise and ridicule. Division of the peer group against itself. Competition. Value labeling attached to students.
Internal division of the student peer group in reference to degree of internalization of classroom norms and values.

Classroom norm to claim responsibility for one's behavior. Black males challenge the authority structure of the classroom. Attempts to invade/control private space/property. Adherence to classroom norm of self-reliance.

Defense of child against peers. Nonverbal threat gestures. This sort of communication reinforces emphasis on the eye over other senses.

Nonverbal requirement of deference. Again, the struggle is for the source of classroom norm/value authority and the control of the children.

Indirect compliance. The child submits without losing "face." Nonpermitted mobility.

Reference to the color of the female student. Awareness of social race/ranking by color.

Explanation by recourse to innate biological differences.

the chair, with him in it, falls with a resounding crash. Students jump at the sudden noise. The male gives the teacher a feeble excuse and "Who, me?" look when she turns to reprimand him. The teacher does not say anything but just glares at him. Now, the boy is back in his chair taunting the girl. He snatches her pencil. She snatches it back. The aide is watching. The boy again snatches the pencil. The girl does not seek help but pauses and pouts as if trying to decide what to do. The aide tells the boy to return the pencil. He slowly rears back on his chair, thrusts out his chin, and looks at the aide, who returns his stare. He makes no move to return the pencil. Again, the aide tells him to give back the pencil. He does not. He makes feeble excuses: she does not need it, or it really is his, or why is *she* picking on *him*! The aide holds out her hand and wiggles her fingers for the student to bring the pencil over to her. The student rears back in his chair and smiles. His cohorts watch intently. The aide again tells him to surrender the pencil. Suddenly, the male jumps up, thrusts the pencil into the aide's hand, and saunters off to the washroom. The pencil falls to the floor. The aide glares at him. While strolling into the washroom, the boy rubs his hands together saying he has to wash the "white cooties" away. The aide picks up the pencil and, sighing, passes it to the girl, who says nothing and buries her head in her book.

Later, in discussing this incident with the observer, the teacher frowns and says, "There are some kids who are just animals. There is just no other way to say it."

A paper airplane quietly sails across the room. The teacher turns around angrily to shout, "All right!" The students sheepishly look at one another and smile. The "fun" is that she does not know who tossed it. The teacher glares at them for several seconds, then turns to her group.

> Denial of autonomy and the mutually supportive student peer group.

The girl the observer had helped is crying. A black male comes from across the room to sit with some other black males across from her. They taunt her as she studiously bends over the encyclopedia, laughing at her for believing in Pandora. To no one in particular she shouts out in anguish, "They're teasing me!" The teacher looks up, frowns at *her*, then turns back to her group. The males sit closer together now. They continue to laugh and point at the girl. At their worst, they actually reach over and laughingly flip the pages as she reads. The girl cries for about five minutes. Occasionally, students turn to see what the noise is about, size up the situation, then turn back to their work. The teacher does not intervene and, in torment, the girl flees to the washroom. The males tauntingly mimic her actions in silent fits of laughter. In five minutes, she comes out and returns to her seat. Composed now, she seems determined to ignore and resist her tormentors. A black female sitting next to her gets up to sit with the boys across from the girl. She ignores them and continues reading the encyclopedia. This continues until the teacher calls the class as a whole to attention.

> Group solidarity among black males. Active assaults on established classroom norms/values.

> The teacher does not defend the child against her peers. Classroom norms of autonomy and self-reliance are reinforced.
> Intrusion into personal space/private property. Dominance behaviors.

> The child signals defeat by relinquishing her territory.
> Adherence to classroom norms of composure under stress, self-control, and task orientation.
> The antagonism is thus with respect to color rather than sex alone.

11:10 A.M. The activity and noise levels are high. Most students have stopped working and frequently get up out of their seats. Others freely talk and carry on personal activities and conversation. One black male says, "Shhhhhh" to another. Quickly and menacingly, the reply is "You shhhhh yourself!" The

> Attempt at peer monitoring of the group. Adherence to established classroom norms/values.
> The internal division of the group is by adherence to norms/values rather than by sex or color.

Self-reliance and self-maintenance are reinforced.

aide watches but makes no effort to intervene, and the teacher works with her reading group.

A white female asks the observer if he would help her. She does not know how to spell *pterodactyl*. Neither does the observer. She goes over to the teacher, who tells her to look it up herself. Having difficulty with the dictionary, she comes back to the observer. The teacher does not intervene. The student sits down next to the observer, and they look for the word.

Adherence to literacy training norm.
Emphasis on student self-reliance and self-maintenance.

Event Transition 3

Nonadherence to customary norms of quietness, regimentation, waiting, and order.

11:30 A.M. The reading groups are dismissed. Students do not heed the teacher's directions or follow her orders. Presently, she shouts at them to get ready for recess, and they rush toward the alcove. They swear at, push, and shove one another as they snatch up their clothing. One student almost knocks down the aide. The teacher yells for them not to rush, but they do not heed her and run out the door. After they are gone, the aide gives the teacher a "What-can-you-do?" look, puts on her coat, and walks to the playground.

The response is ridicule.

Event Transition 4

11:40 A.M. Lunch period. Recess.

Continuing lack of adherence to established classroom norms and values. Incidents here bring into high relief some latent classroom norms and values. Breaking the rule highlights the rule.
Control by power of cessation of activity.

1:00 P.M. Amid a torrent of noise and activity, students burst into the room. Few bother to take off their coats but chase one another around the room, yelling and screaming at the top of their voices. The teacher jumps up and shouts that they will have to go outside and come back in. She cannot be heard over the din. No one is paying her any attention. She screams at them to go outside and to come back in a more quiet and orderly fashion. They straggle out the door, shoving and pushing those who are trying to get in and have yet to hear the teacher say to go back out. Students start throwing snowballs at one another. Finally, they are out and the teacher closes the door. This time, the teacher stands by the door to oversee their entry into the classroom. They are still noisy and loud, and the teacher gives the observer a "What-can-you-do?" look.

Control by focus on the teacher's power to monitor.

Continuing public display of ridiculing and belittling.

It takes the teacher twenty minutes to get them in their seats and reasonably quiet. The aide walks around the classroom trying to keep order and, to her face, students laugh and continue doing as they want. She asks, "Did anyone watch the news this morning?" There are a few grunts. No one had seen the program. They say, "Naw" and "Uh uh" very loudly, joking about the question, prompting giggles from others. The teacher looks over at the observer and gives him a "What-can-you-do?" grimace.

Comparatively more time spent on behavior modification = less time for academics.

Continuing public display of ridiculing and belittling.

Reference to electronic (television) media rather than print (books) media. On the day of observation, this teacher did not stress books and reading as much as did the high session teacher.

"Well," she says, "you all should check it out." She asks how many had seen the Ali-Forman fight on television. No one had. One black male, though, knows about Ali and remarks that the teacher should divorce her husband and marry Ali. Everyone, especially the black males, laughs, and the teacher blushes and says, "All right!"

The student/teacher relationship here is mutually antagonistic and adversarial. Ridiculing.

Physical violence contradicts established norms/values. Ridiculing and belittling.

Event Transition 5

2:00 P.M. The teacher tells the aide that maybe they ought to have a spelldown. The aide announces it, and many students leap from their chairs and begin forming their own line. Other students stand by their desks while others sit on their desks like parked cars. They all ask to be chosen leader. While the aide picks the leaders, a black male starts taking the fire extinguisher from the wall. The teacher

Attempt to control class by changing activity.

Adherence to regimentation.

Game of competition spatially and territorially structured. "Success" and "failure" are publicly displayed.

Important reference to the differential internalization of established classroom norms and the stark polarization of the student peer group.

and aide say nothing. Scrap paper and broken pencils are strewn on the floor. Desks are in disarray, and chairs lie about. A heavy odor of sweat overlies the increasing disorder. Amid the noise, each leader goes to an opposite side of the room and chooses students. Students make "wolf calls," loudly comment on the leaders' choices, and make disparaging remarks about the selected persons. When a black female is chosen, a black male says, "She thinks she so smart anyway." Another black male is trying to open the outside door. No one intervenes. The aide is loudly shouting for the students to stay in line and to be quiet. They pay her no attention. The aide sighs, pauses a second, then proceeds as if nothing has happened. The spelldown finally begins.

Punishment by banishment from the group. Isolation. The assumption is that those children not adhering to established norms/values are past the point of doing so, and they receive less attention from the teacher than do other students.

Other examples of containment attitudes.

The aide, in turn, gives each student a word to spell. If they cannot spell the word, students have to sit down. When a student spells a word correctly, everyone on the team breaks rank to clap and pat him or her on the back. The other team says, "Boooooo" and makes loud catcalls. Two black females suddenly decide they want to do the "bump" (a popular dance) while waiting their turn. Other students run in and out of line chasing one another. The teacher and aide do not intervene. The aide periodically glances at the wall clock.

Event Transition 6

Success/failure as an outcome of the competitive structuring of the game.

Compliance by assumption of authority position and the threat of physical violence.

3:00 P.M. The spelldown is over, and the winning team loudly whoop it up. The teacher stands to tell them, shouting over their voices, to start getting ready. The students do not react to her comand, and she takes out two wooden rulers from her desk and angrily advances to the center of the room. In the background several students say,

"Oh, oh" and run for their seats. The voice and activity levels suddenly drop to zero. The teacher says that she has had enough. Students point at each other, saying it is someone else's fault. This brings on a new round of incriminations as they argue about who did and did not do what to whom. The teacher stands in the center of the room, rulers in her clenched hands, immobile. Sensing they again have won something, students talk loudly and increase their mobility. Slumping, the teacher returns to her desk, puts the rulers away, and tries to tell the class that those not finishing their assignments will have to finish them tomorrow. The teacher shouts at those who have finished their assignments to pass them up to her. Amid a noisy and violent scramble to retrieve their work, students run up to the teacher's desk and throw down their papers. They do not return to their seats but begin putting on their coats. The teacher does not intervene. As they stand in line by the door, there is considerable shoving and pushing. The teacher tries to tell them to put their chairs on top of their desks. Confusion increases as students run back to put up their chairs; some run into students who have gotten their coats and are trying to line up. Of course, students who left the line want their original places back, and others will not let them in. That corner of the room is a mass of shouting, yelling, scuffling, and confused mobility.

    3:15 P.M. The teacher yells at the students to pick up scraps of paper on the floor, but few heed her. She calls students by name, and they angrily protest that the paper is not theirs and, if they do go back, they pick up only a few pieces. Meanwhile, the aide tells them to

Taking seats is an expression of student deference and compliance.

Blame shifting actually reinforces the peer group by diffusing the teacher's power.

Authority positioning. Norms of composure under stress, discipline, and control of the emotions and the body.

Adherence to finishing and completing norm. Expected self-maintenance.

Regimentation. No compliance with order and quietness norms. This pattern of classroom behavior occurred throughout all the days of observation.

The children invariably adhere to the norms/values of ranking and competition.

No compliance with customary norms/values. Students show adherence to their own standards and feelings.

Passive aggression and defiance.

Adherence to classroom norms of self-direction, ranking, and competition.

Public display of belittling and ridiculing. Defiance of the teacher by some students.

Task divisions of labor. Reduction of teacher status by carrying out aide housekeeping tasks, emphasizing neatness and order.

Recurring adult monitoring/structuring of educational experiences. Time/place coordination.

Adherence to order norm.

Self-maintenance and internalization of neatness norm.

Readiness positioning/waiting (self-control).

Compliance/obedience.

Event Transition 1

Recurring status/authority position. Order. Compliance/obedience.

Rotating responsibility training. Administrative tasks. Emphasis on autonomy and individual effort.

put up their chairs correctly; they only *threw* them up. Few comply as most argue over their place in line. The teacher puts her stapler in the drawer, and loudly, so students might hear, she tells the observer she does this because "they" invariably will take it once her back is turned. Students begin leaving before being dismissed, and the teacher vainly tells them to stop. The aide tosses on her coat and runs to catch them.

The door remains partially open. The teacher slumps in her seat, rests a minute, gets up to close the door, then sets about arranging the furniture and picking up the paper on the floor.

A High Classroom Session

8:45 A.M. The teacher is arranging materials and straightening furniture in preparation for the day's activities.

9:00 A.M. Students arrive from their buses, and there is no running or shoving as they enter the room, hang up their coats, and neatly stack their boots in the alcove. They quietly take their seats. One black male comes in and sits down with his coat on, and the teacher tells him to get up, take it off, and hang it up. Although the boy pouts, he immediately obeys.

9:15 A.M. The teacher goes to the front of the room and calls the class to order. The noise and activity cease. She asks a black female to pass out the folders containing the students' class work stacked on the teacher's desk. The class is told to take out any library books from their desks and, if overdue, to bring them to the teacher's desk to be checked out.

The teacher gives out the day's assignments: correct the papers being passed out, study for a spelling test, and give a spelling test to a group of students. The teacher pauses to ask if they understand the assignments and if there are any questions. There are none, and the teacher writes the assignments on the board. When they finish, they are to start composing a short story. The teacher spends several minutes outlining the penmanship and other mechanical faults she found prevalent in their writing. She says that under no circumstances will she accept papers without their name, the subject, and the day's date *neatly* printed in the upper right-hand corner.

9:25 A.M. The teacher and aide call different reading groups to separate tables. The groups are named after the particular textbooks they are reading, such as "Secrets," "Rewards," and "Panoramas." The aide says to her group that if they pass their test today, they will advance to the next book.

The class works on the assignments. Students go to the bathroom or pencil sharpener without asking permission. Their movements are very deliberate and controlled.

9:45 A.M. The teacher calls a new group of students to her table. A white female approaches the teacher requesting an answer to a problem. The teacher firmly asks, "What is the answer?" The girl fidgets, fights to get the answer, then shyly gives it to her. The teacher glares at her and says, "Well, all right!"

The teacher demands that they do their work and do it correctly. Periodically, she interrupts her lesson to tell erring students that they *must* be more careful, and *only* do what

Expected responsibility for personal property.

Expected self-direction. Right/wrong mastery. Literacy training.

Imaginative, creative exercises are always secondary to rote activities.
Emphasis on procedure and obedience training.
Right/wrong mastery.
Emphasis on procedure and conformity to an established model. Autonomy. Time.

Recurring spatial reinforcement of ranked subgroups. Here, the labeling defining the ranked subgroups is made explicit.
Standardized evaluation as basis for ranking and progress in a sequence.
In comparison with the low session, children here exhibit adherence to and compliance with established norms and values. As such, they are permitted more liberties.
Required compliance with procedure. Obedience training. As expected, these children show compliance.
Continuing emphasis on training for self-reliance and problem-solving.

Lack of nurturing and accommodation.
Compare the demands in this high session with the comparative lack of de-

mands in the low session.
Right/wrong mastery.
Obedience training.
Lack of accommodation and nurturing.

Required proof/demonstration. The children here illustrate adherence to several established norms and values.

Emphasis on concentration and task orientation. Obedience training.
Indirect, rhetorical reprimand reinforcing expected self-control.
In comparison with the low session, children are more deferential and passive.

Continuing administrative intrusions and hegemony over individual classrooms.

The classroom norms of concentration and task orientation amid distractions.
Public display to force compliance. Ridiculing. Right/wrong mastery.

Autonomy. Ranking. Peer competition.

she tells them to do. When they make a mistake, she does not yell at them but, in a stern voice, admonishes them to listen and watch as she works through an example. She corrects their mistakes by repeating the directions and telling them to listen more carefully. She will not accept their mistakes.

Students are beginning to finish their board assignments. They get up, push their chairs under their desks, slowly walk to the teacher's desk, put their papers in a metal tray, turn, and walk straight back to their seats.

10:00 A.M. The observer periodically dozes off. The combination of low, murmuring voices, early morning sunlight, and the hum of fluorescent lights proves intoxicating. The students, though, appear alert. Every student is quietly bent over his or her work. The librarylike silence is broken sharply by the teacher's abrupt voice remonstrating a student to pay attention and follow directions. Seeing a number of students not occupied, she says, "Are you ready for the spelling test?" When she responds in this fashion, students avert their gazes, bow their heads, and respond in meek voices.

10:15 A.M. An office assistant walks into the room and casually delivers a message to the teacher. Few students look up from their work.

The teacher corrects papers while students read in her small group. Presently, she gets up, goes to the board, and writes out the names of two black males. Beside their names, she writes the page numbers of their homework on which she found mistakes.

10:25 A.M. The teacher calls a new group of students to her table while the aide dismisses her group and gives individual spelling tests to students. Students receiving a high grade jump out of their seats. One black female receives an A+ and the aide loudly praises her. One black male loudly says, "I won! I won! I'm the champ around here."

Most students form unsupervised groups. The teacher permits normal voice tones and high mobility and intervenes only when they begin to yell and shout.

The black students, especially the males, form the most active groups. Nearly all the white students remain seated at their desks, concentrating on their work and ignore the activity around them. One black male joins a student playing horseshoes. Three black females and two males remain in their seats. A black male and female put together a puzzle on the floor.

The teacher dismisses her group and checks with the aide about the results of her work.

11:00 A.M. The teacher tells the students to take their seats. They put away their materials and get ready to go to the math lab (see Figure 2). The teacher designates a white male to pass out folders taken from a locked file cabinet. The math teacher records the quality and quantity of their work in the folder. Students put on their coats and form a line by the door. The white students habitually gather toward the rear of the line. While waiting in line, a black female shoves another black female. Angrily, the teacher intervenes. Flustered, students accuse each other by pointing fingers and saying someone was out of line. The teacher asks why they are so concerned with *lines*! The students sheepishly

Ranking and differential rewards.
Peer competition for scarce resources is reinforced. The children accept the internal division of the student peer group.
Permitted spontaneous behaviors and mobility as a reward for work.

Differential behaviors by color and sex.
Task orientation/concentration amid distractions.
More expression of nonacademic behavior on the part of some black children.

The teacher does not intervene (expected self-maintenance).

Event Transition 2

Readiness positioning.
Complex scheduling involving spatial mobility. Rotating administrative tasks. Regimentation. Order.
Autonomy. Individual responsibility for progress. Regimentation. Order.
Differential grouping and ranking by color. Waiting. Physical violence occurs.

Ranking and competition are pervasive norms/values. People are often unaware of their own culture (Merton 1957: 60–82).

look at her, but no one says anything. The aide takes the students to the math room. The line is very straight, very orderly, and very quiet.

Adult monitoring and supervision. Adherence to established classroom norms.

Event Transition 3

11:45 A.M. Lunch. Recess.

The peer group is differentiated. Children are having different, specialized educational experiences. Self-maintenance.

The students leave the math lab. Most follow the aide to the lunchroom, but a few come back to the classroom. The teacher stays in her room during the lunch period, and those students who did not finish their morning work can, if they choose, stay during recess to finish it.

Event Transition 4

12:45 P.M. In an orderly line, the students quietly file into the classroom from recess. In an orderly fashion, they take off their coats and hang them in the alcove. There is no shoving or pushing as the students quietly take their seats.

Entry protocol illustrates adherence to procedure and classroom order norms.
Self-control.

Standing up is a change in height/positioning nonverbally signaling forthcoming orders.

The teacher stands up and asks if the class would like to have a "mathdown." The students shout, "Yeeeaaa," smile, and jump up and down in their seats.

Example of conflict between latent and manifest norms. Right/wrong mastery.

The teacher tells them that, today, she is not interested in them *competing* against each other, but she is interested in the *right* answer, emphasizing right, not so much who wins. A mathdown operates like a spelldown except the content is a math problem given by the teacher to which the student must respond. Two students, chosen by the teacher, go to opposite ends of the room and line up against the long wall. In turn, each one calls out the names of students they want to be on their team. Those chosen get up and run, squealing, to their place in line. Students express anguish when a "good" math student is chosen

Emphasis on mathematics. Problem-solving. Rotating responsibility training. Spatial separation and the definition of competing units. Ranking and peer competition.
Public ridicule.
Mobilization of anxiety so children will try harder and compete more fiercely.

by the other side. The students chosen last are anxious because the situation is structured so that everyone knows that the people called last are not considered good risks by their peers. After all the students are chosen, everyone is interested in carefully checking the line and counting to make sure both sides have the same number of students.

Adherence to the notion of equality and the established classroom ideology of group competition.

The teacher shows each student a flash card on which is printed a math problem involving multiplication, addition, subtraction, or division. The student is shown the card for only a few seconds, and if he or she cannot answer the problem, or answers incorrectly, he or she must sit down, and the teacher shows that same card to a student on the opposing team. When a student misses an answer, the team members groan. If an answer is correct, the team applauds. Occasionally, students try to count out the answer on their fingers. The teacher screams, "No finger counting! Give me the answer right off!" Other students are instructed not to help and to answer only in turn. As a student tries to answer, the teammates twist around in frustration, wanting to shout out the answer. When someone misses a question, students sitting down are always asked if they know the answer, and if they do, they are allowed to get back in line. Finally, the last student correctly answers his problem, and teammates rush up to hug him. They all return to their seats.

This activity reinforces rote memorization and recall.

Punishment by banishment from the group and by spatial isolation.

Right/wrong mastery.

Emphasis on rote learning and memorization.

Obedience training.

Automony and self-reliance.

Self-control. Management of emotions.

The children are much more concerned with competition than they are with right answers. Winning results in peer esteem and prestige.

Event Transition 5

1:25 P.M. When all are sitting quietly, the teacher tells them to get their coats and line up by the door for recess. She asks them to be sure to put their pencils in their desks, and several students return to their desks to do so.

Order as required for further activity.

Regimentation. Order.

Expected self-mainte-

nance. Responsibility for private property.
Compliance.
Internalization of ranking/status classroom norms.

Trying to get back in line, though, they find that other students will not let them in. The teacher loudly says she is getting tired of all this talk about lines and whose place is whose in line or that someone stole their place in line! She tells them to let the students in line! The students pout and grumble but do what the teacher says. The aide leads the line to the playground.

Adult monitoring/supervision.

Event Transition 6

Adults permitted more mobility and contact than children.
Self-maintenance and adherence to classroom norms.
Peer monitoring (Goetz 1976: 40) is an elaboration of the rights and obligations flowing from adherence to classroom norms and values. Argument over adherence to competing norm and value systems. Threat of physical violence as control mechanism. In contrast to the previous low sessions, advocates for classroom norms and values prevail.

1:30 P.M. Recess.

2:00 P.M. Shortly before the students arrive, the teacher leaves for an adjoining "portable" to speak with another teacher. The aide is with another teacher this period. Students come in, put their coats and boots away, and take their seats. They look around for the teacher. When she does not immediately appear, they begin talking. A black female tells several students to be quiet. A black male joins in and tells them to sit down. The class watches. The girl says that they are going to get the whole class in trouble, and she does not want to be punished for their actions. Both say they will "beat them up" if they are punished by the teacher. They say the students are acting "like babies," and they act like that only because they are "stupid." The students in question do not back talk but quiet down. When the teacher returns, she smiles and apologizes for being late. Closing the door, she says she had to get the filmstrip they will see this afternoon. The students smile and clap.

Responsibility training (males predominate) involving the operation of machinery.

2:20 P.M. The teacher sets up the screen and projector and asks two black males to operate it. The filmstrip is entitled *The Spirit of Christmas*, and while it is running, the teacher asks questions and asks for the students' comments. At the end of the filmstrip, the students whistle, shout "Yeeeaaaaa," clap, and try to make "V" signs on the screen with their fingers. The teacher shows another filmstrip, *The Meaning of Christmas*. This filmstrip has captions, and students beg the teacher to read them. She lets them, and they gently correct each other's mistakes.

2:50 P.M. At the end of the filmstrip, the teacher tells the black males to put away the projector and screen. She returns to her desk, sits on it, and tells the class that she would like to talk about what they are going to do for Christmas. In anguish, a black female whispers, "Oh no! Not again! I ain't got no money in the bank." The teacher walks around the room calling on students, who give her a list of the things they want for Christmas. For instance, a white female says that she wants a Suzie Homemaker. Several black males say they want the following: clothes, a pocket calculator, a racetrack set, an Erector set, a ten-speed bicycle, a train set, and a basketball pole. Several white males want the following: a scope for a B-B gun, a walkie-talkie, a 7-Up Crime Fighter set, a typewriter, a Steve Scout set, a Rollum' Sockum' set, and a B-B gun.

The teacher calls the observer over to show him some of the students' work. She points out that she wants them to learn how to write neatly without lines to guide them, for they will have to do so in high school. Seeing some of their mistakes, the teacher calls the class to attention and, amid their groans, tells them they are going to have a ten-minute writing assignment as handwriting practice. She gives the students several sentences to write while she goes around looking at their work.

Continuing references to national celebrations.

Approval-seeking. Emphasis on demonstration/proof.
Peer policing of right/wrong mastery.
Rotating housekeeping tasks = responsibility training. Place/activity coordination.
So-called show-and-tell as invasion of privacy.
Association of this national observation with consumerism/economics. Emphasis on consumerism.
Material goods/manufactured products. Integration of educational/economic subsystems. Sexual stereotyping. Contrast between female nurturing toys and male mobility/aggression toys.

Emphasis on procedure and obedience training. Literacy training.

Emphasis on mastery/right answers. Stress on procedure.

Rotating housekeeping tasks = responsibility training. Self-maintenance and self-direction. Manipulation of materials.

Peer competition for teacher rewards.

3:15 P.M. The teacher pauses to ask a black female if she would clean off the boards. The girl gets up, puts away her work, puts her paper on the teacher's desk, goes to the teacher's closet to get the cleaning solution and a rag, and cleans off the blackboards. Students beg the teacher to permit them to clean the boards.

Event Transition 7

Required demonstration/proof.

Exit procedure illustrates compliance with established classroom norms and values. Self-directed (internalized) manner in which separation activities are carried out.

Continuing spatial self-segregation by color. Competition over ranking.

An emphasis on compliance with neatness and cleanliness classroom norms.

Recurrent adult monitoring and supervision. *In loco parentis.*

3:20 P.M. The teacher tells the students to pass their papers up to her desk and prepare to leave. She tells them to be sure to pick up all the scraps of paper on the floor, and they immediately obey. They remove all of the materials from their desk tops, put them in their drawers, pick up loose scraps of paper from the floor, and straighten up the furniture. They are told to put their chairs on their desks and to get their coats. In line, the white students again tend to clump toward the rear. The teacher scans the room and calls back two females who did not properly clean off their desks. They do so.

3:30 P.M. The teacher puts on her coat and takes the students to the buses. She returns to the classroom to finish correcting papers.

The fourth grade level continues and expands upon the student behavioral and attitudinal gap, begun in the third grade, between the high and low sessions. The low session narrative is characterized by the distinctive behavior of black males (1) as well as their spatial isolation (14) in the classroom, by passive student resistance (15) and lack of adherence (7) to customary classroom norms and values, and by an adversarial pattern of relationship between the teacher and most students (13).* These features occur with great frequency in the low ses-

*These paired numbers refer to features of the low/high sessions summarized in Figure C-6, Appendix C.

sion but do not occur at all, on the days of observation, in the high session. The low session spends twice as much time on entry and exit procedures than does the high session, and the low session is characterized by greater fragmentation of the student peer group (11/50).

Prominent classroom characteristics associated with the high session, on the other hand, emphasize academic-related features: student productive activities (50/18), order (48/10) and regimentated activity (30/19), task orientation (33/16) reinforced by the teacher's continued attention to student work (20/13), and the required demonstration of student competence (39/14) and mastery of classroom tasks (51/2). Students routinely adhere to established classroom norms, values (19/1), and procedures (–/4) and, in turn, they continue to be rewarded with more permitted mobility (–/15) and responsibility training (31/11). The high sessions in grades three and four (compare Figures C-5 and C-6 in Appendix C) are more similar than their respective low sessions. The high sessions remain comparatively stable while the low sessions increasingly deviate from previously established classroom norms, values, and procedures.

Major similarities between fourth grade low and high sessions include the continuing classroom emphasis on ranking (2/5), on various forms of student competition (4/3), and on expected student self-maintenance and reliance (5/6). In each session roughly the same amount of time is spent on work-related tasks (see Figure B-6, Appendix B), but for each session the nature of student activity during these work periods is decidedly different. Classroom norms and values are routinized, by the fourth grade, and event and activity patterns exhibit the same configuration. The norms and values required for success in middle grade classroom society and culture are made more apparent through their violation. Dramatic departures from established procedure tend to catch one's eye. The primary violators of established classroom procedure in both high and low sessions are groups of young black males.

Black males continually attempt to dominate the classrooms. These students, however, are not merely being rambunctious; they are rebelling and attacking the value system of the classroom culture. They attack books, literacy, and work, and they consciously interrupt the activities of other students. They attack the social system of the classroom. Autonomy, for example, is a core classroom social norm attacked by those black males whose orientation and interactional frame of reference are toward their own peer group rather than toward the teacher. Extensive efforts are made in early and lower grades to break up the peer bonding tendencies among children, both black and white. Most black male students reject functioning autonomously in the classroom not because of an inability to master classroom norms and values but in defiance of them. The low session is labeled a "problem" class; "problem" means that students do not "behave," and "behave"means that students do not adhere to customary classroom norms and values. A class is deemed "out of control" when its social norms and cultural values are consciously disregarded or defied. Some fourth grade black males and a few white males in many respects are similar to the adolescent Sioux males Rosalie Wax (1967, 1976) studied, who boasted about violating classroom rules and otherwise behaving so as to gain status with respect to their peer group rather than with respect to the teacher. Males in both cases never tattled on each other or otherwise exhibited horizontal competition. Intragroup loyalties in both cases are high. Wax (1967:46) says that schools (that is, classroom society and culture) demand that students behave like "mature adults, which in our culture often means being dull and conformist." They are expected to act, in other words, much like the high session students at West Haven. Students adopting the social and cultural system of the school *ipso facto* become well adapted to the more bureaucratic features of society, but at a price. Wax argues, as does Jules Henry (1955, 1959), that students successfully adapted to classroom life lack independence of thought and creativity. Rebellious Sioux males often simply drop out of school and become casualties because they fail to make the transition to what the school classroom culture and society wants them to become. Theodore Rozsak (1969) coins the term "counterculture" in part to account for the 1960s youth movement's rejection of traditional post–World War II cultural and social norms and values. A youth counterculture is generated in the middle grades, by way of analogy. Two distinct student cultures are formed, and the point of departure for each subgroup is its particular orientation toward the sociocultural system of the classroom. By this point in the process of schooling, students either have accepted the classroom social and cultural system or they are in the process of rejecting it. Students become more homogeneous with respect to behavior and attitude, and both within and between classrooms there is little student mingling across increasingly polarized subgroups. Students in both sessions activate differing norm and value systems and tenaciously hold to their particular sociocultural orientations; the white female, for example, who persists in embracing classroom-relevant symbol systems and mythologies. By not supporting students who are attacked, the teacher throws responsibility onto students themselves for adhering to customary classroom norms and values. During the fourth grade the die is cast on student identification with and allegiance to particular subgroup student ways of life. High session students monitor and police attacks on the classroom culture and society. High session black males and white males peer monitor each other, suggesting that subgroup divisions are not exclusively based on color or sex but are associated with a student's orientation to customary classroom norms and values. In the teacher's absence a majority of the high session students, both black and white, generate their own control structure modeled on customary classroom norms and values. They successfully meet challenges from the counterculture and force compliance with their adopted sociocultural orientation. In the teacher's absence these students *are* the classroom cultural and social system because they carry its norms and values with them. The conditioning and initiation process begun in the preschool is successful for most students in that the classroom culture and society has reproduced itself.

School classrooms also are important settings for student testing of emerging sexual identities (Goetz 1978; Sexton 1969). Classroom culture and society are biased toward females, and the lack of same-sex role models for male students, both black and white, is obvious: "But the school has failed also—failed to offer what the boys from even the most 'deprived' and 'underdeveloped' peoples take as a matter of course—the opportunity to become whole men. . . . Some young people leave . . . school because they are too vital and independent to submit to a dehumanizing situation" (Wax 1967:46). Some middle grade black males behave in ways deemed aggressive by the classroom culture but considered appropriately masculine in the wider culture. West Haven classrooms nurture to an inordinate degree. The job of going to school involves learning to be quiet, orderly, and conformist. For both males and females, tendencies to explore are curtailed sharply. Children are warned: Don't hurt yourself. Don't take chances. Don't get dirty. Children less and less do anything particularly physical or active. The aforementioned tendencies, stereotypically, are considered "feminine" rather than "masculine" (Loeb 1963; Sexton 1969:12–22). Classrooms are harder on males than females and because of the additional impact of color, harder on black males (Haskins 1973; Powdermaker 1970).

What happens to rebellious males? Wax (1967) says Sioux males invariably recognize the classroom assaults on them. The more aggressive boys subtly are pushed out of school (Jackson and Harris 1977; Staples 1975) by a female-oriented sociocultural system. Forms of aggression not sanctioned by classroom norms and values, as witnessed in the early grade sessions, are weeded out. Further sorting out of students can be expected to occur. A primary classroom norm is that students not interfere with the work of others. Some black males and white males, in their attack on the classroom culture and society, prevent other students from working. This is an unforgivable violation of classroom life, and these students and their teachers skirmish until a subtle truce is called. These boys linger on the periphery of upper grade classrooms, where a waiting containment game is played out. Because of compulsory attendance laws these West Haven males, unlike Sioux teenagers, cannot drop out of school at the present time. I believe they would, if they could. Undoubtedly they will when they can because socially and culturally there is no place for them in the classroom. The ideology and mythology of the classroom sociocultural system will remain intact, because dropping out will be interpreted as their own choice.

The sociocultural system of the classroom initially differentially groups students with respect to age and sex. During the middle grades, color becomes an issue among students, and teachers also increasingly refer to students on the stereotypic basis of color in addition to their being either high or low. Fourth grade teachers say white students are more serious and diligent about their work. Black students are "always fooling around," "don't try," and "accept themselves just about as they are." One teacher says black males have come up to her, in seriousness, saying that all they want to be is "a pimp or pusher and to live off women." The teacher says black females frequently mention that all they want from life is to have babies. "Black students have to be shown everything. They have to have everything done for them." A teacher provides an example of a black male who came up to her and asked if he could get money for the lunch ticket he did not use while he was absent. In disbelief, the teacher sat down with the boy and tried to make him see that the school participated in the federal school lunch program and that, in effect, his lunches were free! He would not accept this answer and felt he had money coming because he did not use his ticket. The teacher says he never accepted her explanation and continued to feel something was due him. She says, "They can't reason anything out. They can't make the abstract real. Most of these kids have mentally dropped out by the fourth grade. They've missed a lot of their childhood. These kids have seen things the white kids will not see until they are much older. Maybe never will see. Some of these kids have seen things *I* haven't seen."

The high school was closed for several weeks in 1968 because of demonstrations by black students in favor of being able to use the clenched-fist black power salute in the school. A fourth grade teacher says that over the years there has been considerable "racial progress" in the school. Several years ago, her classes were mostly black as more and more white parents began taking their children out of West Haven classrooms to enroll them in parochial schools in nearby towns. Many found private school tuition too high and reluctantly began sending the children back to West Haven. As noted by the following teacher, white students had to adjust to a predominantly black setting:

> Many of the white students here are migrants from the South. They fear institutions of nearly every sort and therefore do not trust or otherwise relate to or participate in the school. These people are shunned by the long-standing whites in the community. These people consider them poor white trash, you know, and won't associate with them. Most of the white migrants live in the southwestern part of the township and school district, while the other whites live to the north. Earlier on, there weren't a lot of white kids in the classes. If they didn't band together they didn't stand a chance. Still don't sometimes. There was a lot of honky and nigger talk and fights in the hall and such. Several classes had to be broken up, you know, and the white kids removed for their own safety. Now, I have to say that I admired the way those kids stuck up for themselves. They felt, you know, that the school was theirs too.

Classrooms do not cause these attitudes about color. The epithets and color antagonisms expressed in the classrooms are brought to school by the students. Tensions within the community, paralleling the relationship of blacks and whites in the wider society and culture, surface in the classroom. On this matter, the principal said:

> There *are* differences between the black kids. For years black parents taught their children not to display open aggression toward white people. These [mostly high session] middle-class black kids are trained to control their impulses, to adhere strictly to the de-

mands of respectability, to avoid negative interactions with whites, in short, to keep out of trouble. Now, today, many black [mostly low session] youth will not live that type of frustration. Many of our black students are reacting to their rejections and defiance of the larger society. In their reaction to society, which in most cases is an unconscious one, the relationship with their fellow white students in many cases is affected. Many black students feel that since they are rejected both in the home and in the community, the school is their place of control. Many of them are forced to act as adults by taking care of their brothers and sisters in broken homes and even doing the shopping. Then they hear in the community how bad they are. There is bound to be some carryover into the school.

Yet it is rare to witness black students taunting white students in the same fashion as we might expect white students to taunt black students in other desegregated situations. The principal adds:

The white students are required by their position in a minority role to make some great concessions in their way of thinking. In the larger society they view, or are taught to view, their group as superior in every way, and any demands for equality on the part of other groups they see as a threat to their own security. . . . Even if the problems are not real, there is a certain fear among many of the white students. . . . Teaching in [West Haven], which is described as a "disadvantaged area," is difficult for many teachers since the overwhelming majority of [West Haven's] teachers come from middle-class groups. Unfortunately for [West Haven] and the majority of its students, teachers tend to identify with upper-class groups, with their opinions, aspirations, and ways of life because many of them long to be accepted in that stratum. The problems of the community and the problems of teacher identity are producing a negative attitude among [West Haven's] teachers, as the student body shifts to a black majority. This is very important because the teacher is the heart of the classroom and in the last analysis, what teachers play up or ignore will affect the behavior of their students. . . . Many of our teachers are so busy stating that the students cannot learn that they are overlooking the reasons for behavior problems. They are also getting achievement and intelligence confused and letting achievement in the classroom determine their true attitudes toward their students. We have other teachers who bend over backward in their desire to be fair to their students.

Despite the principal's attitude, a prevailing feeling is that if the students do not or will not "behave and act right," as one teacher succinctly put it, they ought to be "put out of school." It is very clear that most teachers believe that consistent behavioral problems, no matter the cause or motivation, should not be tolerated. As the same teacher concluded, "All that stuff takes away from time that could be spent on students who want to learn."

Middle grade teachers feel that West Haven is too concerned, rather than not concerned enough, with so-called low-achieving students. A fourth grade black teacher points to the fact that special reading and mathematics programs are geared to low-achieving students. "Virtually all of the special federal grants we receive are for low achievers." "But," she continues, "low-achieving students themselves do not care much about school. But the school *caters* to them! The low students exert pressure on the high students *not* to achieve, and low-achieving black students bring down the high-achieving black students." "That," she emphasizes, "is why there is compulsory attendance." Another black teacher stresses that, in comparison, "white people don't care about nonachieving white kids, that's why they keep them out of suburban schools!" Black teachers, especially, are very angry about a perceived school emphasis on the plight of low-achieving black students and are outspoken about what they feel is a conspiracy. The conspiracy, perpetuated by the larger white society, is to keep blacks from receiving exceptional training and education. "The kids [primarily black] who can learn are not taught and remain below their capacity," says one teacher, "while the students who act up mostly get kicked out of school anyway. *Nobody* gets a decent education. See, that's the goal. That's how they keep black folks down."

It does not matter whether we agree with these feelings. Many teachers, and all of the black teachers, hold to and act upon them. Several teachers spend most of their classroom time with only a few of their students. These students consciously are singled out to be "saved." Peter Wilson (1973) in his book *Crab Antics* uses the metaphor of crabs in a barrel to talk about what sometimes happens to people trying to escape psychological and material poverty in the Caribbean. When a person puts on the cloak of "respectability" as a means of escape, others latch on and, in also trying to escape, pull them all back down the side of the barrel. In the frantic effort at escape, no one escapes. During the middle grades at West Haven, many teachers consciously override the ideology of perfectibility by intervening to reach in and to help pull out the more "respectable" students. The other students remain, angrily, at the bottom of the barrel.

During the middle grades, students more forcefully are ascribed various roles and statuses in the classroom society: "good" student, "poor" student, "clown," "teacher's pet," and so forth. Differentiated student careers are reinforced during this phase in the process of schooling.

The sociocultural system of the classroom is resistant to change generated from within. Students at West Haven are not successful in trying to alter the customary flow of classroom life. Change is induced externally rather than internally, and grade-to-grade social and cultural changes occur at the instigation of bureaucrats outside the classroom.

The several incidents presented here do not present a complete picture of the continual skirmishing occurring at this grade level, as the classroom sociocultural system fights off the last major challenges to its legitimacy and successful reproduction. Skirmishes are won by the classroom culture and society, in part because the customary system of schooling is so firmly entrenched. Some school systems, though, are particularly subject to successful internal rebellions (Rosenfeld 1971), while others are so well integrated that few students attempt rebellion (Eggan 1956; Hostetler and Huntington 1971). The elementary school classrooms at West Haven do not readily accept sociocultural diversity, counter values and behaviors are suppressed, and the classroom culture and society remain intact. Socioculturally, the classrooms at West Haven are not very tolerant places.

FIFTH AND SIXTH GRADES: ON ONE'S OWN

The upper grades are organized in terms of distinct academic sub-ject areas. Subjects, and the times of subject offerings, rotate between three alternating nine-week marking periods. The state reading specialist gives a placement test to fourth grade students. Several groups of fifth and sixth grade students are formed on the basis of test scores. Although all students take required subjects, separate classes are formed ostensibly on the basis of ability. Subjects taught include mathematics, science, social studies, communication skills, art, physical education, and mathematics. Teachers, students, and academic subject offerings are defined as being either high or low. Teachers are responsible only for subject specialties within major academic areas. Teachers have permanent classrooms, and students change rooms and classes every hour. There are no "contained" classrooms in the upper grades. Several homerooms are provided where students first come in the morning to leave their outerwear and other materials while going from classroom to classroom during the day. Students return to their homerooms in the afternoon to be dismissed from school.

Upper grade classrooms are located in the main building (see Figure 2). Except for the lack of counter and sink areas, these rooms are similar in design to previous classrooms. There is little room-to-room variation in upper grade furniture shape and arrangement. Each classroom is painted either off-white, pale yellow, or pale green; ceilings are off-white or gray acoustic tile, with fluorescent lighting inserts. Upper grade classrooms appear bare devoid of the paraphernalia common to the lower grades. The only visual displays seen exhibit academic subject-related themes; visually at least, the separation of work from play is complete. Upper grade classrooms are stark and functional, and they environmentally help orient students to the more intense task orientation of high school classrooms.

In the low classroom that was observed there are several United States and world wall maps hanging behind and slightly above the teacher's desk; a globe of the world sits on top of the teacher's file cabinet. A bulletin board, on the front wall, displays an elaborate chart diagramming the political structure of the government of the United States. Next to it, a chart pictorially shows all the presidents of the United States. These commercially produced visual displays continue a classroom orientation toward the nation-state; there are no visual references to West Haven's local geographic area or state or regional political figures displayed in the classroom. Various newspaper and magazine clippings of science-related topics, collected by the students, are taped to the blackboards. The physical features of the classroom emphasize the transmission of information through the standardized knowledge in commercially produced workbooks and textbooks. The *World Book Encyclopedia* and science laboratory equipment fill every available shelf and storage space. The second classroom also is stark visually. Pull-down geographic maps hang from the front wall above the teacher's desk. On the front blackboard, a large commercially produced map of nineteenth-century Africa stereotypically conveys pictures of the "typical" Egyptian, bushman, Watusi, and other Africans from each major continental social group and geographic area.

Beginning in the middle grades, a visually apparent shift occurs in the kinds of subject-related classroom materials and physical objects displayed in the classrooms. National sociocultural orientations and traditions still are expressed at West Haven, but there is a cross-grade shift in the physical mediums of their expression (see Figure 9). Classroom materials and physical objects, either commercially or student/teacher-produced, vary by grades. Commercially produced visual references to the national society and culture predominate in the middle and upper grades, while teacher/student-produced materials are concentrated in the early grades. Commercially produced materials and objects are more standardized, of course, than are teacher/student-produced items. Textbooks, clocks, flags, and calendars are mass-produced items standardizing local school classroom environments. More so than not, public school physical references to local community sociocultural traditions are handmade by teachers and students.

A by-product of the cross-grade pattern of distribution of classroom subject-related materials and objects is that, at various levels of age and cognitive development, students *continually* are exposed to national sociocultural orientations and traditions. Different physical items are exhibited at the grade level at which the most efficient sociocultural conditioning occurs. In the early grades, for example, there is pronounced emphasis on the making and display of student-produced art; children participate in the making of national images and symbols. The sociocultural conditioning in the upper grades is more subtle. Informal, contextual teaching and learning is overshadowed by a formal text and subject-oriented standardized curriculum established by federal and state mandate. Standardized, commercially produced classroom maps and globes visually refer to the nation and the world and celebrate and legitimize national events, heroes, and leaders, the political structure of the nation, and the political relationship of the nation to the rest of the world. No matter at what grade or at what age, then, students continually are exposed to the myths, orientations, and paraphernalia symbolic of American national society and culture.

Upper grade furniture shapes and the spatial arrangement of the

Figure 9. Grade-Level Distribution of Classroom Materials*

	P	K	1st	2nd	3rd	4th	5th 6th
Student and/or teacher produced							
Academic products							
Papers							+
Projects							+
Alphabets							
Animals (anthropomorphic)		+	+	+			
Naturalistic/representational		+	+				
Art							
Abstract	+	+	+				
Representational		+	+	+			
Calendars		+	+	+			
Charts							
Achievement							
Number		+					
Holidays							
Scenes		+	+	+	+		
Stereotypes		+	+	+	+		
Symbols		+	+		+		
Posters							
Academic					+		
Graphic					+		
Commercially produced							
Alphabets		+	+	+	+		
Academic products							
Cutouts (magazines, newspapers)							+
Posters			+			+	+
Calendars		+		+		+	+
Clocks	+	+	+	+	+	+	+
Encyclopedias					+	+	+
Flags	+	+	+	+	+	+	+
Holidays							
Scenes		+	+	+	+	+	+
Pictures		+		+	+	+	+
Posters				+	+	+	
Stereotypes				+	+	+	+
Symbols				+	+	+	+
Laboratory apparatus							+
Textbooks					+	+	+
Workbooks					+	+	+
World globes					+	+	+
World maps					+	+	+

* + sign denotes presence.

urniture at West Haven are familiar; they are characteristic of most ɔublic school classrooms (see Figure 10). Upper grade classroom spaces ɪre defined sharply, and the focused arrangement of the furniture, defin-ng a square of five rows and six files, parallels the rectangular shape ɔf the room itself. The teacher's desk is placed in the front center of he room, thereby nonverbally and spatially reinforcing classroom social ɪtatus and role distinctions between teacher and students and between ɪdults and nonadults. The classroom arrangement of the furniture, nore than in previous classrooms, physically reinforces the norm of tudents being in particular seats at particular times. At least a meter's listance separates each student, and student-to-student interactions are ɔontrolled by the spatial environment. To interact at all in this restrictive ɪetting, students must manipulate the distance-reinforcing furniture ar-ʼangement, but they can do so only with the teacher's permission. Up-ɔer grade teachers say that this rank-and-file seating arrangement better ɔocuses student attention on the teacher and on class lessons. Rank-and-ile seating, they say, better permits the orderly transmission of specific nformation to a large group of people.

Within each classroom, though, from preschool through the sixth ʒrade, furniture shape and spatial arrangement reinforce differing pat-erns of student behavior and interaction. In the early grades furniture ɪhape and spatial arrangement condition for cooperative, group pat-ʼerns of student relationship—classroom patterns of interaction norma-ively emphasized by the teachers. During the middle grades this inter-ɪctional orientation to the classroom spatial environment decreases, and ɪn elaboration of spatial conditioning for individualized student tasks, ɪutonomy, and the idea of interchangeability occurs. The upper grade ʼank-and-file seating arrangement is a physical and spatial manifestation ɔf the standardization and emphasis on uniformity characteristic of bu-ʼeaucratically organized societies. The preschool through sixth grade ɔassage through these differing classroom spaces itself is environmental ɔonditioning to the above-mentioned values and behaviors.

In previous grades, students painted pictures or composed displays hat personalized the setting and left their mark on the classroom. In he upper grades, the classroom is a comparatively impersonal setting hrough which students unobtrusively pass.

Upper grade students are ten through twelve years of age. There are ive upper grade teachers and one teacher's aide. Low group sessions in ɪcience and communication skills are taught by a black female in her

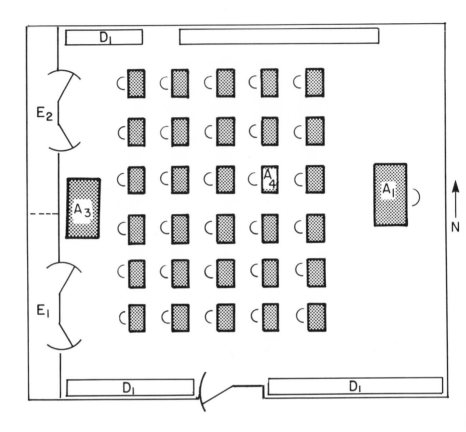

Figure 10. An Upper Grade Classroom

Legend

A_1 = teacher's desk   C = chair
A_3 = classroom activity desk D_1 = bookcases/storage areas
A_4 = student desk E_1 = teacher's closet
                           E_2 = students' closet

early thirties, who has been at West Haven for thirteen years. High groups of fifth and sixth grade students in science and mathematics are taught by a white male in his early thirties, who has been at West Haven for four years.

A Low Classroom Session

Recurrent adult structuring of the formal learning experience.
Housekeeping tasks.
Time/place coordination.
Complexity of scheduling.
Permitted spatial mobility.
At-attention positioning.

At this age/grade level, there is more spatial segregation by color and by sex and less interaction among the peer group as a whole.

Isolation of the classroom from other similar units. Required attendance.
Rotating administrative and housekeeping tasks = responsibility training.

8:45 A.M. The teacher writes out the day's assignments on the board and asks an early arriving white male to help take some chairs off the desks and to distribute materials.

9:00 A.M. Students straggle into the room and tend to cluster in the hallway by the door. The teacher tells them to come in and sit down, but students mill around until she tells them to take their seats.

In this class, there are ten black females, four white females, three black males, and five white males. There is clustering by color and by sex. One black female sits with three white females, and a black male sits with three white males. The males sit in the center rows while the females sit at each end row.

9:10 A.M. When all the students are in their seats, the teacher closes the door. Silently, she takes roll. The pink slip is given to a white female. The teacher says, "It's your turn this week." The girl gets up to put the slip outside the door. A black female is asked to go to the file cabinet for sheets of paper and pass them out to each student.

Event Transition 1

Mathematics training.

The morning assignment involves converting inches to meters and millimeters. The teacher asks the observer to allow students to measure him, then convert his height into meters. The observer stands by the door, and the teacher asks the class members to volunteer to measure the observer. Few volunteer, and the teacher calls on specific students. Though one girl has to stand on a chair, they all find the observer's height to be seventy-two inches. The teacher tells them to convert seventy-two inches into meters. Some students immediately get up to work out the problem on the blackboard, while others work at their desks. Many students work with others, but the noise level is moderate.

Expected self-direction. Norm of task orientation. Permitted mobility and peer interaction.

The teacher walks up and down the aisles looking at the students' work, goading the class into doing more. She says she wants "to see something on your papers" and tells them they would not do *anything* if she did not "get on them." Noticing mistakes she feels they should not be making, her voice and facial gestures echo disapproval. Students are castigated especially for making obvious mistakes.

Recurring adult supervision and monitoring. Right/wrong mastery. Demonstration/proof and task orientation. Belittling/ridiculing.
Reinforcement by threat of withdrawal of affection.
Public praise is differentially distributed.

9:30 A.M. An administrative aide enters the room without knocking. Briefly nodding to the teacher, she asks if any students brought money for the school pictures. As she leaves, a black male asks if he can measure her. The aide sarcastically dismisses the gesture: "I know how tall I am 'n' I don't need nobody measurin' me!" She turns and walks out the door. For a brief moment, the boy does not move. He stares at the door for a minute, then walks back to his desk.

Recurring interruptions indicate the administration's power to supersede the teacher's authority; information about ranking, bureaucracy, and hierarchy.
Public ridicule/belittling.
Nonsupport of classroom norms and values.
Adherence to classroom norms of self-control and composure under stress.

The teacher walks over to her desk and takes out a pocket calculator. Excitedly, several students cluster around her and literally fight to decide who will use the calculator. Periodically, the teacher intervenes to make sure that every student has a chance to "check with the computer."

Manipulation of machine technology. Link between technological and educational subsystems.

9:50 A.M. The teacher looks up to say it is time to go. Immediately and quietly, students return to their desks and gather up their

This complex scheduling places heavy reliance on expected self-reliance and direction.

papers and materials. When the teacher says they are excused, they leap up from their seats and walk quickly to the door. The teacher stands by the door as they leave and as the next class enters.

Event Transition 2

Recurring adult monitoring and supervision.

Halls are a separate sociocultural world and have a different function and set of norms and values existing apart from those of the classroom.

The second period class enters. The noise in the hall is very loud. Students entering the room do not immediately go to their seats but meander around the room until the teacher calls the class to order.

9:58 A.M. In this group, there are seven black females, two white females, five black males, and four white males. There is pronounced sexual segregation, and the spatial segregation by color is more pronounced among the males.

Recurring spatial segregation by color and by sex.

More instances of physical violence in low than in high sessions.
Color and sex as subgroup principles of organization.
This is a significant incident illustrating the manner in which most black males remain at odds with classroom norms and values. Adherence to aggression rather than passivity. Awareness of banishment from group as final punishment.
Bias toward females. Authority positioning. Nonverbal threat gesture.

An altercation breaks out between a black male and a black female. There are hostile words, racial and sexual slurs, and angry exchanges. Quietly, the teacher intervenes by saying that "fighting never resolves anything." The boy retorts that it does and that he will always hit someone back if someone hits him, even a girl. The teacher tries to reason with him and softly tells him that he still should not fight and especially that he should not hit girls. The male is firm in his position and says that is how he feels and that is what he is *always* going to do, even if he gets kicked out of school. The event has no resolution. Offhandedly, the teacher tells the boy, not the girl, to behave himself. She goes back to the front of the room. The boy glares at her back.

Authority positioning is assumed *after* this incident.
Reference to national, ritual celebration. Continu-

The teacher stands in the front of the room and calls the class to attention. A Christmas party is planned for later in the week, and the teacher collects money for milk and ice cream. The teacher then takes roll, calling each student by name, and they either answer, "Here," or "Present." Absences are noted on a pink slip that is placed outside the door to be picked up by a student who then takes it to the office.

> ing required administrative tasks. Rotating administrative tasks = responsibility training.

The students begin working, and the observer is measured. Immediately, ten or so students race to the board while others work at their seats. The teacher does not give out answers to the math problems. Students are supposed to work them out on their own. In walking around and looking at their work she often says, "Close," and walks on.

> These shortened sessions are not amenable to any continuity or finishing of classroom tasks.
> Problem-solving. Self-reliance.
> Monitoring and evaluation. Right/wrong mastery.

10:30 A.M. Slowly, many of the black students begin nonacademic activities. Again, the teacher confines most of her attention to the students, all female, who are working at the board. Three black males and one white male start to nail together a birdhouse at the table. Presently, the white student drops out of the group and stands to one side, watching. The observer asks a neighboring black female what happens to students who do not finish their work. She says the teacher usually makes them stay the next period. What does the next period teacher do if students arrive late? Chewing her gum, she replies, "Nothin'."

> At this age/grade level, responsibility for adhering to task orientation is deemed an individual matter.
> The teacher devotes attention to those students (primarily female) who adhere to classroom norms and values. This pattern is apparent over the entire period of observation.

10:45 A.M. Save one, all the black males are engaged in nonacademic activity; they either work on the birdhouse, talk, or watch others. The white males work quietly at their desks. The females at the board alternately talk and work their problems. The teacher alternates between the white males and the students at the board.

> In effect, these males are not part of the academic classroom environment but are being contained. Little is expected of them.

Most of the noise in the room is made by the black males, and the teacher tells them to be quiet and stop disrupting the class. When

> Instead of telling them to work, the teacher tells the males not to prevent *others*

from working (containment).

Control by threat of physical violence occurs more in the low than in the high sessions. Belittling/ridicule. Norm of self-control. Passivity. Passive aggression. Control by cessation of activity. Finishing. Differential degrees of compliance reflecting differing degrees of adherence to classroom norms and values. Expected self-maintenance.

Show-and-tell public display of private emotions. Lack of privacy. Also, a message that they are doing fifteen things wrong (right/ wrong mastery norm). Emphasis on obedience training and conformity.

Emphasis on order. Differential ranking and rewards. These are rejecting, distancing behaviors possibly expressed.

the noise rises, the teacher goes to her desk, slaps a ruler up and down several times, and stares at the class. The noise level drops. She appeals to them by saying she wants to prepare them for high school and *knows* that they will have to be quiet over there! Several black males mimic her: "Fifty-five." The teacher turns and says, "That's right! Our goal for seventy-six is to be able to sit in one spot for fifty-five minutes." This is met with suppressed groans. Not able to gain absolute quiet, the teacher suggests they begin another activity and finish the math tomorrow. There is some groaning, especially from the males using the calculator. All return to their seats.

The teacher asks students to make up a list of personal resolutions for 1975: fifteen things they could do better, in school, during the coming year. The students groan. Undaunted, the teacher goes on to say she also wants them to make up a list of fifteen things they could do better at home. The students groan more loudly. The teacher coolly responds: "You do not have to like it. Just do it!"

11:00 A.M. The teacher tells the class it is time to go. Immediately, they start talking and gathering up their materials. The teacher goes to stand by the door and dismisses the class by rows, quietest rows first. To avoid being punished for running, the students walk quietly to the door. There is quite a bit of scrap paper on the floor. The third period class enters on their heels, as the teacher picks up pieces of paper from the floor.

Event Transition 3

Bureaucratic structur-

11:05 A.M. The class consists of females because the males go to a separate speech class. The class also has separate physical education sessions. The girls are noisy upon entering and do not immediately take their seats but stand around talking. The teacher closes the door and has to say, "It's time to quiet down now." Speaking in a moderate voice, she says they cannot get started until all are seated, then reprimands them for being out of their seats without permission. As they sit down, they remain restless, frequently talk with one another, fidget, and look around the room.

> ing of sexual segregation. Each group is transmitted different information.

> Required policing of customary norms. Continuing emphasis on order and deference as prelude to further activity.
> These are passive resistance, distancing behaviors. Lack of student involvement.

The teacher silently takes roll, then asks students to hand in their lunch money. This seems an opportunity to talk, and the voice level rises. Several times, the teacher tells them to turn around and be quiet. She says, "That's three times now. Do you want to stay in during the noon hour?"

> Required attendance and administrative tasks. Decline in the *in loco parentis* support functions seen earlier.
> Control by threat of cessation of activity. Play as the children's own "time" (time is a fixed quality and is something to be "used").

There are fifteen black females and four white females in the class. The assignment involves oral presentations, and the teacher has mimeographed Christmas poems for them to read. Going to the front of the room, the teacher pushes together several desks. A portable public address system is set up for the girls to use. By way of example, the teacher presents a dramatic reading of several poems. One girl falls asleep, and several students giggle and point at her. The teacher does not heed them. Before calling on students to read, the teacher says they should try to "show some respect" to those who are reading by being as quiet as possible.

> Recurring references to national celebrations.

> Creative exercises are subordinate to other types of exercises. Rejecting, distancing postures. Public ridicule/belittling.

The teacher calls students to stand behind the desks to read a few poems. The girls are flustered and shy about coming to the front of the room but also are anxious to show off while reading. As each girl reads her poem

> Public display of skills. Demonstration/proof.

> Peer competition.

Children here are reading at lower levels than in the high group.

Coaction and support mark this activity as more play than work.

Sequencing of classroom activity according to a priori school time schedule rather than how long the activity takes.

Peer competition. Punishment by banishment from the group and by spatial isolation. Right/wrong mastery.

Peer competition. Ridicule. Demonstration/proof.

Expected self-maintenance.

Regimentation and self-direction. Required deference to authority. Order.

Neatness and order. Recurring housekeeping tasks.

Partial compliance/obedience. Differential adherence to classroom norms and values.

Event Transition 4

Age/grade-related permitted mobility and self-direction. Self-reliance.

over the public address system, there is a tendency to read each word slowly without expressing the content. At the end of each recitation, the girls loudly clap and praise the speaker.

The teacher looks at the clock and says there are several minutes left to begin another activity. She says they are going to play the City Game, and the girls clap and shout. Randomly, the teacher calls on a student to give the name of any city. Then that student calls on another student, who gives the name of a city beginning with the same first letter, for instance, Ann Arbor and Anaheim. If the second student cannot do this, she is eliminated, and the first student calls another. The girls enjoy this game and preen when they get a right answer. When someone misses a question, there are faint but audible murmurs of "stupid." Then, *these* students raise their hands to give the right answer. As a student struggles with trying to think of a city, there is always a thatch of hands waving in the air.

11:50 A.M. The teacher asks students to put up their materials and prepare to leave. The noise level increases, and they automatically form a line by the door. The teacher shouts that they have yet to be dismissed and orders them to straighten up their chairs and desks and to pick up the paper on the floor. When the door is opened, noise from the hall bursts into the room. Some students do what the teacher ordered. Others do not.

12:00 P.M. Lunch. Recess.

In the upper grades, students do not have recess as such but can go outside if they choose. Most students, especially during winter, go to the multipurpose room after lunch (see Figure 2), where they structure activities of their own choosing. Others return to the homeroom to work on various assignments.

Event Transition 5

12:45 P.M. The fourth period class wanders in after the lunch and recess period. Most of the students take their seats, but a few stand around talking. There are three white females, three white males, five black males, and six black females in this session, and students cluster by color but not by sex. The black males and females sit together, and there is interaction within these groups but not between them. White females sit together, but white males interact with one another least of all.

These student clusterings are self-selected. In these upper grade classrooms there are few instances of assigned seating.

After taking and posting roll, the teacher tells the students that they are going to work on metrics. She goes to the board and writes down five conversion problems involving multiplying .54 by two-digit numbers.

Required attendance and administrative tasks. Problem-solving. Mathematics training.

Students become increasingly noisy once the teacher's back is turned. Some students immediately start working, but others hesitate as if looking for something to do. Some students, mostly black females, go to the board to work out the math problems. The white males and females work in their seats while the black males begin talking among themselves.

Indicating differential adherence to classroom norms. The teacher permits the self-selection of classroom activities. Individual responsibility for one's level of classroom participation.

1:10 P.M. A black female from the high school, a student volunteer, walks in and goes to help the people at the board.

Continuing unscheduled interruptions. No aides are assigned to the upper grades.

Many of the students, especially the black males, engage in nonacademic activities. One boy works on a poem for a Christmas card. Looking very bored, a girl reads a magazine. Several students watch others. The mobility

Increasing student contact with other age grades. More intricate participation in the sociocultural system of the school as a whole.

The pattern is for the teacher to spend time with the children, primarily with females, self-selecting adherence to established classroom norms and values. Control by physical constraint. Control by appeal to the emotion of pleasing the teacher. Appeal to norm of self-control. Authority positioning. Peer monitoring = differential adherence to norms and values.

The important point here is that this defiance is permitted. Some failure to internalize classroom norms and values is accepted.

Emphasis on specialized knowledge apart from basic training in literacy and mathematics.

Rejecting, distancing behaviors. Nonparticipation in the established classroom system. The children are required to be physically present but distance themselves by passive withdrawal. This is the only way classroom norms permit the legitimate expression of the children's feelings. The anger and rage here are clear, but there are classroom norms against their direct expression.

and noise levels increase, as some students begin shouting at one another and running around the room. The teacher does not intervene but very intensely works with the girls at the board.

1:25 P.M. The teacher tells the students to take their seats because they are going to work on some science problems. Students loudly groan, and several minutes elapse before everyone is seated and fairly quiet. In correcting their behavior, the teacher does not yell but looks disappointed and displeased. Standing in front of the room with her arms crossed, she waits for them to be quiet. Eventually, people yell at one another to be quiet. The teacher asks a white female to pass out the textbooks. When the teacher tells them to open their books to the section on the human nervous system, some do and others, mainly the black males, do not. Several of the black males sit with their books closed, defiant looks on their faces. The teacher does not intervene.

The teacher asks the class some questions about the human nervous system. Many students are not paying attention but look out the window, play with their shoes, fiddle with their pencils, or merely gaze about the room. When the teacher asks a black male a question, he is found not to be on the right page. A black female blurts out, "They ain't even listenin'!" The students who *do* answer repeatedly guess at what the teacher wants. When they answer incorrectly, the teacher groans, starts to slam her book shut, and looks at them disgustedly. The class is very silent. The teacher's tone of voice and gestures unmistakably imply that the students are stupid. Several students are looking at the wall clock. The teacher is getting no response from the class. She calls on them, and they turn their heads to one side to avoid her gaze. The teacher grows hostile and angry but finally looks at the clock and says it is time to go.

The classroom explodes in a sudden frenzy of noise and activity. Books are slammed down on desks, chairs are pushed back, and everyone runs for the door. The teacher yells after them but to no avail. In several seconds, every student is out the door. Briefly, the teacher stands in the center of the room blankly looking at the door. Textbooks are strewn helter skelter, there are broken bits of chalk ground into the floor, closet doors are open, hangers lie on the floor, nearly every chair is out from its desk, there is quite a bit of paper on the floor, the desks are not straight, and the noise from the hall is deafening. When the fifth period class arrives, the teacher is still straightening the room.

Clockwatching signals that students have to be here, even if against their will.

The children act legitimately because they are no longer under this teacher's time/space jurisdiction.

The lack of customary separation procedures signals a lack of identification with and attachment to the classroom setting.

Neatness and cleanliness norms.

Event Transition 6

1:35 P.M. Between classes, the hall door is left open, and homeroom students frequently come into the room, put in or take things from the closet, and leave. The doorway and the front of the room are usually congested. This group, though, squeezes through the crowd to take their seats quietly. Several black males run into the room, and the teacher tells them to go back out and then enter more quietly. Without any back talk, they follow her order. Closing the door, the teacher smiles and thanks the students for taking their seats.

As a whole, students are told to finish the resolutions begun this morning. The students groan. Waiting for them to be quiet, the

Expected self-maintenance.

Different groups vary in their adherence to classroom norms and values. The student peer group has become more clearly ranked and stratified.

Reinforcement of adherence to classroom norms and values by a pleasing-the-teacher response. Differential rewards. Literacy training.

Emphasis on finishing/completing despite a fractured time/activity scheduling. Authority posturing.

Implied threat. Solicitude for others is counter to the autonomy norm. One of several latent norm conflicts in the classroom culture.

Ridicule/belittling. Implied lack of self-discipline.

Nonverbal threat gesture forcing compliance. Ridicule/belittling.

Nonadherence to classroom norms and values.

Ridicule/belittling. Neatness and order. Emphasis on autonomy and self-reliance.

Autonomy.

Recurring spatial expression of student subgrouping.

Autonomy. Ranking. Evaluation by universalistic standards (tests and grades).

Ridicule. Public display of personal matters. Lack of student privacy.

Right of access of administrative representative.

teacher stands by the door with her arms folded. Students, mostly females, yell at the class to be quiet. The teacher gives them a long, sarcastic look and says that "someday you are going to have to learn to be considerate of others." The teacher repeats the assignment and says that, when they finish, she wants them to look up one or two famous events or people to prepare for a report. Disparagingly, she adds that they were supposed to have started on this assignment last week. Several students groan, but she stares at them until they are silent. As the students take out their materials, the teacher offhandedly says that they will one day regret their attitudes and that they have not yet learned to take proper advantage of school. Students silently walk to the encyclopedias, and the teacher tells them to handle the books carefully and to straighten them up when they are finished. A black male complains that he cannot find the "C" volume. The teacher does not intervene.

While these activities are in progress, the teacher begins giving individualized reading tests. She calls several students to the table at the rear of the room. In particular, she works with a white female whose performance on recent tests has not been good. The teacher pauses to tell the observer that she sometimes does not know what to do with "some students." In disbelief, she says that the girl does not know what a theater is. She has never seen a movie. The teacher blankly stares at the observer.

Suddenly, a white female student worker from the office walks into the room. She tells the teacher she forgot to fill out an attendance slip. Grumbling, the teacher quickly takes roll.

2:30 P.M. Several students suddenly get

up and leave the room. A white female explains to the observer that some students have a reading class today. No discernible notice is otherwise taken of their departure.

In working on their assignments, students form informal groups. This is permitted though the teacher says, "If you can't talk softly, then don't talk at all," and "No, Brenda, you can't work with anybody because you talk constantly." Students talk softly, and soon everyone is working on his or her assignment.

2:55 P.M. The teacher finishes the reading tests. A few more students get up and leave the room. The white female explains to the observer that she thinks these students have band practice.

3:00 P.M. As the teacher dismisses her reading group and as students finish their assignments, the classroom becomes a homeroom for those students having no place else to go or nothing else to do. The teacher encourages the remaining students to read. The observer helps several students with their reading assignments. The teacher is at her desk reading. The room is quiet.

3:15 P.M. The teacher tells the remaining students it is time to go and to put their chairs on top of their desks and to clean off the table tops. In a sudden and startling burst of noise and activity, the class comes alive. For several seconds, the noise is deafening.

The teacher frowns and quietly says she is not going to tolerate all this noise. Two misplaced chairs crash to the floor. The teacher tells the offending students to place their chairs "properly" on top of their desks. Other students put on their coats and stand by their

Permitted mobility. Expected self-direction.
Acclimation to a segmented student peer group. Personalized scheduling.
Permitted student co-action.
Control by threat of cessation of activity. Primacy of task orientation and work. Isolation as punishment. Compliance. Task orientation.

Time/space coordination. Children are responsible for their personal schedules and exhibit a high degree of expected self-maintenance.

Increasing containment activity.
Increasing specialization. Different students are having different educational experiences and are transmitted different information in different spatial areas.

Event Transition 7

Time/activity coordination.
Recurring housekeeping tasks.

Ridicule.
Manifestation of feelings of mutual rejection. The children temper their desire to escape the class-

room until formally outside the jurisdiction of the teacher. Ridicule/belittling.

Waiting. Regimentation. Order. Access on the basis of rank.
Recurring adult monitoring. Continuing adherence to classroom norms of regimentation and order.

Here, the teacher does not accommodate the children by preparing materials. Emphasis on self-maintenance.
Time/space coordination.
Compare with the spontaneous clustering seen in the lower grades. Self-direction and adherence to classroom norms.
Recurring upper grade spatial segregation by color and by sex.
Spatial bias favoring females sitting closer to the teacher. In comparison with the low sessions, notice the student self-direction.

Required attendance. Administrative tasks.
Recurring rotating administrative task (bias toward females).

desks. Disgustedly, the teacher says, "OK," and the students burst from the room and half run down the hall. Two more chairs fall from their tables. Giving the observer a "What-can-you-do?" look, the teacher stoops to pick them up. Scanning the room, the teacher gathers her belongings and locks the door behind her. The students are waiting, in line, for the teacher. Everyone waits as the lower grades pass, then the teacher goes to the head of the line to accompany her students to the buses. Everyone walks inside the yellow line on the hall floor.

A High Classroom Session

8:45 A.M. The teacher reads at his desk until students begin arriving.

9:00 A.M. In a quiet and orderly fashion, students begin arriving from the buses. They arrive individually, or in same-sex groups, and hang their coats in the closet, each time carefully closing the doors behind them, and go to specific seats.

In this homeroom and first period mathematics class, there are four white males, six black males, six black females, and three white females. The four white males immediately cluster in the far corner of the room, three black males sit in a cluster in the center of the room, another three sit in the far front corner, and all the females sit toward the front of the room.

At his desk, the teacher takes roll by scanning the room. A white female is asked to post the note outside the door. The teacher writes hall passes dismissing several students to go to the office (see Figure 2) to purchase lunch tickets.

Presently, a black female passes back homework the teacher has corrected. Shortly thereafter, students go to the teacher's desk to go over their work with him. The teacher has not called the class to attention, yet the session obviously has begun.

There is a continual stream of students going to the teacher's desk. The great majority of the students surrounding the teacher are female.

The teacher goes over each student's paper. As the session proceeds, chairs are moved and student spacing is polarized. Toward the rear of the room, a few males, mostly white, sit just in front of the observer. Black males are strung out toward the rear and along the sides of the room. All of the females cluster near the teacher's side. In seating themselves, students form a rough X-shape. It is as if there are two classrooms.

There is little contact between the males in the rear of the room and the females toward the front. The females interact with one another, but there is little interaction between females and males. Black males frequently interact with one another, but the white male remains isolated.

9:35 A.M. The teacher breaks free of the girls around him and tells the class to turn in their book reports. He says, "You may check your papers." The observer asks a black male the meaning of this remark. He says they check their own work by going up to the teacher's desk and looking at his answer sheet. They correct their papers, if necessary, then take them to the teacher, who records the score.

Event Transition 1

Right/wrong mastery.
Notice the spatial deference—children approach the teacher, rather than vice versa.

Self-direction. Adherence to/internalization of classroom procedure norm. Differential spatial organization by sex/sex segregation.
The females and the teacher form the "classroom" while the males remain interactionally peripheral. This is a recurring spatial pattern in upper grades/classrooms.

This pattern is self-selected but reinforced by the teacher's nonintervention. The pattern is consistent and occurs throughout the observation period.

Literacy training.
Autonomy and student responsibility training.
This pattern of self-direction does not occur in the low sessions.
Ranking by universalistic standards (standardized grades and evaluations).

Permitted spontaneity among the females.

The students signal "time" by passive, nonverbal means. Authority sanction. Order.

Adherence to classroom behavioral norms. "Inside"/"outside" voices.

9:45 A.M. Most of the girls around the teacher's desk finish their assignments and quietly talk.

The background noise level rises, and the teacher looks up from his work to say, "You may go." Students grab their books, begin talking more openly, then walk out the door.

Event Transition 2

Hallways are transitional zones (Van Gennep 1960:18) free from customary classroom norms and values.

Recurring spatial clustering by sex and by color. Female proximity to (male) source of classroom authority.

At-attention waiting positioning required for further activity. Required attendance and administrative tasks.

Control by implied threat. Ranking. Public ridicule.

Expected self-direction. Individual accountability.

Required deference. Public display of ranking. Evaluation by universal standards. Expected self-maintenance. Autonomy. Self-direction.

9:50 A.M. The second period class enters. There is congestion by the door, and the exchange of classes is noisy. The hallway is very noisy. Students quietly take their seats and begin talking with one another. In this group, there are four white males, seven black females, four white females, and five black males. The white students enter and immediately go to their seats. They sit in the back of the room just in front of the observer. The black males also sit in the back of the room but along the sides of the walls. Again, the females, both black and white, cluster toward the front of the room.

When all the students are seated, the teacher closes the door and takes roll. The noise and activity levels are low; the class is orderly and quiet.

The teacher goes to his desk, picks up a paper, and says, "These people are in trouble." He reads the names of students who have not turned in all their tests. There is a flurry of activity as students rummage through their belongings trying to find their papers. The teacher sits down at his desk and, one by one, students take their papers to him. The teacher records their work and gives out new assignments. Students silently work on their assignments until their names are called.

The teacher tells several students, mostly female, to help others, mostly male, with their work. He assigns the more "advanced" students to help others.

Differential responsibility training. Classroom bias toward females. Public display of ranking.

A miniclass of girls forms around the teacher's desk. Students coming up to him with questions lounge around while waiting their turn. The males remain in the back of the room and rarely go up to the teacher's desk except when called. Several black males are not paying attention. They look out the windows, around the room, or stare at each other. They are not creating a disturbance, and the teacher does not intervene.

Adherence to classroom norms of waiting and regimentation.
Continuing differential classroom interaction patterns by sex.
Spatial placement and interaction patterns are manifestations of differing degrees of involvement in the classroom culture and society.

Several students leave the room. The teacher does not look up. The observer leans over to ask a black male where they are going. To band practice, he says.

Individual responsibility for time/activity coordination. Permitted mobility.

The teacher interrupts the class to tell students to return library books, and several students go up to his desk. He makes out a pass for them, and they pick up their books and leave the room.

Increasing levels of elective subject areas.
Another administrative task. Expected self-maintenance.

The females around the teacher are whining and complaining about the work, yet coyly smiling at the teacher. The teacher says they have to find the answer themselves. The teacher says, "I want this work done before class is over. You have six minutes." A chorus of female voices whines: "Six minutes! I can't do this in six minutes!" The males sit and silently watch, slightly smiling. The teacher responds, "That's because you've been talking instead of working." Whining all the way, several girls come up to his desk for help. Calmly, the teacher goes over the assignment with

Passes are sanctions to cross the hallways and to enter the high school building.
These girls are practicing sex-role behaviors on the only adult male they have so far encountered. Males are on the periphery of this semisexual banter between the girls and the teacher.
Task-orientation and self-control are reinforced.
Problem-solving rather than rote procedures.

Notice the difference in interaction when males are involved.

Right/wrong mastery. Public ridicule/belittling.

Females are reinforced for the classroom norm of composure under stress and not giving up, while males are not at all similarly encouraged.

These nurturant behaviors are similar to interactions more common to the lower grades.

Emphasis on self-discipline and concentration.

Recurring unscheduled interruptions.

Internalization of classroom procedure. Self-direction.

In comparison with the low sessions, a greater emphasis on order and compliance. The females receive greater opportunity to display knowledge and thus be deemed "competent" (Gearing 1973; Ogbu 1979).

Required production of products. Demonstration/proof.

Expected responsibility for private property. Regimentation. Order.

Adherence to estab-

them, and he tries to get them to think through the problem to find their mistakes. A black male comes up to the teacher's desk. The teacher looks at his work, then loudly and angrily tells him that he will have to do the work over because he did not take the time initially to do it right. The boy slowly walks back to his seat, his head down. He slams his paper on the desk, falls into his seat, and pouts. A black female whines to the teacher that she wants to get an "A," but that the work is too hard. The teacher, in the midst of other work, softly tells her to continue working and not to give up. She asks if she could "Pllleeeaaassse" finish tomorrow. In an even voice, he responds that she can finish the three problems in two minutes. The teacher and the girl do not look at each other but carry out this dialogue with their heads in their work.

Several students enter the room. The observer asks a white male who they are. He says they are returning from band practice. The teacher and students take no notice of them as they get textbooks and sit down.

10:25 A.M. The teacher looks up and says, "You may check your papers." Students scurry to his desk. The females in the front of the room pull their chairs up closer to it. A noticeable spatial gap in the middle of the room separates the girls and the teacher, the black males strung out along the sides of the room, and the black and white males in the back of the room.

10:30 A.M. The teacher calls for students' papers, and the noise and activity levels increase. Students bring their work to his desk and prepare to leave. They put up their materials and gather the books they will take to other classes. By rows, the teacher randomly dismisses the group. They get up slowly, push their chairs under their desks, and leave the room.

lished classroom norms and values.

Event Transition 3

The homeroom students return for spelling work, minus those students not scheduled for it. There are ten black females, seven white males, seven white females, and seven black males. All the females sit in the first two rows, pulling their chairs close to the teacher's desk. The males are scattered all over the room. When the observer asks a white female which ones are the fifth graders, she points out that the sixth graders sit in the first two rows. The teacher takes roll and posts the slip outside the door.

Literacy training.
Increasing fragmentation of the student peer group.
Characteristic spatial subgrouping by sex.
Age/grading and ranking are expressed by degrees of distance from the teacher (authority).

The teacher asks a black female to aid him. They go to the board and write out a list of words. Turning, the teacher says that he will ask them both for the meaning of and a synonym for each word. Students raise their hands to answer. The teacher listens to several students' responses, then gives the correct answer, if it has not been given. Several males shout out the answers, and the teacher sternly tells them to raise their hands when they want to talk.

Regularly rotating administrative tasks = responsibility training (female bias). Literacy training. Deference norm.
Right/wrong mastery.
Continuing emphasis on procedure and the denial of spontaneity. Deference.

11:00 A.M. The teacher tells the students to take out their language books. At this point, several students get up and leave the room. No one takes notice of them. In giving assignments, the teacher refers to each student's particular reading level. For instance, he says, "You Galaxies . . . you Rainbows."

Private property. Literacy training.
Time/space coordination of individual scheduling.
Public display of ranked subgrouping ostensibly on the basis of universal criteria (performance on standardized tests).

In some detail, the teacher reviews the directions for this particular assignment. He tells a white female, "I don't know why they

Obedience training. Following orders to the exclusion of personal judgment. Compliance. Creative exercises are secondary. Show-and-tell incidents involving the display of personal throughts and feelings. Lack of privacy.

[the textbook] want you to do that. It's kind of silly, but do it anyway." The student asked a question about the directions and appears confused but accepts the teacher's admonition. As the students begin their assignment, the teacher tells them that they also will have to write another short story titled "My Most Embarrassing Moment." There are a few groans, and the teacher tells them to get to work. Students work quietly and individually. The teacher sits at his desk correcting papers.

Self-direction and self-maintenance.
Task orientation and the classroom norm of concentration amid distractions.
Time/activity coordination.
Play as a reward for work. Adherence to classroom norms. Neatness and order.
Authority positioning. Monitoring.

Several students who previously left the room return and quietly take empty seats. Though they are frequent and prominent, neither the teacher nor the students take apparent notice of these goings and comings.

11:45 A.M. The teacher reminds them they have fifteen minutes left and says they can go to recess only if their chairs and desks are arranged properly. In a sudden flurry of activity, they straighten the furniture and pick up stray paper from the floor. The teacher stands in front of the room watching, his arms folded over his chest. When finished, they gather up their papers and books and stand by their desks. They raise their hands and wave them in the air. One by one, in no appreciable order, the teacher calls them by name, signaling that they can leave. They grab their coats from the closet and run out the door. Occasionally, the teacher turns to glare at a student, nonverbally telling him or her to slow down.

Regimentation. Waiting. Peer competition. Deference. Regimentation.

Nonverbal reinforcement of classroom order norm. Reinforcement of expected self-discipline.
Spatial separation indicates rank and status.

During the lunch hour, the teacher stays in his classroom eating and reading. The door is closed.

Event Transition 4

12:00 P.M. Lunch. Recess.

12:40 P.M. Students enter, throw their coats in the closet, gather up books and materials from their desks, then rush out the door to another class.

The teacher sits at his desk, reading, and waiting for students to arrive. The fifth period math students enter in a quiet and orderly fashion, go directly to their seats, and quietly talk among themselves. Several students, especially the females, say hello to the teacher, but most sit down and quietly wait for class to begin. There are five white males, three black males, four white females, and five black females. There is a spatial gap between the males and the females; females sit toward the front of the room and males toward the rear. The teacher closes the door, silently takes roll, and posts the note outside the door. The teacher gives no assignments or directions, but on the way back to his desk merely says, "Get to work."

Students immediately begin working. Finishing their work, they take their papers to the teacher's desk to check the answer sheet, return to their desks to correct any mistakes, then take the paper back to the teacher. The teacher either points out other mistakes or approves the work by saying, "Excellent" or "OK."

As the class progresses, students ask the teacher if they can go to the bathroom, or if they can go get a drink of water. The teacher rarely refuses such requests. They go out of the room one at a time. Upon entering they ask, "Who's ready to go?" Hands go up, and someone else is picked. The classroom noise level remains very low.

Today, a white female has finished all the assignments and tests in her particular book.

Expected self-maintenance of individual time/activity coordination. Spatial mobility.

Waiting.

We see these entry behaviors only among the females. Waiting.

Customary spatial clustering by sex. Differential degrees of physical closeness and interaction with the teacher. Required attendance. Mathematics training. Expected student self-direction.

Obedience and task orientation. Required products. Demonstration/proof of mastery. Right/wrong mastery. Disappearance of classroom standards based on pleasing the teacher and increasing occurrence of standards based on universal criteria (grades).

Permission requesting. Adherence to deference and propriety norms. In this high session, children gain practice in leadership roles.

Ranking and differential grouping on the basis of

(ostensibly) universal criteria. A hierarchy of progress and achievement is valued.

Time/activity coordination. Expected self-maintenance.

The teacher says, "Class, Deena finished her green book today." Most of the students, especially the females, clap for Deena.

1:30 P.M. The teacher says it is time to go. Students gather up their books and materials, and the teacher says, "You may go." The students straggle out the door. Several girls smile good-bye to the teacher. He smiles good-bye.

Event Transition 5

Self-monitoring and self-maintenance. Literacy training.
Permitted spatial mobility.
Again we see a high degree of adherence to established norms and values in high sessions. High students have less adult monitoring and are given more opportunities for responsibility than low students.
Differential subgrouping and ranking.
Adherence to classroom norm of not interrupting work.

Required products. Demonstration/proof of mastery.
Emphasis on order and procedure. Deference.
Continuing ready obedience and compliance among high students.
Literacy training. Expected self-direction.
Females are given re-

The sixth period class enters. Some half run into the room. They are very noisy and were playing in the hall while waiting for the previous class to be dismissed. Yet once inside the room, they quietly and directly go to their seats. This is the homeroom section, and they have language this session.

The teacher briefly leaves the room on an errand. While he is gone, the noise level in the classroom does not change even though students quietly talk and visit among themselves. Several students start reading on their own.

The teacher returns, goes straight to his desk, and sits down. Roll is taken and posted. No directions or assignments are given, yet most students are reading from three different texts. It is extremely quiet. When a student leans over to talk with another student, it is always in a whisper.

As students finish reading, they go up to the teacher's desk. At one point, he turns to them to say, "There are too many of you up here at once. Go sit down and raise your hands if you want to come up." The students immediately obey.

2:10 P.M. As students are checked on their reading assignments, the teacher says he would like them to begin a writing assignment on "unusual authors." He does not elaborate but tells the students to get busy. A black female passes back the papers corrected by the teacher. She tends to stop, or is stopped, by other females. They chat and giggle. The noise level briefly increases. The teacher says, "Keep it down! Some people are still reading." The noise level decreases. Another pile-up occurs by the teacher's desk. Waiting their turn, students tend to roam around the room at will, sometimes talking with other students. Large amounts of unsupervised activity are permitted.

2:30 P.M. The teacher looks up to say, "OK, band people, you may go." Noisily, several students gather up their materials and books, push their chairs in, put their papers on the teacher's desk, and leave.

3:00 P.M. Many of the students have left for other classes and activities, and only ten students remain in the room. The teacher sits at his desk surrounded by students. Several groups of two or three students are seated in various spots around the room. As they work, the teacher banters back and forth with the class. He asks students if they saw the "Missiles of October" on television last night. A few had. Most had not. The teacher stresses that "violence begets violence." Violence is bad. They seem interested in the concept, and a small debate starts. Many of the black males do not agree with the teacher, and many politely laugh off his remarks. The teacher launches into a minilecture on the futility of war. The students do not argue with him but return to their work or sit quietly.

3:20 P.M. The teacher tells the students that it is almost time to leave. They are told to straighten the furniture. In the back of the

sponsibility-training administrative tasks. Females interact more with each other than males do.

Waiting. Permitted mobility as a reward for work.

The teacher also is subordinate to the demands of scheduling. The source of control now is more clearly outside the classroom.

Fragmentation of the peer group. No common educational experiences at this grade level. Different students are taught and learn different bodies of knowledge.
Reference to mass media.
The teacher is reinforcing ideology and moral principles. The opposition by the black males indicates another norm and value system at work. Notice that these males are not as active in their confrontation as are males in the low sessions.

After this interchange, the teacher assumes an authority position. Neatness and order.

Permitted nonacademic activity among black males. Place/activity coordination. Acceptance of established classroom procedure. The "best" group in the building is also the most deferential and compliant. These children are the "best" because the school sees in them the most complete expression of a seven-year process of sociocultural conditioning.

room, several black males quietly play checkers and a football-like game but are told to put the games back in the closet. Everyone is asked to put his or her chair on top of the desks. In so doing students shout, "Inspection! Inspection!" There is a high level of general excitement. Students are eager to please the teacher and look toward him with eager anticipation. Smiling, he looks at them and says, "Get ready!" The students run to get their coats and line up by the door. They appear restrained, receptive, and orderly. Scanning the room, the teacher looks at them and says, "OK." He stands by the door until the lower grades pass, then takes the students to the buses. They walk in single file inside the yellow line.

There is a cluster of related classroom features associated with the more complex scheduling pattern of the upper grades. These features include: more equitable patterns of student mobility (18/14) for both low and high sessions; an emphasis on various forms of coordination (8/8) and student coaction (24/42);* the use of conscripted student labor to help with administrative tasks (7/11); and attention to required student attendance (13/23). Both low and high sessions also emphasize: expected student self-maintenance and self-reliance (2/7); expected student mastery (4/10) of classroom tasks (11/29); order (3/6); various forms of ranking (10/3); and required student compliance and obedience (15/13) to teacher directives. Lower ranking features include: an ongoing emphasis on student self-control (21/28); the ideal if not the reality of student autonomy (23/24); various forms of regimentation (31/22); and required student demonstration and proof of competence (28/25). The upper grade way of classroom life highlights the further fragmentation of the student peer group (26/45), mostly around factors of color (5/31) and sex (16/5).

The social and cultural system of the elementary school classrooms

*These paired numbers refer to features of low/high sessions summarized in Figure C-7, Appendix C.

actively manage and set norms for relationships between the male and female students. Within separate classroom spaces males and females are taught, and presumably learn, quite different things. In addition to self-selected sex segregation (33/16) occurring through the manipulation of classroom seating patterns, formal segregation is characteristic of upper grade classrooms and increases with succeeding levels of schooling. During secondary schooling at West Haven, patterns of segregation by sex become more evident in automotive and wood "shop" (male) classes, sports (male), home economics (female), and art and music classes (primarily female). Increasingly, different bodies of classroom knowledge and subject areas are associated with either males or females. This situation is not peculiar to public schooling in the United States. Vai- and Mandingo-speaking peoples in the Liberia/Sierra Leone areas of West Africa (Watkins 1943), for example, traditionally separate children, by sex, into different village areas for a year to eighteen months when they approach adolescence. The boys' group is termed the Poro; the girls' group, the Sande. Males are trained in civil affairs important to the operation of the villages; females are trained in domestic duties such as learning various ways of preserving food and caring for children. In Nichū, Japan (Singleton 1967:75), elementary schooling traditionally is characterized by alternate seating for boys and girls on opposite sides of the classroom. In Rebhausen, Germany (Warren 1967:64), girls are expected to attend a separate, two-year home economics school after completing the sixth grade. From the upper elementary grades on, classrooms customarily are divided spatially with respect to the sex of the student.

Both upper grade sessions at West Haven Elementary School show a classroom bias toward females (16/5), with the bias here strongly expressed with respect to the presence of the male teacher in the high session. Routinely girls are delegated to carry out classroom housekeeping chores with their attendant responsibility training. The girls seem to enjoy school life much more than the boys, who are pushed to the social and physical periphery of the classrooms. There is a haremlike quality to the high classroom sessions as the male teacher, crowding out younger males, is surrounded by prepubescent females. In the early secondary grades, though, male students begin challenging male teacher hegemony over these females by more aggressively interrupting their conversations, taking risks to malign the teacher verbally, and initiating, to female amusement, displays of bravado in the classroom.

From grade level to grade level, high and low sessions *between* grade levels grow more similar than do high and low sessions *within* each grade level. In fourth (Figure C-6, Appendix C) and fifth/sixth (Figure C-7, Appendix C) grade low sessions, for example, public ridicule (8/1) continues as a frequently occurring feature of classroom life. Students continue to be more watched and monitored (9/14) by the teacher, and there is less classroom emphasis on literacy training (26/65). On the other hand, fourth and fifth grade high sessions continue to emphasize student adherence to/internalization of customary classroom norms and values (1/2), expected student self-maintenance and self-reliance (6/7), literacy training (27/9), and the expected mastery of classroom tasks (2/10). From grade level to grade level, high session students consistently exhibit greater permitted mobility (15/14) and responsibility training (11/12) as rewards for compliance and obedience (8/13). This cross-grade patterning to classroom culture and society demonstrates the castelike and classlike nature of elementary schooling. Beginning with the kindergarten sessions students are tracked and, during the upper grades, the tracks diverge widely. Dysfunctional classroom behavior and some academic failure, mostly among the "poor students," are accepted, and despite their performance the teacher of the low session knows these students will be passed on to high school. "They will just have to keep working with them over there," she shrugs. The teacher is sincere and well-meaning but feels "locked-in" and despairs of effecting meaningful changes in "the system." The separation of "good" and "poor" students, in any case, is complete, and students move to the more serious subject-area tracking of secondary schooling.

The summary profile for the upper grade low session in Figure C-7, Appendix C, shows more classroom emphasis being placed on the public ridicule of students by the teacher (1) than in the high session (36). Horizontal hostility in the form of students actively belittling each other (19/–) is significant in the low session but not in the high session. The low session also exhibits greater monitoring and supervision (12/40) of students by the teacher (14/30) than does the high session. In comparison with the low session, the summary profile for the high session emphasizes the following: expected student self-direction (1/22) associated with teacher monitoring (40/12) and authority positioning (30/14); expected student obedience (34/67) and adherence to/internalization of classroom norms and values (2/38); a greater degree of student deference (4/27) to and waiting (18/74) on the teacher; more attention to literacy training (9/65) and procedure (15/–); and the teacher/student generation of classroom products (20/–).

Through the process of schooling from preschool through the upper grades as revealed in these selected narratives, there is a gradual reduction in the number of discrete classroom events. The kindergarten session, for example, exhibits eight major events, the fourth grade exhibits six, and the upper grade classroom sessions exhibit only three (see Figures in Appendix B). The upper grade session event profile reveals a major transformation akin to the transformation from preschool/kindergarten to the first grade. In comparison with the fourth grade sessions (see Figure B-6, Appendix B), the amount of upper grade classroom session time spent on work activities almost doubles from 38 to 67 percent for the low session and from 43 to 74 percent for the high session (see Figure B-7, Appendix B). The upper grade high session spends more classroom time on work-related activities (74 percent) than does any other classroom session observed over the process of schooling. There is a 4 percent decrease in time spent on entry/exit procedures for both high and low sessions, in comparison with the fourth grade, associated with the increased student mobility (18/14) characteristic of the upper grades. The number of identified classroom features expressed in the upper grade sessions is slightly higher (419) when compared with the fourth grade sessions (343). There is more going on, more different kinds of activity occurring, in the upper grade sessions. There is a slight reduction in time spent on meals/recess, from 20 to 11 percent in the low session and from 15 to 11 percent in the high session, again in comparison with the fourth grade. The upper grade profile parallels event and activity patterns routinely associated with the high school classroom culture and society at West Haven and is conditioning to that phase in the process of schooling as a rite of passage.

The upper grade classroom way of life is characterized by loss of an earlier, more holistic teaching and learning environment with the advent of a more complex pattern of scheduling classes. Like bits of chaff in the wind, students are faced with increasing dislocation. The temporal and spatial context of classroom life is fragmented. Students come and go according to personal schedule. Transience and impermanence are the rule. Classrooms are differentiated and specialized, and neither teacher nor students remain the organizational center of attention. Upper grade classrooms cease to provide an organizational frame of reference for student events and activities, in comparison with previous grade leve classroom life. Emphasis is placed instead on coordinating time between classrooms as distinct spatiotemporal points (8/8). Time itself, the schedule, is paramount. Students must adopt a new spatiotemporal orientation in assimilating the upper grade classroom way of life. In the lower grades, the basic classroom time unit is the school day. In the upper grades, it is the hour. Time has shrunk. Classroom space declines in importance with respect to the out-of-class mobility characterizing the upper grade students. Students are required to make major emotional, conceptual, and relational changes and adaptations over the early grade through upper grade classroom process of schooling. Although fit preparation for the way of life in our discontinuous (Bennis and Slater 1968; Benedict 1938), mobile (Scrupski 1975) society, the contextual lesson in the upper grades is that nothing is permanent. The only constant is change itself.

Teachers lose a great deal of power with the advent of this more complex pattern of scheduling classes, and they directly influence less and less of what goes on in the classrooms. In "contained" rooms teachers controlled time, space, strategic resources, and student mobility. Comparatively more upper grade teacher time is spent on required bureaucratic tasks such as taking roll, collecting lunch money, and filling out permission slips for individual student activities. Actual classroom session time spent on academics may amount to no more than thirty minutes, less in some instances because of bureaucratic intrusions and disruptive students. Students are conditioned to these political, bureaucratic facts of classroom life through being conscripted to help with administrative tasks. Students increasingly are drawn into networks filtering in from outside the classroom. A student getting up to go to an extracurricular, or elective, activity interrupts the continuity of the classroom. Students owe more allegiance to their subjects and to their schedules than they do to any particular teacher or classroom. Very little upper grade teacher interview comment on disruptive school behaviors and attitudes focuses on students themselves or their home environment. Invariably, the culprit mentioned is the upper grade pattern of schooling. Upper grade teachers are vehement in saying, as one did, that "all this moving around is really not in the best interests of the children." Why, I ask. "Well, the kids are unnaturally isolated from each other. Changing classes is bad for their social development. There are so many problems in the hallways because that is the only place where they can be social." The teacher of the low group says that the class rotation system is "pathologically disadvantageous" to students. "They don't have one room or teacher they are responsible to," she says. "This means I can't really set firm rules for them because they might be different from another teacher's. Plus it's more difficult to enforce rules with them getting up to go to another class as soon as you get things organized. You know, we [teachers] don't coordinate too much of anything. Everybody is in their own room doing their own thing. The kids learn to play one teacher against another, as far as rules go. So it's difficult to enforce rules." Yet another teacher feels the upper grade pattern fosters "nonrelatedness" and leads to student "self-centered, irresponsible behavior." The problem is that students ought to be able to "learn from each other more." Teachers recognize that the further along in school students move, the less opportunity they have for sustained contact with each other. Everyone is alway moving around. "Children," one teacher says, "ought to be required to be in *one* room with *one* teacher, because it makes them feel more secure with the school." The high teacher does not like to see "the kids shuffled around like chickens! They can do all that moving around when they get to high school. These kids have too many choices, you know. Too much freedom. There are too many electives; they are confused by the freedom of all these electives."

Hallways invariably are mentioned when adult school personnel talk about lingering student behavior and attitude problems in the upper grades. Hallway behavior is not much of an issue in the early and middle grades because students are required most of the time to be in their ("contained") classrooms. Upper grade students, because of the scheduling system, spend a lot of time in the hallways. The principal faces a continuing problem of trying to get upper grade teachers to monitor the hallways better. Upper grade teachers view themselves as "subject" rather than "contained" classroom oriented, and they do not feel students moving between classes are their responsibility. Upper grade students, in addition, are removed spatially form the monitoring view of persons in the principal's office (see Figure 2). The upper grades, literally, are the end of the assembly line, and this level of schooling is viewed by teachers as conscious preparation for secondary school. Upper grade teachers and students view themselves as separate from the rest of the people in the building. Physically, though, the upper grades still are in the building and exist in a limbo state of not being truly elementary or truly secondary. Student behavior in the upper grade hallways is the same as observed in secondary school hallways—noisy, disorderly, and spontaneous (Sitton 1980). "Acting crazy" is the way several upper grade teachers term it. Hallways, though, moderate the emphasis on quietness, order, and the denial of spontaneity associated with classrooms. They provide an important opposition to the customary norms and values of the classroom and are safety valves balancing out the tensions and emotions generated in the classroom sociocultural system. Upper grade students creatively make over hallway spaces for their own purposes. Information is exchanged, social bonds reinforced, and future plans made during scheduled student passes through the hallways. Upper grade students momentarily are suspended from classroom reality while going from one place to another. Student behaviors say that customary classroom norms and values ought not apply here. Alternate patterns of behavior also become more extreme during lunch period. If not monitored, students may start dancing in the halls, while becoming more boisterous and interactive. Hallways elicit spontaneity, and these important *between* times and spaces even out the often overpowering drives reinforced in the regular classroom world. Administrators at West Haven, whether in the secondary building or in the upper elementary grades, undoubtedly will continue to experience difficulty trying to make expected student behavior in hallways exactly the same as expected student behavior in the classrooms.

Most of what customarily is thought of as "schooling" occurs from the first through the fourth grade levels. Most of the content teachings and learnings of schooling occur in lower and middle grade classrooms, during the transitional phase of the process of schooling. Although sociocultural conditioning takes place in every classroom, important core social and cultural information is presented to students during the early and upper grades. The early grades and the upper grades are similar in that both initiate students into ways of life characteristic of succeeding levels of schooling; initiation into middle grade patterns of classroom life occur during the early grades, and initiation into middle (seventh and eighth grade) and secondary high school patterns of classroom life occur during the upper grades.

Elementary schooling at West Haven, in summary, is a process of transition and change; the classroom experiences children undergo always are in preparation for something. This is the existential reality of initiation and rite of passage:

For groups, as well as for individuals, life itself means to separate and to be reunited, to change form and condition, to die and to be reborn. It is to act and to cease, to wait and rest, and then begin acting again, but in a different way. And there are always new thresholds to cross: the thresholds of summer and winter, of a season or a year, of a month or a night; the thresholds of birth, adolescence, maturity, and old age; the threshold of death and that of the afterlife—for those who believe in it. [Van Gennep 1960: 189–190, 194.]

Education, in whatever guise, is initiation and rite of passage preparing children for life. Sequence, transformation, becoming: these are the true human lessons. And these human lessons do appear in public schooling in contemporary America, if we are careful to look for them.

PART III

Epilogue

6

Education and the Lessons of Classroom Life

True education incarnates the permanent search of people to-gether with others for their be-coming more fully human in the world in which they exist.

Paulo Freire,
Education for Critical Consciousness

Children are required to spend more than seven thousand hours of their lives in elementary school classrooms similar to the ones at West Haven. Most of us do not have ongoing access to classrooms. Every weekday morning throughout the United States, we relinquish children to school buildings into which we ourselves only occasionally are permit-ted. This study presents a glimpse, albeit brief, of the customary class-room way of life associated with public schooling. Then too, teachers and administrators ostensibly familiar with classroom life need to stand back and take a more studied look at the nature of the setting in which they are continually immersed. Teachers, especially, are isolated physi-cally within individual classrooms and grade levels and rarely have a whole picture of the school experiences children undergo before and after those students are in their care. Finally, these descriptions of class-room life will be of use to those who shape school policy and practice. My message is that it is important to conceptualize schooling from three interrelated points of view: as a process of social and cultural condition-ing; as a process of initiation and rite of passage; and as a process aiding the continuity of heterogeneous societies like our own.

The character of public schooling will be misconstrued if, in our thinking and in our research policy, we deemphasize the social and cul-tural aspects of classroom life. When schooling comes to mind, for ex-ample, so also do pictures of teacher/student interactions and a formal curriculum of instruction. Schooling = content. This conception of

251

schooling preoccupies educational research and is a primary focus of efforts directed at improving classroom life. The nature of classroom life, though, does not flow primarily from the mouths of teachers or from the words in a text but lies silently within the form of schooling itself. What we term schooling is an interrelated set of features, and effective efforts at school improvement require attending to the way of life of schooling as a whole. School intervention and change have proved a difficult matter, in part, because what we as a society continually choose to teach young people, what we consciously and unconsciously transmit to them, is in fact what we believe important and of value. Superficial changes such as open classroom use of interaction-reinforcing round tables will conflict with contextual messages about autonomy that cling to standardized testing procedures. We must be consistent in the content and context messages we send children in school classrooms. Structural changes, real context changes, in the social and cultural fabric of classroom life would signal that, nationally, we are changing ourselves socially and culturally. Until we are ready to make real context changes involving the structure of schooling, we must remain content to define "school improvement" as curriculum change and less hostile teacher/student classroom interactions.

Viewing classroom life as initiation and rite of passage directs attention to schooling as a process occurring through time and over space. When we study individual classrooms we are studying aspects of schooling, not schooling itself. Schooling has less to do with pedagogy than we might think. The spatiotemporal process of schooling is sociocultural conditioning. The school experiences children undergo initiate them into the culture and society of the classroom and serve as rite of passage preparation for life in the wider society and culture. All of this takes time and a great deal of energy on the part of those involved. Conceptualizing schooling as initiation and rite of passage focuses attention on ritual ceremony, symbol, and myth as important features of classroom life—features routinely studied when we research forms of education in societies other than our own. Schooling also ought to be conceptualized as an institution adapted to the educational requirements of stratified state societies like our own. Classrooms are small sociocultural systems. The character of classroom life is meshed with and cannot effectively be considered apart from the characteristics of the wider social and cultural life, both local and national, in which they occur. This means that efforts directed at school improvement must be a matter of national as well as local concern. Individual public school systems are not exclusively state and local entities, and to argue otherwise is to seriously misread the nature of the educational system in our society. Efforts to decentralize federal involvement in schooling will continue to center on politics and economics rather than matters more social and cultural. Local public schools will remain under both overt and subtle pressure to produce young people adapted to the work and mission of the national society. As such, we must make certain that our national social and cultural life is what we want it to be, so that our public school classroom social and cultural life also will be what we want it to be.

Initially I asked what way of life, values, and habits of mind children at West Haven are initiated into and conditioned to adhere to. What behaviors, patterns of social relationship, ideas, and objects constitute classroom life and consistently are emphasized? A few significant features frequently occur throughout the sessions sampled observationally, as against a variety of features less frequently occurring (see Figure 11). Only 136 features occur in these sessions, not an especially high number considering the many separate events and activities described in the classroom narratives. The first twelve features listed in Figure 11 occur with more than half the frequency of all the classroom features. These first twelve features represent the social and cultural themes on which the process of elementary schooling at West Haven places emphasis. The event and activity pattern of elementary school classroom life at West Haven is highly repetitive, and primarily conditions students to the following: ideas about the importance of order and ranking (1/2);* adherence to regimentation (12) and following set procedures (5/8); self-control (3), self-maintenance and self-reliance (4); autonomy in personal behavior and adherence (6) to an ideology of individualism amid competition for scarce resources (9) and the expected mastery (11) of set tasks; and responsibility training (10) for helping to maintain the special classroom spaces in which schooling occurs. The power of sociocultural conditioning lies in redundancy, and primary features and themes of classroom life are expressed again and again in different ways. These primary features are not pedagogical but are attitudinal and behavioral. Literacy training (19), training in mathematics (95), problem solving (73), classroom attention to work (27), and the production of materials (43) receive less overall emphasis.

*The numbers in parenthesis refer to features listed in Figure 11.

Figure 11. Preschool through Upper Grade Classroom Session Characteristics and Their Frequency of Occurrence

	Frequency*
1. Order	117
2. Ranking	113
3. Self-Control	98
4. Self-Maintenance/Reliance	94
5. Compliance/Obedience	90
6. Internalization (of norms/procedures)	83
7. Autonomy/Individualism	77
8. Procedure/Sequencing	70
9. Competition 10. Responsibility Training (housekeeping tasks)	68 (136)
11. Right/Wrong Mastery	67
12. Regimentation	61
13. Adult Monitoring/Supervision	56
14. Task Orientation/Concentration	48
15. Deference (deferential positioning/permission requesting) 16. Waiting/Waiting Positions	47 (94)

*Frequency = frequency of occurrence of each numbered characteristic

Figure 11. (continued)

	Frequency
17. Coordination (place/activity; place/item; space/activity; time/activity) 18. Neatness	44 (88)
19. Literacy Training	42
20. Self-Direction	41
21. Public Ridicule (teacher belittling/sarcasm)	39
22. Demonstration/Proof (of knowledge/skill) 23. Property (orientation toward private)	38 (76)
24. Mobility/Permitted Mobility	37
25. Public Displays	33
26. Violence 27. Work	32 (64)
28. Differential Grouping 29. National (celebrations; legends; observations; orientation; mythology)	31 (62)
30. Denial of Spontaneity 31. Evaluation 32. Safety/Care of the Body	30 (90)
33. At-Attention/Attention Position (readiness position) 34. Authority Positioning (teacher)	29 (58)
35. Food (rituals; socialization)	28
36. Confinement/Containment (subgroup/individuals/spatial)	27

Figure 11. (continued)

	Frequency
37. Sex (spatial separation/segregation by) 38. Work/Play (separation of)	26 (52)
39. Cleanliness 40. Spatial (segregation/isolation)	25 (50)
41. Lineality	25
42. Finishing (completing) 43. Products	23 (46)
44. Sex (socialization; stereotyping) 45. Spontaneity	22 (44)
46. Administrative Tasks (student/teacher) 47. Obedience Training (following orders) 48. Pleasing the Teacher	20 (60)
49. Black Male Behavior (differential behaviors/isolation of black males) 50. Internal Division (by students) of Peer Group (horizontal aggression)	19 (38)
51. Housekeeping 52. *In Loco Parentis*	18 (36)
53. Color (conflicts/race/segregation by/spatial separation by) 54. Machine Technology	17 (34)
55. Cessation of Activity (teacher control by) 56. Scheduling (complexity/fragmentation of) 57. Threat Gestures (nonverbal)	16 (48)
58. Entry Rituals/Ritualized Greetings 59. Lack of Adherence (to norms/values) 60. Nurturing 61. Violation of Norms/Norm-Breaking	15 (60)

Figure 11. (continued)

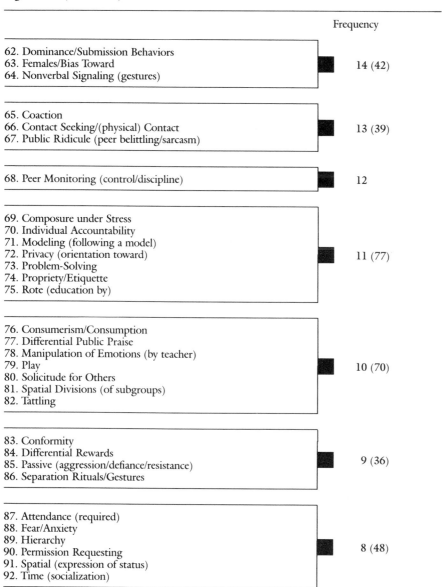

	Frequency
62. Dominance/Submission Behaviors 63. Females/Bias Toward 64. Nonverbal Signaling (gestures)	14 (42)
65. Coaction 66. Contact Seeking/(physical) Contact 67. Public Ridicule (peer belittling/sarcasm)	13 (39)
68. Peer Monitoring (control/discipline)	12
69. Composure under Stress 70. Individual Accountability 71. Modeling (following a model) 72. Privacy (orientation toward) 73. Problem-Solving 74. Propriety/Etiquette 75. Rote (education by)	11 (77)
76. Consumerism/Consumption 77. Differential Public Praise 78. Manipulation of Emotions (by teacher) 79. Play 80. Solicitude for Others 81. Spatial Divisions (of subgroups) 82. Tattling	10 (70)
83. Conformity 84. Differential Rewards 85. Passive (aggression/defiance/resistance) 86. Separation Rituals/Gestures	9 (36)
87. Attendance (required) 88. Fear/Anxiety 89. Hierarchy 90. Permission Requesting 91. Spatial (expression of status) 92. Time (socialization)	8 (48)

Figure 11. (continued)

	Frequency
93. Differential Adherence to/Internalization of Norms 94. Labeling 95. Mathematics Training 96. Moral Instruction/Moralizing 97. Quietness	7 (35)
98. Behavior Modification 99. Creativity/Imagination (subordination of)	6 (12)
100. Defiance (of norms/values) 101. Games 102. Newness 103. Progress 104. Task Division of Labor 105. Toilet Rituals/Procedures 106. Universalistic Standards/Criteria	5 (35)
107. Administrative Hegemony/Control 108. Adversarial Relationships (peer aggression/vertical hostility) 109. Age/Role Privileges (age/role stereotyping; age/status privileges) 110. Anthropomorphism 111. Guilt (as control mechanism) 112. Mass Media (electronic; print) 113. Public Praise (differential rewards) 114. Sharing	4 (32)
115. Accommodation 116. Approval Seeking 117. "Don't Give Up" (persistence) 118. Stimulus/Response Conditioning	3 (12)
119. Choice/Permitted Choice 120. Cooperation 121. Success/Failure (permitted "failure")	2 (6)

Figure 11. (continued)

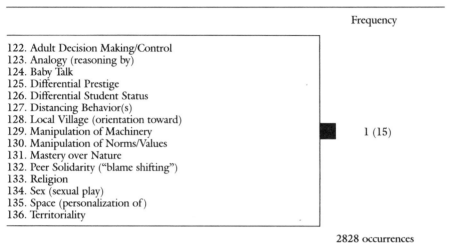

Frequency

122. Adult Decision Making/Control
123. Analogy (reasoning by)
124. Baby Talk
125. Differential Prestige
126. Differential Student Status
127. Distancing Behavior(s)
128. Local Village (orientation toward)
129. Manipulation of Machinery   1 (15)
130. Manipulation of Norms/Values
131. Mastery over Nature
132. Peer Solidarity ("blame shifting")
133. Religion
134. Sex (sexual play)
135. Space (personalization of)
136. Territoriality

2828 occurrences

Debating whether classroom life at West Haven is "good" or "bad" depends on what one thinks schooling ought to do to children and what one feels children ought to become as a result of their classroom experiences. I am not concerned with whether or not children at West Haven are being well taught; for the most part, they are. There is room for concern, though, about the kind of social and cultural conditioning taking place in West Haven classrooms.

The fifteenth-century French essayist Michel de Montaigne observed, correctly, "The most important difficulty of human science is the education of children." Montaigne, though, had in mind the education of children rather than their instrumental training. Our society, I think, at present is not especially interested in children or in their true education. Philippe Aries, writing in *Centuries of Childhood*, suggests that collectively we do not value children that much or yet consider them full human beings, as historically used to be the case. True or not, it is obvious that across any domain within our society anyone having extensive contact with children—homemakers or teachers, for example—is ascribed low socioeconomic status. This lack of concern again is seen in the way we attend to our educational system. Periodic national spasms of concern with the state of public schooling are reflex reactions. Around the turn of the century, public schools were charged with preparing the children of immigrants for the industrial work routine developing in this country. After World War II and into the 1950s, public schools were charged with training children to meet the perceived technological threat of the Soviet space program. Presently, the hue and cry is that public school systems are not preparing children to meet the perceived threat of Japanese microelectronic and scientific developments. Over the last hundred years it is evident that between paroxysms of largely instrumental concern about education we show very little concern with, pay little attention to the health of, or devote adequate national resources to the care of public schooling. We are more concerned, to paraphrase the late President Kennedy, with what our children and schools can do for us than with what we can do for them. The concern in the final analysis always is that our children are not being well trained, not that they are being less than well educated.

Training is guidance for adherence to a prepared course of instruction for some instrumental end. Training is autocratic and is associated with conditioned obedience and lack of choice in response. Education, on the other hand, is concerned with teaching how to learn, not prescribing exactly what is to be learned. Education inherently is democratic, and the essence of true education is choice. Education probes issues of what is worth knowing, rather than issues of what knowing is worth. Education says that how we are taught to live is the answer to questions of what is worthwhile to do and to be in life, making education the most serious of human activities. True education is rare and, as Paulo Freire notes, is a process of consciousness raising for the fulfillment of human potential—a process for helping us understand what we are so that we can be fully what we already are.

Childrearing in many so-called "primitive" societies is a much more fundamental matter than it is in our society. In most of these societies education is a process for gaining metaphysical wisdom rather than merely a process of receiving information. Among the traditional Hano Tewa, a group of Pueblo Native Americans in the southwest United States (Dozier 1966:81–82), for example, children understand that well being is dependent on their maintaining a proper relationship with nature:

> The Hano Tewa hold a world view generally characteristic of all the Pueblos. This is the premise that man and the universe are in a kind of balance and that all things are interrelated. There is no dichotomy between good and bad; evil is simply a disturbance in the

equilibrium which exists between man and the universe. The activity world of man, of the natural environment of plants and animals; the inanimate world of earth, rocks, and dead vegetable matter; the ethereal world of wind, clouds, rain, and snow; even the
"thought world" of human beings are all believed to be in a state of
balance. . . . There is no evidence that Hano itself was ever an anxi-
ety-ridden community or that it ever was rent with internal strife.

I am not promoting nostalgic romanticism but reporting a sane point of
view that our school system should consider embracing as we see our
children looking toward the possibility of destruction of life on earth, if
not destruction of the earth itself—a possibility our educational system
has helped to create. Mercia Eliade (Eliade 1958:x) remarked that initiation and rite of passage in such societies "both were sacred matters
educating people into the nature of their link with the metaphysical
world. The world is a divine work, and everything becomes significant.
That was the meaning of education." We should keep education separate
from religion, of course, but I lament the manner in which we neither
permit school children awareness of the significance of education nor
reinforce the almost sacred delight in life with which they seem to be
born. Perhaps I ask too much but many days I sat in the back row of
West Haven secondary school classrooms thinking about the students
with whom I had spoken, and all of whom had complained of feeling
lost in school. In part, they feel this way because they are not offered and
have yet to find for themselves any vital life meaning to the experiences
they have in school classrooms. The true meaning of education is not in
information exchange or sociocultural conditioning but in understanding, through experience, something of life itself. Black Elk, a holy man
of the Oglala Sioux (Niehardt 1961:212), reminds us that schooling has
no power for children because it does not offer understandings of significance: "it is from understanding that power comes; and the power in
the ceremony [for children] was in understanding what it meant."

There is much we can learn, about nature and power for example,
from cultures other than our own. The fundamental lesson is that we
need to attend more to the education than to the training of our children. We have an advantage over these societies, as I see it, in that
contemporary heterogeneous societies offer the greatest possibility for
achieving freedom through education. Children in Sioux, Tewa, Tiwi, or
Inuit societies traditionally could not unlearn their culture or experiment

with adopting other, possibly better, points of view leading to deeper understanding of life. What did the Sioux know of Tiwi childrearing practices or world views? We have the possibility of our children's borrowing at will from other times and places in order to help them resolve some of the more persistent and constraining contradictions in our culture. They have the opportunity to denounce those parts of our way of life that are not worthy of transmission across generations and to search for ways to help each other become more fully human. (Thomas Ruggles was wrong; some children do not have to be conditioned to contentedly accept a life of toil.) This is occurring in parts of our society, and I hope it will occur in our school system as well.

As human beings we do not fully depend on biology or genetics to determine what we are or what we are to be, as do other animals. Our reliance on culture, ways of being that are taught and learned rather than inherited, means that we and our children can be anything we or they feel is worth being. Education, we must increasingly realize, is our ultimate freedom. Schools and classroom life can change, or they can stay the same.

Appendix A
A Cross-Cultural
Outline of Education by Jules Henry*

I. On what does the educational process focus?

1. Environment (other than human)
   1. Flora
   2. Fauna
   3. Climate
   4. Geographical features
   5. Anthropomorphized flora
   6. Anthropomorphized fauna
   7. Anthropomorphized or zoomorphized machines
   8. Anthropomorphized or zoomorphized natural phenomena other than flora or fauna (winds, rivers, mountains, etc.)
   9. Space
   10. Time
   11. Motion
   12. Space-time-motion
   13. The world view of the culture
      1. Isolate-static
      2. Communicate-changing
         1. Engulfing
      3. Hostile or pacific
         1. Hostile
         2. Pacific
      3. Selectively hostile or pacific
   4. Geographical position of places studied
      1. Near: own town, state or province, village, tribe
      2. Near-distant: other states or provinces, nation in general; other villages or tribes
      3. Distant: other lands
   5. Temporal position
      1. Immediate
      2. Contemporary
      3. Near past
      4. Distant past
      5. Mythological past
   14. Clothing
   15. Food
   16. Transportation and communication

2a. Values
   1. Good and bad: moral rules
   2. Work, success, failure
   3. Being on time
   4. Culture
   5. Proper dress

*Reprinted from *Current Anthropology* 1 (1960):269–72.

263

6. Strength, activity, power
7. Beating the game
8. Politeness, tact
9. Cooperation, helpfulness, togetherness
10. Patriotism
11. Cleanliness, orderliness
12. Thrift, saving, don't waste
13. Parents are good
14. Prettiness, beauty
15. Love
16. Mother, motherhood
17. Happiness
18. Competitiveness
19. Equality
20. Novelty, excitement
21. Pride
22. Knowledge as value
23. The "beautiful person"
24. Private property
25. Democracy
26. Family
27. Responsibility
28. Generosity, doing more than required, non-commercialism
29. The state
30. Deference
31. Enlightened self-interest
32. Independence, toughness
33. Physical intactness
34. Sense of emergency
35. Constancy
36. Solicitude for others, kindness
37. Composure under stress
38. Courage
39. Knowledge as means to an end
40. Compromise
41. Fun, relaxation
42. Friends, friendship, faithfulness
43. Fairness
44. Flattery, empty praise
45. Honor (integrity), personal autonomy
46. Self-restraint
47. Trying hard, don't give up
48. Fame, ambition
49. Honesty
50. Prestige
51. Niceness, likeableness
52. Respect for authority
53. Excitement
54. Gentleness, non-violence
55. Speed, alertness
56. Sacredness, etc., of parents
57. Flexibility
58. Modesty
59. Tolerance
60. Freedom
61. Peace
62. Progress
63. Wealth
64. U.S.A.
65. Loyalty
66. Money, greed, etc., are corrupting
67. Smartness, cleverness, thinking
68. Profit
69. Size
2*b*. Value conflict
3. Institutions
  1. Social structure
  2. Religion
  3. Economic system
4. Technology, machines
5. Reading, writing, and arithmetic
6. Social manipulation
  1. Recognition-seeking behavior
  2. Manipulation of others
  3. Manipulation of self
7. Responsibility
8. How to compete
9. How to take care of others
10. Use of the mind
  1. How to think
  2. Disjunction
    1. When to disjoin
    2. How to disjoin
    3. From what to disjoin
  3. Concentration
    1. Interest stimulation defining purpose; motivation
    2. Force
    3. Shutting out external stimuli
    4. Visualization

5. Focused retention
4. Preparation of the mind
5. "Mental discipline"
11. Body parts or functions
   1. The voice
   2. The sphincters
   3. Care of the body (like getting enough rest)
   4. Posture
   5. How to relax
   6. The mouth
12. Art
13. History
14. Some other facts about which information is communicated
   1. About systems of rewards and punishments
   2. About what the culture promises its members
   3. About permitted and forbidden activities
   4. About how to get pleasure and avoid pain
   5. About whom to love and whom to hate
   6. How to handle frustration
   7. The difference between the real and the manifest (this refers to situations in which an effort is deliberately made to enable the child to see "behind" the obvious)
   8. About death
   9. About sex relations
   10. About race, class, or ethnic differences
15*a*. Instruction in identifiable adult tasks
15*b*. Teaching about adult tasks
16. Scientific abstractions
17. Science (general)
18. Routine procedures
19. Childish handiwork
20. Cultural stereotypes
21. Warfare and associated activities
22. Safety
23. Songs, music
24. Mythology

25. The object system
26. Games
27. Cultural fictions

II. How is the information communicated (teaching methods)?

   1. By imitation
   2. By setting an example
   3. By instruction in schools, ceremonials, or other formal institutions
   4. By use of punishments
   5. By use of rewards
   6. Problem-solving
   7. Guided recall
   8. Giving the child tasks to perform beyond his immediate capacity
      1. Jamming the machine
   9. Mechanical devices
   10. By kinesthetic association
   11. By experiment
      1. By teacher
      2. By pupil
   12. By doing
   13. By symbolic association
   14. By dramatization
   15. By games or other play
   16*a*. By threats
   16*b*. By trials
   17. By irrelevant association
   18. By relevant association
   19. Through art
      1. Graphic
      2. Music, general
      3. Songs
      4. Literature (stories, myths, tales, etc.)
   20. By stating the opposite of the truth ("Water's a solid, isn't it?"); writing antonyms
   21. By holding up adult ideals
   22. Acting in undifferentiated unison
   23. Physical force
   24. By positive or negative assertion
   25. Repetition
   26. By specifically relating information to the child's own body, bodily function, or experience
   27*a*. Through ego-inflation

27b. Through ego-deflation
28. Through use of humor
29. By telling
30. By watching
31. By listening
32. Question and answer
    1. Teacher question, pupil answer
    2. Pupil question, teacher answer
33. Holding up class, ethnic, national,
    or religious ideals
34. By doing something on his own
35a. By repeating the child's error to him
35b. By repeating the child's correct
    answer
36. By accusing
37. By following a model
    1. Human
    2. Non-human
38. By comparison
39. By filling in a missing part
40. By associative naming (e.g., a book
    mentions gingham as a mate-
    rial, and teacher asks students if
    they can name other materials)
41. By identifying an object (like going
    to the board and underlining "a
    noun" in a sentence)
42a. By group discussion
42b. By class discussion
43. Physical manipulation
    1. Bodily manipulation
    2. Bodily mutilation and other
       physical stresses
44. Rote memory
45. By working together with a student
    (as when teacher and student
    work together to make a bat-
    tery, or as when teacher and
    student go over reference
    books together)
46. Through special exhibits
47. By having children read substantive
    materials (e.g., reading the
    chemistry lesson in the reader)
48. By putting the child on his mettle
    ("Now let's see how well you
    can read.")
49. Through group projects
50. By giving procedural instructions
51. By demanding proof

52. Through reports by students
53. By pairing (e.g., one child gives a
    word and calls on another child
    to give a sentence with the
    word; one child gives the state
    and another gives the capital)
54. By asking for volunteers
55. Through isolating the subject

III. Who educates?

    1. Males or females?
    2. Relatives or others?
    3. On which age group does the bur-
       den of education fall?
       1. Peers
          1. Boy
          2. Girl
       2. Older children
          1. Male
          2. Female
       3. Adolescents
          1. Male
          2. Female
       4. Adults
          1. Male or female
          2. Younger or older
          3. Married or unmarried
       5. Others
    4. Is education by "successful" people?
    5. What rewards accrue to the
       educator?
       1. Enhanced status
       2. Material rewards
       3. Emotional satisfactions
    6. Are there education specialists?
    7. Does the educator wear distinctive
       dress or other insignia?
    8. Is the educator of the same or of a
       different social group from that
       of the person being educated?
       (national, racial, class, etc.)

IV. How does the person being educated
    participate? (What is his attitude?)

    1. Accepting
    2. Rejecting, resistive
    3. Bored, indifferent
    4. Defiant
    5. Inattentive

6. Social closeness of teacher and child
7. Social distance of teacher and child
8. Finds the process painful?
9. Finds the process gratifying?
10a. Competitively
10b. Cooperatively
11a. With inappropriate laughter
11b. Ridiculing peers
12. Laughter at humor of peers or teacher
13. Overt docility
14. Eagerly
   1. Facial expression
   2. Hand-raising
   3. Talking out
   4. Heightened bodily tonus
15. Through making independent decisions and suggestions
16. Asks for clarification, direction, etc.
17. Through spontaneous contributions or other demonstrations not precisely within the context of the lesson
18. Through spontaneous contributions within the context of the lesson
19. Attentively
20. Spontaneously humorous
21. Spontaneously expressive
22. Approaches teacher physically
23. Mobile—free
24. Immobile—constricted
25. Through performing special assigned tasks
26a. Hostile to peers
26b. Protective of peers
27. Diversion to peers
28. Anxiously
29. Disjoined hand-raising
30. By whispering to teacher
31. Laughs at peers
32. Corrects teacher
33a. Disruptively
33b. Critically
34. By carping criticism
35. By praising work of peers
36. Dishonesty, cheating, lying, etc.
37. Attempts to maintain order
38. Guiltily
39. With sense of inadequacy
40. With sense of adequacy

41. By copying from peers
42. Attempts to control the class
43. No response
44. Uses teacher's last name
45. Uses teacher's first name
46. Calls out to teacher
47. Uses kinship term
48. By public performance

V. How does the educator participate? (What is his attitude?)

  1. Eagerly
    1. Facial expression
    2. Bodily movement
    3. Tone of voice
    4. Heightened bodily tonus
  2. Bored, uninterested, etc.
  3. Embarrassed
  4a. Dominative
  4b. Integrative
  5. Insecure
  6. Politely
  7. Enjoys correct response
  8. Resents incorrect response
  9. Can't tell
  10. Seeks physical contact with person being educated
  11. Acceptance of blame
  12. Putting decisions up to the children
  13. Discouraging
  14. Encouraging
  15. Hostile, ridiculing, sarcastic, belittling
  16. Relatively mobile
  17. Relatively immobile
  18. Personalizing
    1. Use of request sentence with name
    2. Use of name only
    3. Use of hand-name technique
    4. Use of equalizing, leveling term like "comrade"
  19. Depersonalizing
    1. Use of class seating plan for recitation in succession
    2. Use of "next" or some such impersonal device
    3. Use of "you" instead of name
    4. Pointing, nodding, looking

20. Irritable
21. Accepts approach
22. Repels approach
23. Accepting of child's spontaneous expressions
24. Rejecting of child's spontaneous expressions
25. Humorous
26. Handles anxiety, hostility, discomfort, etc.
27. Acts and/or talks as if child's self-image is fragile
28. Acts and/or talks as if child's self-image is irrelevant
29. Defends child against peers
30. Responds to non-verbal cue other than hand-raising
31. Excessively polite
32. Keeps word
33. Fails to keep word
34. Praises and rewards realistically
35. Praises and rewards indiscriminately
36. Critical (does not point out good things in student's work)
37. Does not reward correct answer or good performance
38. Does not punish incorrect answer or poor performance
39. Acknowledges own error
40. Uses affectional terms like "honey" or "dear"
41. Awakens anticipation ("Now we are going to get some nice new books.")
42. The inclusive plural

VI. Are some things taught to some and not to others?

1. Do different age groups learn different things?
2. Do the sexes learn different things?
3. Are different groups taught different things?

VII. Discontinuities in the educational process

1. Discontinuities between age-periods
    1. In regard to techniques
    2. In regard to values

2. How do all these apply between the sexes?
    1. Are discontinuities different for boys and girls?
    2. The secrecy of initiation rites

VIII. What limits the quantity and quality of information a child receives from a teacher?

1. Methods of teaching
2. Available time
3. Quality of equipment
4. Distance from the object
5. Ignorance or error of teacher
6. Stereotyping of the object
7. Failure of teacher to correct pupil's mistakes
8. Failure of teacher to indicate whether the pupil's answers are right or wrong
9. Failure of teacher to respond to a question
10. General vagueness or fumbling of the teacher

IX. What forms of conduct control (discipline) are used?

1. Relaxed
2. Tight
3. Sense of propriety
4. Affectivity
5. Reprimand
    1. Direct
    2. Gentle
    3. Mixed ("We like for you to have an opinion but it is childish for you to shout out your numbers like that.")
    4. Impersonal ("Some of you are holding us up.")
6. Ridicule
7. Exhortation ("How can I teach you if you keep making so much noise?")
8. Command
9. Command question or request
10. "We" technique
11. Instilling guilt

12. Cessation of activity
13. Group sanction
14. Threat
15. Putting the child on his mettle
16. Non-verbal signal
17. Reward
18. Promise of reward
19. Special stratagems
20. Awakening fear
21. Using a higher power
    1. Human
    2. Non-human
22. Exclusion
23. Punishment
24. Encourages peer-group control

X. What is the relation between the intent and the results of education?

1. Relatively high correlation between intention and results
2. Relatively low correlation between intention and results

XI. What self-conceptions seem reinforced?

1. Ego-forming factors
    1. Syntonic: praise, support, status inflation
        1. Grandiose self-conception
        2. Dystonic: blame, shame, guilt, fright, exclusion, depersonalization

XII. How long does the process of formal education last?

Appendix B
Percentages of Session Time Spent on Classroom Events

Figure B-1. Percentage of Preschool Session Time Spent on Classroom Events

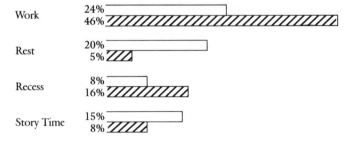

Play	47%
Story Time	16%
Meals	17%
Entry/Exit	13%
Rest	7%

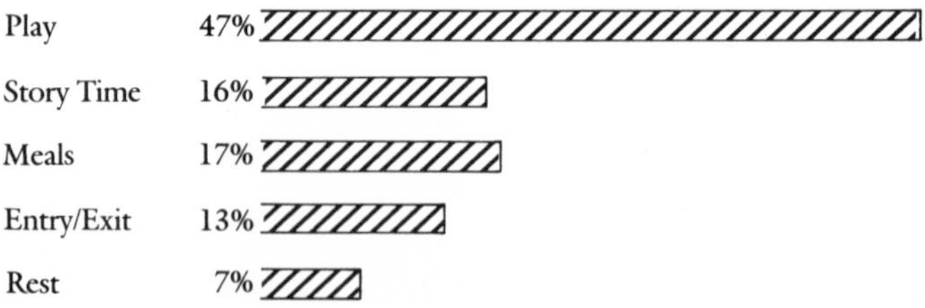

Figure B-2. Percentage of Kindergarten Session Time Spent on Classroom Events

Work	24% / 46%
Rest	20% / 5%
Recess	8% / 16%
Story Time	15% / 8%

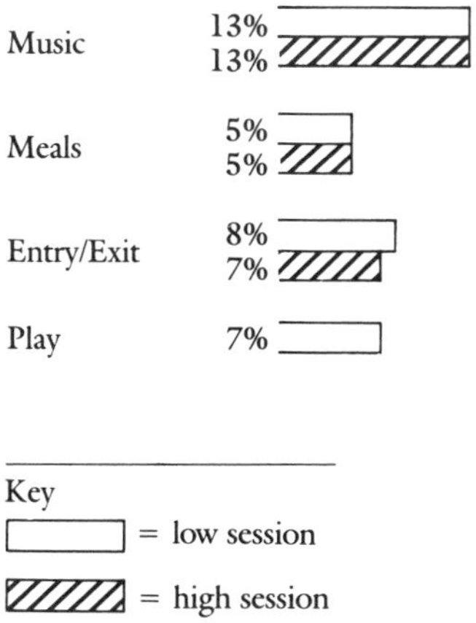

Music   13%
        13% ///////

Meals   5%
        5% ///

Entry/Exit 8%
            7% /////

Play   7% [   ]

Key
[   ] = low session
/////// = high session

Figure B-3. Percentage of First Grade Session Time Spent on Classroom Events

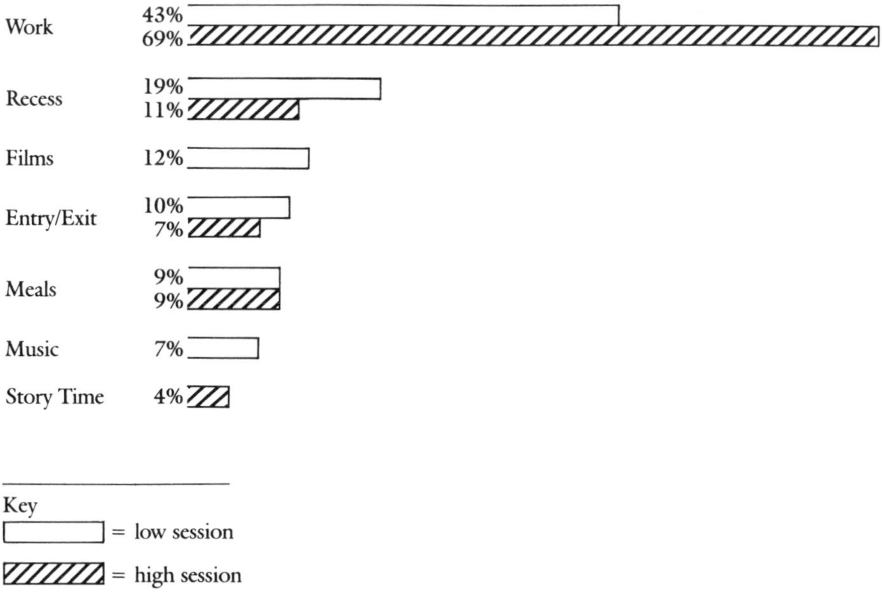

Work   43%
        69% ///

Recess 19%
        11% ///////

Films   12% [   ]

Entry/Exit 10%
            7% /////

Meals   9%
        9% ///////

Music   7% [   ]

Story Time 4% ////

Key
[   ] = low session
/////// = high session

Figure B-4. Percentage of Second Grade Session Time Spent on Classroom Events

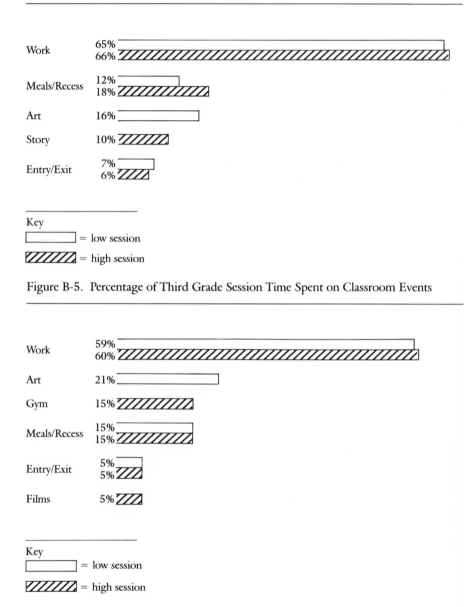

Work   65%
        66%

Meals/Recess   12%
                18%

Art   16%

Story   10%

Entry/Exit   7%
              6%

Key
☐ = low session
▨ = high session

Figure B-5. Percentage of Third Grade Session Time Spent on Classroom Events

Work   59%
        60%

Art   21%

Gym   15%

Meals/Recess   15%
                15%

Entry/Exit   5%
              5%

Films   5%

Key
☐ = low session
▨ = high session

Figure B-6. Percentage of Fourth Grade Session Time Spent on Classroom Events

Work	38% 43%	
Entry/Exit	26% 11%	
Meals/Recess	20% 15%	
Mathdown	15%	
Spelldown	16%	
Films	16%	

Key
☐ = low session
▧ = high session

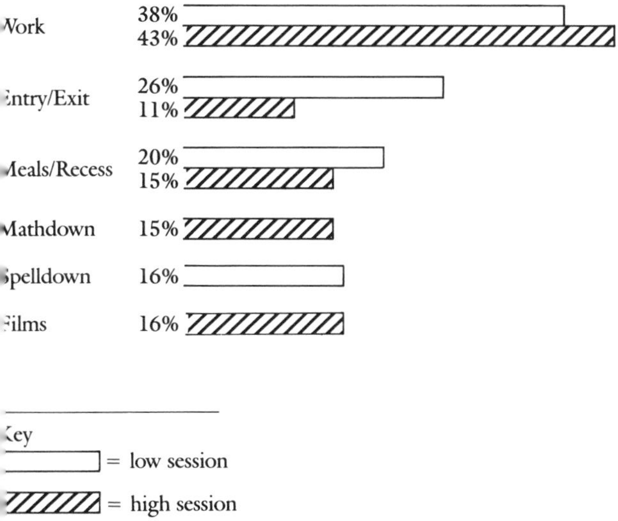

Figure B-7. Percentage of Upper Grade Session Time Spent on Classroom Events

Work	67% 74%	
Entry/Exit	22% 15%	
Meals/Recess	11% 11%	

Key
☐ = low session
▧ = high session

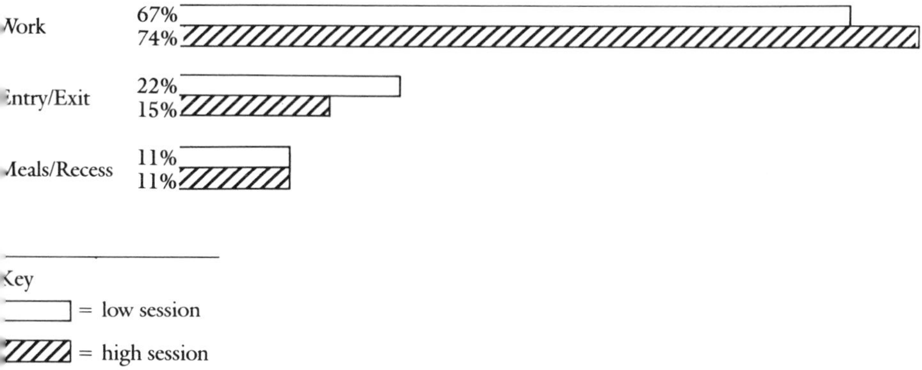

Appendix C
Summaries of the Characteristics of the Classroom Sessions

Figure C-1. Preschool Session Characteristics and Their Frequency of Occurrence*

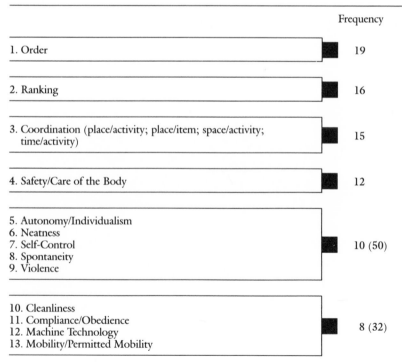

	Frequency
1. Order	19
2. Ranking	16
3. Coordination (place/activity; place/item; space/activity; time/activity)	15
4. Safety/Care of the Body	12
5. Autonomy/Individualism 6. Neatness 7. Self-Control 8. Spontaneity 9. Violence	10 (50)
10. Cleanliness 11. Compliance/Obedience 12. Machine Technology 13. Mobility/Permitted Mobility	8 (32)

*Frequency = frequency of occurrence of each trait

Figure C-1. (continued)

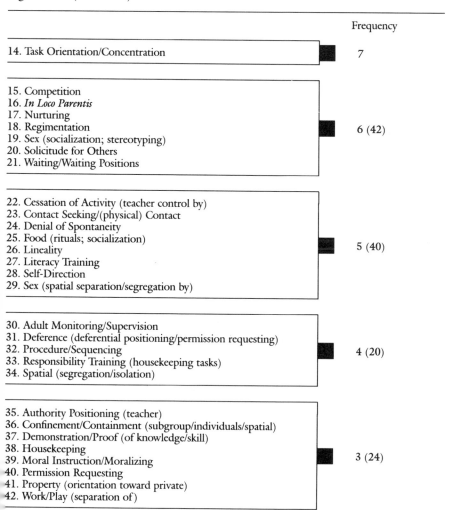

Frequency

14. Task Orientation/Concentration — 7

15. Competition
16. *In Loco Parentis*
17. Nurturing
18. Regimentation
19. Sex (socialization; stereotyping)
20. Solicitude for Others
21. Waiting/Waiting Positions

6 (42)

22. Cessation of Activity (teacher control by)
23. Contact Seeking/(physical) Contact
24. Denial of Spontaneity
25. Food (rituals; socialization)
26. Lineality
27. Literacy Training
28. Self-Direction
29. Sex (spatial separation/segregation by)

5 (40)

30. Adult Monitoring/Supervision
31. Deference (deferential positioning/permission requesting)
32. Procedure/Sequencing
33. Responsibility Training (housekeeping tasks)
34. Spatial (segregation/isolation)

4 (20)

35. Authority Positioning (teacher)
36. Confinement/Containment (subgroup/individuals/spatial)
37. Demonstration/Proof (of knowledge/skill)
38. Housekeeping
39. Moral Instruction/Moralizing
40. Permission Requesting
41. Property (orientation toward private)
42. Work/Play (separation of)

3 (24)

Figure C-1. (continued)

Frequency

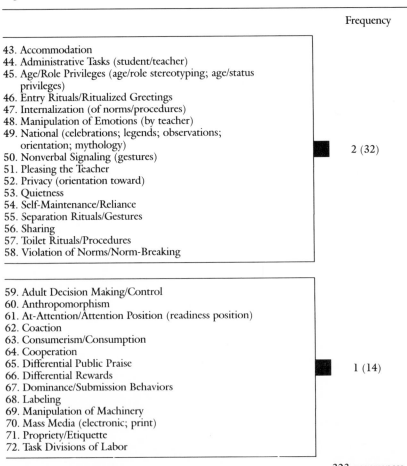

43. Accommodation
44. Administrative Tasks (student/teacher)
45. Age/Role Privileges (age/role stereotyping; age/status privileges)
46. Entry Rituals/Ritualized Greetings
47. Internalization (of norms/procedures)
48. Manipulation of Emotions (by teacher)
49. National (celebrations; legends; observations; orientation; mythology)
50. Nonverbal Signaling (gestures)
51. Pleasing the Teacher
52. Privacy (orientation toward)
53. Quietness
54. Self-Maintenance/Reliance
55. Separation Rituals/Gestures
56. Sharing
57. Toilet Rituals/Procedures
58. Violation of Norms/Norm-Breaking

2 (32)

59. Adult Decision Making/Control
60. Anthropomorphism
61. At-Attention/Attention Position (readiness position)
62. Coaction
63. Consumerism/Consumption
64. Cooperation
65. Differential Public Praise
66. Differential Rewards
67. Dominance/Submission Behaviors
68. Labeling
69. Manipulation of Machinery
70. Mass Media (electronic; print)
71. Propriety/Etiquette
72. Task Divisions of Labor

1 (14)

323 occurrences

ıure C-2. Kindergarten Session Characteristics and Their Frequency of Occurrence*

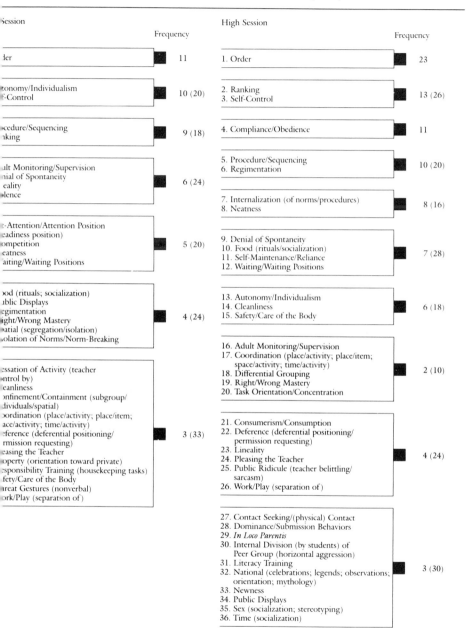

...ession	Frequency	High Session	Frequency
...der	11	1. Order	23
...tonomy/Individualism ...f-Control	10 (20)	2. Ranking 3. Self-Control	13 (26)
...ocedure/Sequencing ...nking	9 (18)	4. Compliance/Obedience	11
...ult Monitoring/Supervision ...nial of Spontaneity ...eality ...lence	6 (24)	5. Procedure/Sequencing 6. Regimentation	10 (20)
...t-Attention/Attention Position ...eadiness position) ...ompetition ...eatness ...aiting/Waiting Positions	5 (20)	7. Internalization (of norms/procedures) 8. Neatness	8 (16)
		9. Denial of Spontaneity 10. Food (rituals/socialization) 11. Self-Maintenance/Reliance 12. Waiting/Waiting Positions	7 (28)
...ood (rituals; socialization) ...ublic Displays ...egimentation ...ight/Wrong Mastery ...atial (segregation/isolation) ...olation of Norms/Norm-Breaking	4 (24)	13. Autonomy/Individualism 14. Cleanliness 15. Safety/Care of the Body	6 (18)
...essation of Activity (teacher ...ontrol by) ...eanliness ...onfinement/Containment (subgroup/ ...dividuals/spatial) ...oordination (place/activity; place/item; ...ace/activity; time/activity)		16. Adult Monitoring/Supervision 17. Coordination (place/activity; place/item; space/activity; time/activity) 18. Differential Grouping 19. Right/Wrong Mastery 20. Task Orientation/Concentration	2 (10)
...eference (deferential positioning/ ...rmission requesting) ...easing the Teacher ...operty (orientation toward private) ...esponsibility Training (housekeeping tasks) ...fety/Care of the Body ...reat Gestures (nonverbal) ...ork/Play (separation of)	3 (33)	21. Consumerism/Consumption 22. Deference (deferential positioning/ permission requesting) 23. Lineality 24. Pleasing the Teacher 25. Public Ridicule (teacher belittling/ sarcasm) 26. Work/Play (separation of)	4 (24)
		27. Contact Seeking/(physical) Contact 28. Dominance/Submission Behaviors 29. *In Loco Parentis* 30. Internal Division (by students) of Peer Group (horizontal aggression) 31. Literacy Training 32. National (celebrations; legends; observations; orientation; mythology) 33. Newness 34. Public Displays 35. Sex (socialization; stereotyping) 36. Time (socialization)	3 (30)

...quency = frequency of occurrence of each trait

Figure C-2. (continued)

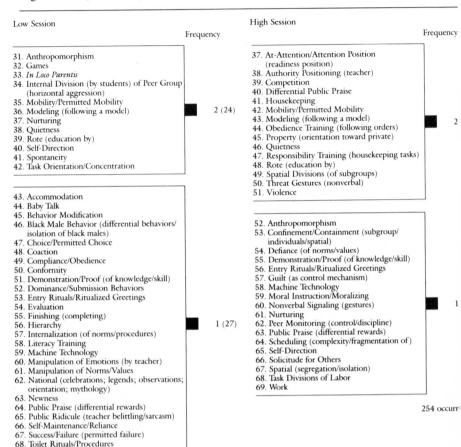

Low Session	Frequency
31. Anthropomorphism	
32. Games	
33. *In Loco Parentis*	
34. Internal Division (by students) of Peer Group (horizontal aggression)	
35. Mobility/Permitted Mobility	
36. Modeling (following a model)	2 (24)
37. Nurturing	
38. Quietness	
39. Rote (education by)	
40. Self-Direction	
41. Spontaneity	
42. Task Orientation/Concentration	

	Frequency
43. Accommodation	
44. Baby Talk	
45. Behavior Modification	
46. Black Male Behavior (differential behaviors/ isolation of black males)	
47. Choice/Permitted Choice	
48. Coaction	
49. Compliance/Obedience	
50. Conformity	
51. Demonstration/Proof (of knowledge/skill)	
52. Dominance/Submission Behaviors	
53. Entry Rituals/Ritualized Greetings	
54. Evaluation	
55. Finishing (completing)	
56. Hierarchy	1 (27)
57. Internalization (of norms/procedures)	
58. Literacy Training	
59. Machine Technology	
60. Manipulation of Emotions (by teacher)	
61. Manipulation of Norms/Values	
62. National (celebrations; legends; observations; orientation; mythology)	
63. Newness	
64. Public Praise (differential rewards)	
65. Public Ridicule (teacher belittling/sarcasm)	
66. Self-Maintenance/Reliance	
67. Success/Failure (permitted failure)	
68. Toilet Rituals/Procedures	
69. Work	

201 occurrences

High Session	Frequency
37. At-Attention/Attention Position (readiness position)	
38. Authority Positioning (teacher)	
39. Competition	
40. Differential Public Praise	
41. Housekeeping	
42. Mobility/Permitted Mobility	
43. Modeling (following a model)	2
44. Obedience Training (following orders)	
45. Property (orientation toward private)	
46. Quietness	
47. Responsibility Training (housekeeping tasks)	
48. Rote (education by)	
49. Spatial Divisions (of subgroups)	
50. Threat Gestures (nonverbal)	
51. Violence	

	Frequency
52. Anthropomorphism	
53. Confinement/Containment (subgroup/ individuals/spatial)	
54. Defiance (of norms/values)	
55. Demonstration/Proof (of knowledge/skill)	
56. Entry Rituals/Ritualized Greetings	
57. Guilt (as control mechanism)	
58. Machine Technology	
59. Moral Instruction/Moralizing	
60. Nonverbal Signaling (gestures)	1
61. Nurturing	
62. Peer Monitoring (control/discipline)	
63. Public Praise (differential rewards)	
64. Scheduling (complexity/fragmentation of)	
65. Self-Direction	
66. Solicitude for Others	
67. Spatial (segregation/isolation)	
68. Task Divisions of Labor	
69. Work	

254 occurr

Figure C-3. First Grade Session Characteristics and Their Frequency of Occurrence*

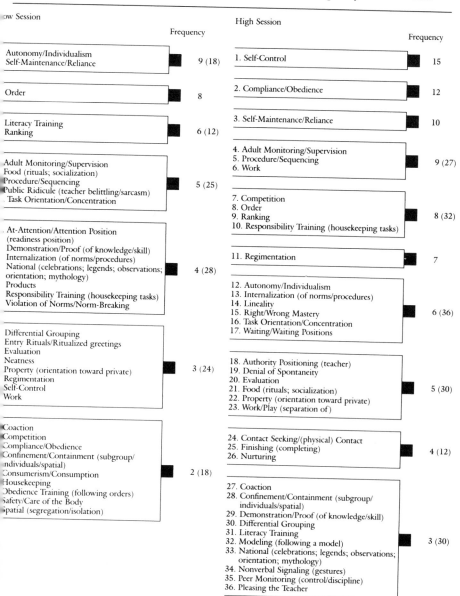

ow Session

	Frequency
Autonomy/Individualism Self-Maintenance/Reliance	9 (18)
Order	8
Literacy Training Ranking	6 (12)
Adult Monitoring/Supervision Food (rituals; socialization) Procedure/Sequencing Public Ridicule (teacher belittling/sarcasm) Task Orientation/Concentration	5 (25)
At-Attention/Attention Position (readiness position) Demonstration/Proof (of knowledge/skill) Internalization (of norms/procedures) National (celebrations; legends; observations; orientation; mythology) Products Responsibility Training (housekeeping tasks) Violation of Norms/Norm-Breaking	4 (28)
Differential Grouping Entry Rituals/Ritualized greetings Evaluation Neatness Property (orientation toward private) Regimentation Self-Control Work	3 (24)
Coaction Competition Compliance/Obedience Confinement/Containment (subgroup/ individuals/spatial) Consumerism/Consumption Housekeeping Obedience Training (following orders) Safety/Care of the Body Spatial (segregation/isolation)	2 (18)

High Session

	Frequency
1. Self-Control	15
2. Compliance/Obedience	12
3. Self-Maintenance/Reliance	10
4. Adult Monitoring/Supervision 5. Procedure/Sequencing 6. Work	9 (27)
7. Competition 8. Order 9. Ranking 10. Responsibility Training (housekeeping tasks)	8 (32)
11. Regimentation	7
12. Autonomy/Individualism 13. Internalization (of norms/procedures) 14. Lineality 15. Right/Wrong Mastery 16. Task Orientation/Concentration 17. Waiting/Waiting Positions	6 (36)
18. Authority Positioning (teacher) 19. Denial of Spontaneity 20. Evaluation 21. Food (rituals; socialization) 22. Property (orientation toward private) 23. Work/Play (separation of)	5 (30)
24. Contact Seeking/(physical) Contact 25. Finishing (completing) 26. Nurturing	4 (12)
27. Coaction 28. Confinement/Containment (subgroup/ individuals/spatial) 29. Demonstration/Proof (of knowledge/skill) 30. Differential Grouping 31. Literacy Training 32. Modeling (following a model) 33. National (celebrations; legends; observations; orientation; mythology) 34. Nonverbal Signaling (gestures) 35. Peer Monitoring (control/discipline) 36. Pleasing the Teacher	3 (30)

*Frequency = frequency of occurrence of each trait

Figure C-3. (continued)

Low Session	Frequency
35. Administrative Hegemony/Control	
36. Age/Role Privileges (age/role stereotyping; age/status privileges)	
37. Authority Positioning (teacher)	
38. Behavior Modification	
39. Black Male Behavior (differential behaviors/ isolation of black males)	
40. Cessation of Activity (teacher control by)	
41. Cleanliness	
42. Contact Seeking/(physical) Contact	
43. Deference (Deferential positioning/ permission requesting)	
44. Denial of Spontaneity	
45. Differential Public Praise	
46. Differential Rewards	
47. Finishing (completing)	
48. *In Loco Parentis*	
49. Internal Division (by students) of Peer Group (horizontal aggression)	▮ 1 (33)
50. Labeling	
51. Lineality	
52. Local Village (orientation toward)	
53. Machine Technology	
54. Mobility/Permitted Mobility	
55. Nonverbal Signaling (gestures)	
56. Peer Monitoring (control/discipline)	
57. Privacy (orientation toward)	
58. Pleasing the Teacher	
59. Public Displays	
60. Religion	
61. Right/Wrong Mastery	
62. Rote (education by)	
63. Sex (socialization; stereotyping)	
64. Spatial Divisions (of subgroups)	
65. Tattling	
66. Violence	
67. Waiting/Waiting Positions	

166 occurrences

High Session	Frequency
37. Administrative Tasks (student/teacher)	
38. At-Attention/Attention Position (readiness position)	
39. Conformity	
40. Consumerism/Consumption	
41. Coordination (place/activity; place/item; space/activity; time/activity)	
42. Deference (deferential positioning/permission requesting)	▮ 2 (2
43. Differential Rewards	
44. Entry Rituals/Ritualized Greetings	
45. Fear/Anxiety	
46. Neatness	
47. Propriety/Etiquette	
48. Public Praise (differential rewards)	
49. Public Ridicule (teacher belittling/sarcasm)	
50. Safety/Care of the Body	
51. Black Male Behavior (differential behaviors/ isolation of black males)	
52. Cessation of Activity (teacher control by)	
53. Housekeeping	
54. *In Loco Parentis*	
55. Individual Accountability	
56. Labeling	
57. Manipulation of Emotions (by teacher)	
58. Mathematics Training	
59. Mobility/Permitted Mobility	
60. Newness	
61. Obedience Training (following orders)	
62. Play	
63. Privacy (orientation toward)	▮ 1
64. Problem-Solving	
65. Products	
66. Progress	
67. Public Displays	
68. Scheduling (complexity/fragmentation of)	
69. Self-Direction	
70. Separation Rituals/Gestures	
71. Sex (socialization; stereotyping)	
72. Space (personalization of)	
73. Spatial (segregation/isolation)	
74. Spatial Divisions (of subgroups)	
75. Task Divisions of Labor	
76. Tattling	
77. Time (socialization)	
78. Violation of Norms/Norm-Breaking	

267 occurre

Figure C-4. Second Grade Session Characteristics and Their Frequency of Occurrence*

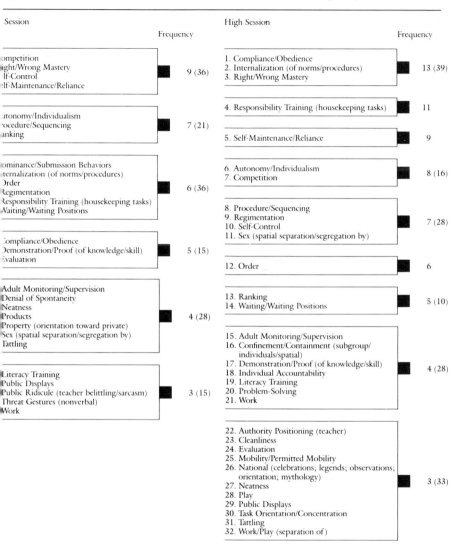

Session	Frequency	High Session	Frequency
Competition Right/Wrong Mastery Self-Control Self-Maintenance/Reliance	9 (36)	1. Compliance/Obedience 2. Internalization (of norms/procedures) 3. Right/Wrong Mastery	13 (39)
Autonomy/Individualism Procedure/Sequencing Ranking	7 (21)	4. Responsibility Training (housekeeping tasks)	11
		5. Self-Maintenance/Reliance	9
Dominance/Submission Behaviors Internalization (of norms/procedures) Order Regimentation Responsibility Training (housekeeping tasks) Waiting/Waiting Positions	6 (36)	6. Autonomy/Individualism 7. Competition	8 (16)
Compliance/Obedience Demonstration/Proof (of knowledge/skill) Evaluation	5 (15)	8. Procedure/Sequencing 9. Regimentation 10. Self-Control 11. Sex (spatial separation/segregation by)	7 (28)
		12. Order	6
Adult Monitoring/Supervision Denial of Spontaneity Neatness Products Property (orientation toward private) Sex (spatial separation/segregation by) Tattling	4 (28)	13. Ranking 14. Waiting/Waiting Positions	5 (10)
Literacy Training Public Displays Public Ridicule (teacher belittling/sarcasm) Threat Gestures (nonverbal) Work	3 (15)	15. Adult Monitoring/Supervision 16. Confinement/Containment (subgroup/ individuals/spatial) 17. Demonstration/Proof (of knowledge/skill) 18. Individual Accountability 19. Literacy Training 20. Problem-Solving 21. Work	4 (28)
		22. Authority Positioning (teacher) 23. Cleanliness 24. Evaluation 25. Mobility/Permitted Mobility 26. National (celebrations; legends; observations; orientation; mythology) 27. Neatness 28. Play 29. Public Displays 30. Task Orientation/Concentration 31. Tattling 32. Work/Play (separation of)	3 (33)

*Frequency = frequency of occurrence of each item

Figure C-4. (continued)

Low Session	Frequency

29. At-Attention/Attention Position (readiness position)
30. Cleanliness
31. Composure under Stress
32. Conformity
33. Deference (deferential positioning/permission requesting)
34. Differential Grouping
35. Differential Public Praise
36. Differential Rewards
37. Finishing (completing)
38. Guilt (as control mechanism)
39. Individual Accountability   2 (42)
40. Internal Division (by students) of Peer Group (horizontal aggression)
41. Lack of Adherence (to norms/values)
42. Mobility/Permitted Mobility
43. Moral Instruction/Moralizing
44. Scheduling (complexity/fragmentation of)
45. Self-Direction
46. Sex (socialization; stereotyping)
47. Spatial (segregation/isolation)
48. Task Orientation/Concentration
49. Violence

50. Administrative Tasks (student/teacher)
51. Approval Seeking
52. Authority Positioning (teacher)
53. Behavior Modification
54. Cessation of Activity (teacher control by)
55. Confinement/Containment (subgroup/ individuals/spatial)
56. Cooperation
57. Entry Rituals/Ritualized Greetings
58. Lineality
59. Manipulation of Emotions (by teacher)
60. National (celebrations; legends; observations; orientation; mythology)
61. Nonverbal Signaling (gestures)   1 (25)
62. Play
63. Pleasing the Teacher
64. Privacy (orientation toward)
65. Problem-Solving
66. Propriety/Etiquette
67. Sharing
68. Solicitude for Others
69. Spatial Divisions (of subgroups)
70. Spontaneity
71. Stimulus/Response Conditioning
72. Time (socialization)
73. Toilet Rituals/Procedures
74. Work/Play (separation of)

218 occurrences

High Session	Frequency

33. At-Attention/Attention Position (readiness position)
34. Black Male Behavior (differential behaviors/ isolation of black males)
35. Coaction
36. Color (conflicts/race/segregation by/ spatial separation by)
37. Conformity
38. Deference (deferential positioning/permission requesting)
39. Differential Public Praise
40. Finishing (completing)   2
41. Food (rituals; socialization)
42. Hierarchy
43. Modeling (following a model)
44. Products
45. Public Ridicule (teacher belittling/sarcasm)
46. Rote (education by)
47. Separation Rituals/Gestures
48. Sex (socialization; stereotyping)
49. Spatial (expression of status)
50. Spatial Divisions (of subgroups)
51. Violence

52. Composure under Stress
53. Coordination (place/activity; place/item; space/activity; time/activity)
54. Creativity/Imagination (subordination of)
55. Defiance (of norms/values)
56. Differential Grouping
57. Dominance/Submission Behaviors
58. Entry Rituals/Ritualized Greetings
59. Fear/Anxiety
60. Females/Bias Toward
61. Games
62. Housekeeping
63. Internal Division (by students) of Peer Group (horizontal aggression)
64. Lack of Adherence (to norms/values)
65. Lineality
66. Machine Technology   1
67. Manipulation of Emotions (by teacher)
68. Mass Media (electronic; print)
69. Mathematics Training
70. Nonverbal Signaling (gestures)
71. Obedience Training (following orders)
72. Permission Requesting
73. Pleasing the Teacher
74. Privacy (orientation toward)
75. Property (orientation toward private)
76. Quietness
77. Self-Direction
78. Sharing
79. Spontaneity
80. Threat Gestures (nonverbal)
81. Time (socialization)
82. Violation of Norms/Norm-Breaking

249 occurrences

Figure C-5. Third Grade Session Characteristics and Their Frequency of Occurrence*

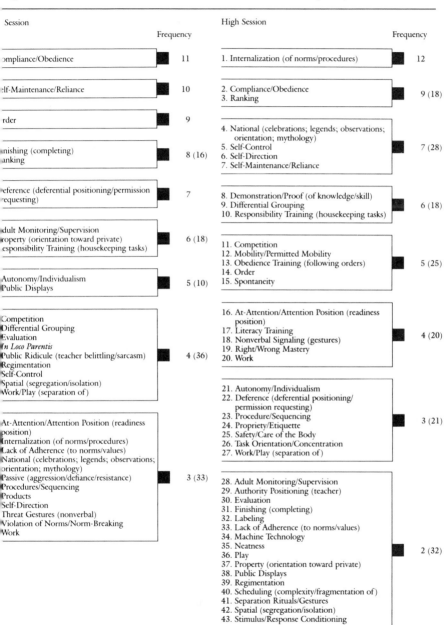

Session	Frequency	High Session	Frequency
ompliance/Obedience	11	1. Internalization (of norms/procedures)	12
elf-Maintenance/Reliance	10	2. Compliance/Obedience 3. Ranking	9 (18)
rder	9	4. National (celebrations; legends; observations; orientation; mythology) 5. Self-Control 6. Self-Direction 7. Self-Maintenance/Reliance	7 (28)
nishing (completing) anking	8 (16)		
eference (deferential positioning/permission requesting)	7	8. Demonstration/Proof (of knowledge/skill) 9. Differential Grouping 10. Responsibility Training (housekeeping tasks)	6 (18)
dult Monitoring/Supervision roperty (orientation toward private) esponsibility Training (housekeeping tasks)	6 (18)	11. Competition 12. Mobility/Permitted Mobility 13. Obedience Training (following orders) 14. Order 15. Spontaneity	5 (25)
Autonomy/Individualism Public Displays	5 (10)		
Competition Differential Grouping Evaluation In Loco Parentis Public Ridicule (teacher belittling/sarcasm) Regimentation Self-Control Spatial (segregation/isolation) Work/Play (separation of)	4 (36)	16. At-Attention/Attention Position (readiness position) 17. Literacy Training 18. Nonverbal Signaling (gestures) 19. Right/Wrong Mastery 20. Work	4 (20)
At-Attention/Attention Position (readiness position) Internalization (of norms/procedures) Lack of Adherence (to norms/values) National (celebrations; legends; observations; orientation; mythology) Passive (aggression/defiance/resistance) Procedures/Sequencing Products Self-Direction Threat Gestures (nonverbal) Violation of Norms/Norm-Breaking Work	3 (33)	21. Autonomy/Individualism 22. Deference (deferential positioning/ permission requesting) 23. Procedure/Sequencing 24. Propriety/Etiquette 25. Safety/Care of the Body 26. Task Orientation/Concentration 27. Work/Play (separation of)	3 (21)
		28. Adult Monitoring/Supervision 29. Authority Positioning (teacher) 30. Evaluation 31. Finishing (completing) 32. Labeling 33. Lack of Adherence (to norms/values) 34. Machine Technology 35. Neatness 36. Play 37. Property (orientation toward private) 38. Public Displays 39. Regimentation 40. Scheduling (complexity/fragmentation of) 41. Separation Rituals/Gestures 42. Spatial (segregation/isolation) 43. Stimulus/Response Conditioning	2 (32)

equency = frequency of occurrences of each trait

Figure C-5. (continued)

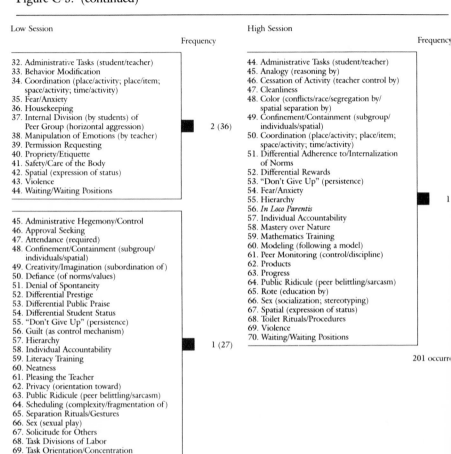

Low Session

Frequency

High Session

Frequency

32. Administrative Tasks (student/teacher)
33. Behavior Modification
34. Coordination (place/activity; place/item; space/activity; time/activity)
35. Fear/Anxiety
36. Housekeeping
37. Internal Division (by students) of Peer Group (horizontal aggression)
38. Manipulation of Emotions (by teacher)
39. Permission Requesting
40. Propriety/Etiquette
41. Safety/Care of the Body
42. Spatial (expression of status)
43. Violence
44. Waiting/Waiting Positions

2 (36)

45. Administrative Hegemony/Control
46. Approval Seeking
47. Attendance (required)
48. Confinement/Containment (subgroup/ individuals/spatial)
49. Creativity/Imagination (subordination of)
50. Defiance (of norms/values)
51. Denial of Spontaneity
52. Differential Prestige
53. Differential Public Praise
54. Differential Student Status
55. "Don't Give Up" (persistence)
56. Guilt (as control mechanism)
57. Hierarchy
58. Individual Accountability
59. Literacy Training
60. Neatness
61. Pleasing the Teacher
62. Privacy (orientation toward)
63. Public Ridicule (peer belittling/sarcasm)
64. Scheduling (complexity/fragmentation of)
65. Separation Rituals/Gestures
66. Sex (sexual play)
67. Solicitude for Others
68. Task Divisions of Labor
69. Task Orientation/Concentration
70. Tattling
71. Territoriality

1 (27)

213 occurrences

44. Administrative Tasks (student/teacher)
45. Analogy (reasoning by)
46. Cessation of Activity (teacher control by)
47. Cleanliness
48. Color (conflicts/race/segregation by/ spatial separation by)
49. Confinement/Containment (subgroup/ individuals/spatial)
50. Coordination (place/activity; place/item; space/activity; time/activity)
51. Differential Adherence to/Internalization of Norms
52. Differential Rewards
53. "Don't Give Up" (persistence)
54. Fear/Anxiety
55. Hierarchy
56. *In Loco Parentis*
57. Individual Accountability
58. Mastery over Nature
59. Mathematics Training
60. Modeling (following a model)
61. Peer Monitoring (control/discipline)
62. Products
63. Progress
64. Public Ridicule (peer belittling/sarcasm)
65. Rote (education by)
66. Sex (socialization; stereotyping)
67. Spatial (expression of status)
68. Toilet Rituals/Procedures
69. Violence
70. Waiting/Waiting Positions

1

201 occurre

Figure C-6.   Fourth Grade Session Characteristics and Their Frequency of Occurrence*

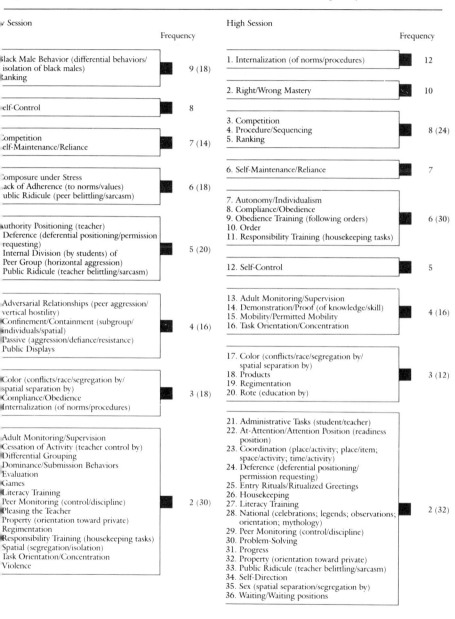

Figure C-6. (continued)

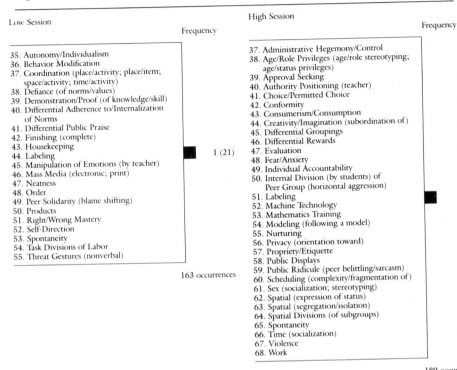

Low Session

Frequency

35. Autonomy/Individualism
36. Behavior Modification
37. Coordination (place/activity; place/item; space/activity; time/activity)
38. Defiance (of norms/values)
39. Demonstration/Proof (of knowledge/skill)
40. Differential Adherence to/Internalization of Norms
41. Differential Public Praise
42. Finishing (complete)
43. Housekeeping
44. Labeling
45. Manipulation of Emotions (by teacher)
46. Mass Media (electronic; print)
47. Neatness
48. Order
49. Peer Solidarity (blame shifting)
50. Products
51. Right/Wrong Mastery
52. Self-Direction
53. Spontaneity
54. Task Divisions of Labor
55. Threat Gestures (nonverbal)

1 (21)

163 occurrences

High Session

Frequency

37. Administrative Hegemony/Control
38. Age/Role Privileges (age/role stereotyping; age/status privileges)
39. Approval Seeking
40. Authority Positioning (teacher)
41. Choice/Permitted Choice
42. Conformity
43. Consumerism/Consumption
44. Creativity/Imagination (subordination of)
45. Differential Groupings
46. Differential Rewards
47. Evaluation
48. Fear/Anxiety
49. Individual Accountability
50. Internal Division (by students) of Peer Group (horizontal aggression)
51. Labeling
52. Machine Technology
53. Mathematics Training
54. Modeling (following a model)
55. Nurturing
56. Privacy (orientation toward)
57. Propriety/Etiquette
58. Public Displays
59. Public Ridicule (peer belittling/sarcasm)
60. Scheduling (complexity/fragmentation of)
61. Sex (socialization; stereotyping)
62. Spatial (expression of status)
63. Spatial (segregation/isolation)
64. Spatial Divisions (of subgroups)
65. Spontaneity
66. Time (socialization)
67. Violence
68. Work

180 occurrences

Figure C-7.   Upper Grade Session Characteristics and Their Frequency of Occurrence*

Session	Frequency	High Session	Frequency
ublic Ridicule (teacher belittling/sarcasm)	9	1. Self-Direction	12
elf-Maintenance/Reliance	8	2. Internalization (of norms/procedures)	11
Order / ight/Wrong Mastery	7	3. Ranking	10
olor (conflicts/race/segregation by/ spatial separation by) / cheduling (complexity/fragmentation of)	6 (18)	4. Deference (deferential positioning/permission requesting) / 5. Females/Bias Toward	9 (18)
dministrative Tasks (student/teacher) / oordination (place/activity; place/item; space/activity; time/activity) / ifferential Adherence to/Internalization of Norms / Ranking / Task Orientation/Concentration	5 (25)	6. Order / 7. Self-Maintenance/Reliance	8 (16)
		8. Coordination (place/activity; place/item; space/activity; time/activity) / 9. Literacy Training / 10. Right/Wrong Mastery	7 (21)
Adult Monitoring/Supervision / Attendance (required) / Authority Positioning (teacher) / Compliance/Obedience / Females/Bias Toward / Housekeeping / Mobility/Permitted Mobility / Public Ridicule (peer belittling/sarcasm) / Responsibility Training (housekeeping tasks) / Self-Control / Self-Direction	4 (44)	11. Administrative Tasks (student/teacher) / 12. Responsibility Training (housekeeping tasks)	6 (12)
		13. Compliance/Obedience / 14. Mobility/Permitted Mobility / 15. Procedures/Sequencing / 16. Sex (spatial separation/segregation by) / 17. Universalistic Standards/Criteria / 18. Waiting/Waiting Positions	5 (30)
Autonomy/Individualism / Coaction / Competition / Confinement/Containment (subgroup/ individuals/spatial) / Deference (deferential positioning/permission requesting) / Demonstration/Proof (of knowledge/skill) / Evaluation / Neatness / Regimentation / Sex (socialization; stereotyping) / Sex (spatial separation/segregation by)	3 (33)	19. Black Male Behavior (differential behaviors/ isolation of black males) / 20. Products / 21. Public Displays / 22. Regimentation	4 (16)
		23. Attendance (required) / 24. Autonomy/Individualism / 25. Demonstration/Proof (of knowledge/skill) / 26. Differential Grouping / 27. Property (orientation toward private) / 28. Self-Control / 29. Task Orientation/Concentration	3 (21)

*Frequency = frequency of occurrence of each trait

Figure C-7. (continued)

Low Session	Frequency
34. Cessation of Activity (teacher control by)	
35. Entry Rituals/Ritualized Greetings	
36. Finishing (completing)	
37. Hierarchy	
38. Internalization (of norms/procedures)	
39. Machine Technology	
40. Mathematics Training	
41. National (celebrations; legends; observations; orientation; mythology)	
42. Peer Monitoring (control/discipline)	2 (36)
43. Pleasing the Teacher	
44. Privacy (orientation toward)	
45. Problem-Solving	
46. Property (orientation toward private)	
47. Public Displays	
48. Spatial (expression of status)	
49. Spatial (segregation/isolation)	
50. Threat Gestures (nonverbal)	
51. Violence	

52. Administrative Hegemony/Control	
53. At-Attention/Attention Position (readiness position)	
54. Black Male Behavior (differential behaviors/ isolation of black males)	
55. Cleanliness	
56. Composure under Stress	
57. Conformity	
58. Creativity/Imagination (subordination of)	
59. Defiance (of norms/values)	
60. Differential Grouping	
61. Differential Rewards	
62. Distancing Behavior(s)	
63. Fear/Anxiety	1 (24)
64. Internal Division (by students) of Peer Group (horizontal aggression)	
65. Literacy Training	
66. Manipulation of Emotions (by teacher)	
67. Obedience Training (following orders)	
68. Passive (aggression/defiance/resistance)	
69. Play	
70. Solicitude for Others	
71. Spatial Divisions (of subgroups)	
72. Success/Failure (permitted failure)	
73. Waiting/Waiting Positions	
74. Work	
75. Work/Play (Separation of)	

204 occurrences

High Session	Frequency
30. Authority Positioning (teacher)	
31. Color (conflicts/race/segregation by/ spatial separation by)	
32. Creativity/Imagination (subordination of)	
33. Neatness	
34. Obedience Training (following orders)	2
35. Permission Requesting	
36. Public Ridicule (teacher belittling/sarcasm)	
37. Scheduling (complexity/fragmentation of)	
38. Sex (socialization; stereotyping)	
39. Work	

40. Adult Monitoring/Supervision	
41. At-Attention/Attention Position (readiness position)	
42. Coaction	
43. Competition	
44. Composure under Stress	
45. Confinement/Containment (subgroup/ individuals/spatial)	
46. Denial of Spontaneity	
47. "Don't Give Up" (persistence)	
48. Evaluation	
49. Hierarchy	
50. Individual Accountability	
51. Internal Division (by students) of Peer Group (horizontal aggression)	
52. Mass Media (electronic; print)	1
53. Mathematics Training	
54. Moral Instruction/Moralizing	
55. Nonverbal Signaling (Gestures)	
56. Nurturing	
57. Passive (aggression/defiance/resistance)	
58. Privacy (orientation toward)	
59. Problem-Solving	
60. Progress	
61. Propriety/Etiquette	
62. Separation Rituals/Gestures	
63. Spatial Divisions (of subgroups)	
64. Spontaneity	
65. Threat Gestures (nonverbal)	
66. Time (socialization)	
67. Work/Play (separation of)	

215 occurre

Glossary

Age Grade/Age Set Fixed social categories, based on age by which people are classified and organized, constitute age grades. An age set is the actual group of individuals, of similar age and sex, as a unit moving through the (rite of passage) various levels of a culturally defined age grade.

Anthropomorphism The ascription of human characteristics to nonhuman objects, in particular, the transfer of human qualities to animals.

Bureaucracy A form of organization characterized by hierarchical authority structure and explicit procedural rules. Bureaucratic organizations provide for the efficient coordination of large numbers of people and/or things.

Caste A hereditary, intermarrying group of people possessing a common name and associated with specific occupations. Caste customarily is applied to the system of stratification found in traditional India in which social and cultural status distinctions are ascribed at birth, caste groups are arranged hierarchically and vary with respect to prestige, and cross-caste mobility is limited. Caste refers to those sociocultural systems exhibiting rigid stratification (see also *class*; *status*; *stratification*).

Class A level, or position, in a hierarchically organized social system. Class membership is ascribed at birth. A class society, in comparison with a caste society, offers the possibility of mobility between sociocultural status levels (see also *caste*; *status*; *stratification*).

Culture Shared patterns of and for learned behavior transmitted extragenetically from generation to generation consti-

tuting the total lifeway of a group of people. Culture is the pattern (as well as the rules underlying the pattern) of the way a group of people integrates physical objects, beliefs, and ideas and actual behavior. Culture can be apprehended by studying the manner in which people transmit information across generations (see also *society*).

Culture Theme Core principles underlying and occurring in different interactions of behavior, ideas, and physical objects, which recur often enough to form a discernible pattern.

Dominance Hierarchy Among nonhuman primates, a dominance hierarchy often is defined by reference to priority of access to some necessary or desirable item (food, sex, and so on). Priority of access often is associated with successful aggressive encounters with others resulting in the establishment of a rank ordering in the group. Though associated primarily with males, dominance hierarchies also occur among females (see also *primate*).

Ecology/Cultural Ecology The relationship and the study of the relationship between individuals, populations, and their natural or built environments. Cultural ecology primarily is connected with the relationship between sociocultural systems and their natural environment.

Education General teaching and learning within a social and cultural context, at both conscious and unconscious levels. Education is distinct from schooling (see also *schools*).

Egalitarianism A form of political economy in which all persons of a given age/sex category have equal access to resources, goods, services, and prestige (see also *rank*; *stratification*).

289

Enculturation The general category and process of teaching and learning consciously and unconsciously preparing children, primarily, for adherence to the specific way of life of the social group into which they are born. The transmission of culture from one generation to another generation (see also *culture*; *socialization*).

Ethnography The description of a sociocultural system as comprised of a group of people's customary patterns of behaviors, ideas, and physical objects, as primarily based on first hand observation and empirical research.

Function/Functionalism A mode of analysis by which social and cultural events and activities are explained in terms of the service they perform in the ongoing life of the system as a whole. *Manifest functions* are overt and are recognized by participants in the sociocultural system. *Latent functions* are covert, mostly unconscious, and are not recognized by most participants in the sociocultural system but are uncovered by analysis of the entire sociocultural system.

Informants Knowledgeable people who volunteer or who are employed by cultural anthropologists to provide information about their society and culture.

Initiation Patterned events and activities to which a person is presented and must undergo for permitted entrance into some social or cultural group. Initiation usually is associated with age groups and age sets and is the beginning phase in a rite of passage to advanced levels of status and participation in the group. Initiation confers eligibility for one to be presented with restricted information, knowledge, and experience.

Kinship/Descent Kinship refers to the internal definitions of relatedness existing among people within any sociocultural system. Kin are all persons considered to be "relatives." Descent refers to the rules connecting individuals with particular sets of kinfolk, owing to a known or presumed common ancestry.

Kiva Among the Hopi and Zuni Native Americans, a group exclusive to males through which sacred knowledge about the supranatural is stored and transmitted. During their rites of passage ceremony into the *kiva* society, young boys are told accounts of the founding of the world, the coming of humans, and the nature of feared and revered supranatural beings. Male *kiva* members are the spiritual caretakers of the community. The ceremonial, semicircular underground chamber where boys are taken to complete their initiation also is termed a *kiva*.

Nation-State Centralized political system (state) composed of a socially stratified, heterogeneous population occupying a specific territory (nation).

Norm There are two meanings to this term: first, a norm refers to the shared standards of a social group to which members are expected to adhere; second, a norm is a statistical average.

Nuclear Family A family group consisting of a couple, usually married and coresidential, and their children.

Rank The hierarchical ordering and evaluation of individuals or groups constituting a society or social group. A ranked society is organized around differences in positions of prestige but does not place limits on access to basic life resources as a result of differences in prestige (see also *egalitarianism*; *stratification*).

Rite of Passage Rite of passage is the sequence individuals must observe and to which they must adhere in their biological passage through human culture in general and through individual cultures in particular. Rite of passage refers to the manner in which all societies organize and demarcate phases in the individual life cycle, and it marks changes in levels of participation and status in the sociocultural system. The idea of rite of passage postulates that individuals, on their passage through life, cannot stand apart from the fact of their immersion in the life of their society and culture.

Ritual Behavior that is stereotyped, predictable, prescribed, communicative, and noninstrumental. Ritual behaviors adhere to an invariable sequence. Important cultural themes are activated through ritual, and individuals often are connected to the sacred. Rituals do not have an effect on the physical world but only on the world of sociocultural meaning.

Role The cultural rules for behavior appropriate to a particular status/social position (see also *status*).

School A bureaucratic educational institution associated with a certain group of nation-states characterized by specialized personnel, permanent physical structures, standardized texts and stereotyped means of instruction, a formal curriculum, and manifest objectives standardized for all students. A latent function of schooling is education for various levels of participation in large-scale, stratified societies.

Socialization Preparation of children, in particular, to assume a status and role in a social group. General teaching and learning activities oriented toward participation in extant social groups and institutions (see also *enculturation*).

Society A group of people occupying a distinct territory who share a common language, set of customs, and persist over time (see also *culture*).

State A form of political organization in which an entire society is organized around a centralized authority at the apex of an administrative bureaucracy (see also *egalitarianism*; *rank*).

Status A position in a hierarchy or in a so-

cial structure. Status positions carry with them certain rights, duties, and obligations termed roles. Different status positions are associated with different amounts of prestige, or relative value, with respect to other status positions. There are two types of status: achieved and ascribed. An achieved status is a position of voluntary social membership attained through one's own efforts. An ascribed status is a position of involuntary social membership assigned by sociocultural stereotypes, on bases such as sex, age, and color (see also *role*; *stereotype*).

Stereotype A sociocultural system's ascription of fixed, immutable personality and behavioral characteristics to all the members of a group, regardless of the reality of individual variations. Stereotypes customarily are defined with respect to characteristics associated with the color, religion, sex, nationality, or ethnic origin of groups. The stereotypic characterizations of particular groups can be either positive or negative.

Stratification The division of a society into a hierarchically ordered series of social strata, the members of which exhibit differing degrees of access to the strategic resources, goods, or services of the society as a whole (see also *egalitarianism*; *rank*).

Symbol Signs without a natural or necessary association with the meanings attributed to them. Anything that stands for or represents some other thing with which it has no intrinsic connection.

Totem/Totemism An object, plant, or animal symbolically associated with particular individuals or groups.

Universalism/Particularism Particularism refers to processes of cultural conditioning oriented toward education for participation in localized groups such as a family, kin network, household, or village. Universalism refers to processes of sociocultural conditioning for participation in supralocal groups such as nonkin employment networks and national-level bureaucracies.

Value The qualities of an idea, thing, behavior, or person that make it more, or less, desirable than other ideas, things, behaviors, or persons. Attributes of relative worth, merit, usefulness, or importance.

References Cited

Arensburg, Conrad M., and Arthur H. Niehoff
1964 "American Cultural Values." In *Introducing Social Change: A Manual for Americans Overseas*. Conrad M. Arensburg and Arthur H. Niehoff, eds. Pp. 153–83. Chicago: Aldine.

Austin, M. R.
1976 "A Description of the Maori Marse." In *The Mutual Interaction of People and Their Built Environment: A Cross-Cultural Perspective*. Amos Rapoport, ed. Pp. 229–41. The Hague: Mouton.

Balikci, Asen
1970 *The Netsilik Eskimo*. Garden City, N. Y.: Natural History Press.

Baratz, Stephen S., and Joan C. Baratz
1970 "Early Childhood Intervention: The Social Science Base of Institutional Racism." *Harvard Educational Review* 40:29–50.

Barker, Roger G., and Louise S. Barker
1961 "Behavior Units for the Comparative Study of Culture." In *Studying Personality Cross-Culturally*. Bert Kaplan, ed. Pp. 456–76. Evanston, Ill.: Row, Peterson.

Becker, Howard S.
1961 "Schools and Systems of Stratification." In *Education, Economy, and Society: A Reader in the Sociology of Education*. A. H. Halsey, Jean Floud, and C. Arnold Anderson, eds. Pp. 93–104. New York: Free Press.

Benedict, Ruth
1938 "Continuities and Discontinuities in Cultural Conditioning." *Psychiatry* 1:161–67.

Bennis, Warren G., and Philip E. Slater
1968 *The Temporary Society*. New York: Harper & Row.

Bernstein, Basil
1977 "Class and Pedagogies: Visible and Invisible." In *Power and Ideology in Education*. Jerome Karabel and A. H. Halsey, eds. Pp. 511–34. New York: Oxford University Press.

Bourdieu, Pierre
1973a "The Berber House, or the World Reversed." In *Rules and Meanings*. Mary Douglas, ed. Pp. 98–110. London: Penguin.
1973b "Cultural Reproduction and Social Reproduction." In *Knowledge, Education, and Social Change*. Richard Brown, ed. Pp. 71–112. London: Tavistock.

Bourdieu, Pierre, and Jean-Claude Passeron
1977 *Reproduction in Education, Society and Culture*. London: Sage.

Bowles, Samuel
1977 "Unequal Education and the Reproduction of the Social Division of Labor." In *Power and Ideology in Education*. Jerome Karabel and A. H. Halsey, eds. Pp. 137–53. New York: Oxford University Press.
1972 "Schooling and Inequality from Generation to Generation." *Journal of Political Economy* 80:219–51.

Bowles, Samuel, and Herbert Gintis
1976 *Schooling in Capitalist America*. New York: Basic Books.

Brown, Judith K.
1963 "A Cross-Cultural Study of Female Initiation Rites." *American Anthropologist* 65:837–53.

Burnett, Jacquetta Hill
1969 "Ceremony, Rites, and Economy in the Student System of an American High School." *Human Organization* 28:1–10.
1970 "Culture of the School: A Con-

struct for Research and Explanation in Education." *Council on Anthropology and Education Newsletter* 1:4–13.

1976 "Event Description and Analysis in the Microethnography of Urban Classrooms." In *Educational Patterns and Cultural Configurations: The Anthropology of Education.* Joan I. Roberts and Sherrie K. Akinsanya, eds. Pp. 288–98. New York: David McKay.

Campbell, Bernard G.
1974 *Human Evolution: An Introduction to Man's Adaptations.* Chicago: Aldine.

Carnoy, Martin
1974 *Education as Cultural Imperialism.* New York: David McKay.

Carnoy, Martin, and Jorge Werthein
1977 "Socialist Ideology and the Transformation of Cuban Education." In *Power and Ideology in Education.* Jerome Karabel and A. H. Halsey, eds. Pp. 573–89. New York: Oxford University Press.

Carpenter, Edmund
1973 *Eskimo Realities.* New York: Holt, Rinehart and Winston.

Carpenter, Edmund, Frederick Varley, and Robert Flaherty
1959 *Eskimo.* Toronto: University of Toronto Press.

Carroll, Michael P.
1982 "The Logic of Anglo-American Meals." *Journal of American Culture* 5:36–45.

Cohen, Yehudi A.
1964 *The Transition from Childhood to Adolescence: Cross-Cultural Studies of Initiation Ceremonies, Legal Systems, and Incest Taboos.* Chicago: Aldine.

1970 "Schools and Civilizational States." In *The Social Sciences and the Comparative Study of Educational Systems.* Joseph Fischer, ed. Pp. 55–147. Scranton, Pa.: International Textbook Company.

1971 "The Shaping of Men's Minds:

Adaptations to Imperatives of Culture." In *Anthropological Perspectives on Education.* Murray L. Wax, Stanley Diamond, and Fred O. Gearing, eds. Pp. 19–50. New York: Basic Books.

1975 "The State System, Schooling, and Cognitive and Motivational Patterns." In *Social Forces and Schooling: An Anthropological Perspective.* Nobou Kenneth Shimahara and Adam Scrupski, eds. Pp. 103–40. New York: David McKay.

Collier, John, Jr.
1973 *Alaskan Eskimo Education: A Film Analysis of Cultural Confrontation in the Schools.* New York: Holt, Rinehart and Winston.

Comitas, Lambros
1973 "Education and Social Stratification in Contemporary Bolivia." In *Cultural Relevance and Educational Issues: Readings in Anthropology and Education.* Francis A. J. Ianni and Edward Storey, eds. Pp. 402–18. Boston: Little, Brown.

Cusick, Philip A.
1973 *Inside High School: The Student's World.* New York: Holt, Rinehart and Winston.

DeCarlo, Giancarlo
1969 "Why/How to Build Buildings." *Harvard Educational Review* 39:12–35.

Dobbert, Marion L.
1975 "Another Route to a General Theory of Cultural Transmission: A Systems Model." *Council on Anthropology and Education Quarterly* 6:22–26.

Douglas, Mary
1975 *Implicit Meanings.* London: Routledge & Kegan Paul.

Dozier, Edward P.
1966 *Hano: A Tewa Indian Community in Arizona.* New York: Holt, Rinehart and Winston.

Dreeben, Robert
1968 *On What Is Learned in School.*

Reading, Mass.: Addison-Wesley.

Dubois, Cora
1955 "The Dominant Value Profile of American Culture." *American Anthropologist* 57:1232–39.

Dumont, Robert V., Jr., and Murray L. Wax
1969 "Cherokee School Society and the Intercultural Classroom." *Human Organization* 28:217–26.

Dundes, Alan
1968 *Every Man His Way*. Englewood Cliffs, N.J.: Prentice-Hall.

Eddy, Elizabeth M.
1965 *Walk the White Line: A Profile of Urban Education*. New York: Anchor Books, Doubleday.
1969 *Becoming a Teacher: The Passage to Professional Status*. New York: Teachers College Press.

Eggan, Dorothy
1956 "Instruction and Affect in Hopi Cultural Continuity." *Southwestern Journal of Anthropology* 12:347–70.

Ehman, Lee H.
1980 "The American School in the Political Socialization Process." *Review of Education Research* 50:99–119.

Eliade, Mircea
1958 *Rites and Symbols of Initiation: The Mysteries of Birth and Rebirth*. New York: Harper Torchbooks, Harper & Row.
1959 *The Sacred and the Profane: The Nature of Religion*. New York: Harcourt, Brace & World.

Freire, Paulo
1973 *Education for Critical Consciousness*. New York: Seabury Press.

Fried, Morton H.
1960 "On the Evolution of Social Stratification and the State." In *Culture in History*. Stanley Diamond, ed. Pp. 713–31. New York: Columbia University Press.
1967 *The Evolution of Political Society: An Essay in Political Anthropology*. New York: Random House.

Fuller, Wayne E.

1983 *The Old Country School: The Story of Rural Education in the Middle West*. Chicago: University of Chicago Press.

Gearing, Frederick O.
1973 "Where We Are and Where We Might Go: Steps toward a General Theory of Cultural Transmission." *Council on Anthropology and Education Newsletter* 4:1–10.

Gladwin, Thomas
1970 *East Is a Big Bird: Navigation and Logic on a Puluwat Atoll*. Cambridge, Mass.: Harvard University Press.

Gluckman, Max
1962 *Essays on the Ritual of Social Relations*. Manchester: Manchester University Press.

Goetz, Judith P.
1976 "Behavioral Configurations in the Classroom: A Case Study." *Journal of Research and Development in Education* 9:36–49.
1978 "Theoretical Approaches to the Study of Sex-Role Culture in Schools." *Anthropology and Education Quarterly* 9:3–21.

Goodenough, Ward H.
1976 "Multiculturalism as the Normal Human Experience." *Anthropology and Education Quarterly* 7:4–6.

Griaule, Marcel, and Germaine Deterlen
1954 "The Dogon." In *African Worlds: Studies in the Cosmological Ideas and Social Values of African Peoples*. Daryll Forde, ed. Pp. 83–110. London: Oxford University Press.

Gump, Paul V., with Lawrence R. Good
1976 "Environments Operating in Open Space and Traditionally Designed Schools." *Journal of Architectural Research* 5:20–27.

Hall, Edward T.
1959 *The Silent Language*. Greenwich, Conn.: Premier Books, Fawcett.
1969 *The Hidden Dimension*. Garden City, N.Y.: Anchor Books, Doubleday.

Hart, C. W. M., and Arnold R. Pilling

1960 *The Tiwi of North Australia*. New York: Holt, Rinehart and Winston.

Haskins, Jim, ed.
1973 *Black Manifesto for Education*. New York: William Morrow.

Hatch, Elvin
1979. *Biography of a Small Town*. New York: Columbia University Press.

Henry, Jules
1955 "Docility, or Giving the Teacher What She Wants." *Journal of Social Issues* 2:33–41.
1957 "Attitude Organization in Elementary School Classrooms." *American Journal of Orthopsychiatry* 27:117–33.
1959 "The Problem of Spontaneity, Initiative, and Creativity in Suburban Classrooms." *American Journal of Orthopsychiatry* 29:266–79.
1960 "A Cross-Cultural Outline of Education." *Current Anthropology* 1:267–305.
1963 *Culture against Man*. New York: Random House.
1966 "A Theory for the Anthropological Analysis of American Culture." *Anthropological Quarterly* 39:90–109.

Herzog, John D.
1975 "The Socialization of Juveniles in Primate and Foraging Societies: Implications for Contemporary Education." *Council on Anthropology and Education Quarterly* 5:12–17.

Hostetler, John A.
1974 "Education in Communitarian Societies—The Old Order Amish and the Hutterian Bretheran." In *Education and Cultural Process: Toward an Anthropology of Education*. George D. Spindler, ed. Pp. 119–38. New York: Holt, Rinehart and Winston.

Hostetler, John A., and Gertrude E. Huntington
1971 *Children in Amish Society: Socialization and Community Accultura-*

tion. New York: Holt, Rinehart and Winston.

Hsu, Francis L. K.
1972 "American Core Value and National Character." In *Psychological Anthropology*. Francis L. K. Hsu, ed. Pp. 241–62. Cambridge, Mass.: Schenkman.

Hunter-Anderson, Rosalind
1977 "A Theoretical Approach to House Form." In *For Theory Building in Archaeology*. Lewis R. Binford, ed. Pp. 287–315. New York: Academic Press.

Illich, Ivan
1973 "The Futility of Schooling in Latin America." In *To See Ourselves: Anthropology and Modern Social Issues*. Thomas Weaver, ed. Pp. 320–26. Glenview, Ill.: Scott, Foresman.

Inkeles, Alex
1966 "Social Structure and the Socialization of Competence." *Harvard Educational Review* 36:265–83.

Jackson, Jacquelyne J., and Larry C. Harris
1977 "'You May Be Normal When You Come Here, But You Won't Be When You leave,' or Herman: The Pushout." *Black Scholar* 8:2–11.

Jackson, Philip W.
1968 *Life in Classrooms*. New York: Holt, Rinehart and Winston.

Kramer, Samuel Noah
1959 *History Begins at Sumer*. Garden City, N.Y.: Doubleday.

Kuper, Hilda
1972 "The Language of Sites and the Politics of Space." *American Anthropologist* 74:411–25.

Lacey, Colin
1970 *Hightown Grammar: The School as a Social System*. Manchester: Manchester University Press.

Lancy, David F.
1975 "The Social Organization of Learning: Initiation Rituals and Public Schooling." *Human Organi-*

zation 34:371–80.

Leach, Edmund
1976 *Culture and Communication: The Logic by Which Symbols Are Connected.* Cambridge: Cambridge University Press.

Leacock, Eleanor Burke
1969 *Teaching and Learning in City Schools: A Comparative Study.* New York: Basic Books.

LeCompte, Margaret
1978 "Learning to Work: The Hidden Curriculum of the Classroom." *Anthropology and Education Quarterly* 9:22–37.

Lee, Dorothy
1959 "Codifications of Reality: Lineal and Nonlineal." In *Freedom and Culture*, by Dorothy Lee. Pp. 105–120. Englewood Cliffs, N.J.: Prentice-Hall.

Lippitt, Ronald, and Martin Gold
1959 "Classroom Structures as a Mental Health Problem." *Journal of Social Issues* 15:40–49.

Loeb, Martin B.
1963 "Social Role and Sexual Identity in Adolescent Males: A Study of Culturally Provided Deprivation." In *Education and Culture: Anthropological Approaches.* George D. Spindler, ed. Pp. 284–330. New York: Holt, Rinehart and Winston.

McDermott, Ray P.
1974 "Achieving School Failure: An Anthropological Approach to Illiteracy and Social Stratification." In *Education and Cultural Process.* George D. Spindler, ed. Pp. 82–118. New York: Holt, Rinehart and Winston.
1977 "Social Relations as Contexts for Learning in School." *Harvard Educational Review* 47:198–213.

McDermott, Ray P., and Kenneth Gospodinoff
1976 "Social Contexts for Ethnic Borders and School Failure." Paper presented at the First International Conference on Nonverbal Behavior, Ontario Institute for Studies in Education, Toronto, Canada.

McGiffert, Michael
1963 "Selected Writings on American National Character." *American Quarterly* 15:271–88.

McLuhan, Marshall
1964 *Understanding Media: The Extensions of Man.* New York: Signet Books, New American Library.

Marc, Oliver
1977 *Psychology of the House.* London: Thames and Hudson.

Marrou, H. I.
1964 *A History of Education in Antiquity.* Translated by George Lamb. New York: Mentor Books, New American Library.

Mayer, Martin
1961 *The Schools.* New York: Harper & Brothers.

Mead, Margaret
1971 "Early Childhood Experiences and Later Education in Complex Cultures." In *Anthropological Perspectives on Education.* Murray L. Wax, Stanley Diamond, and Fred O. Gearing, eds. Pp. 67–90. New York: David McKay.

Merton, Robert K.
1957 *Social Theory and Social Structure.* New York: Free Press.

Miner, Horace
1956 "Body Ritual among the Nacirema." *American Anthropologist* 58:503–7.

Moore, Alexander
1981 "Basilicas and King Posts: A Proxemic and Symbolic Event Analysis of Competing Public Architecture among the San Blas Cuna." *American Ethnologist* 50:259–77.

Moore, G. Alexander, Jr.
1967 *Realities of Urban Classrooms: Observations in Elementary Schools.* Garden City, N.Y.: Anchor Books, Doubleday.

298 References Cited

1976 "Alternative Attempts at Instruction in Atchalan." In *Schooling in the Cultural Context: Anthropological Studies of Education*. Joan I. Roberts and Sherrie K. Akinsanya, eds. Pp. 65–84. New York: David McKay.

Niehardt, John
1961 *Black Elk Speaks: Being the Life Story of a Holy Man of the Oglala Sioux*. Lincoln: University of Nebraska Press.

Ogbu, John U.
1974 *The Next Generation: An Ethnography of Education in an Urban Neighborhood*. New York: Academic Press.
1978 *Minority Education and Caste: The American System in Cross-Cultural Perspective*. New York: Academic Press.
1979 "Social Stratification and the Socialization of Competence." *Anthropology and Education Quarterly* 10:3–20.
1982 "Cultural Discontinuities and Schooling." *Anthropology and Education Quarterly* 13:290–307.

Osmund, Humphrey
1957 "Function as the Basis of Psychiatric Ward Design." *Mental Hospitals* (architectural supplement) April, pp. 23–29.

Parsons, Talcott
1951 *The Social System*. New York: The Free Press.

Paul, Robert A.
1976 "The Sherpa Temple as a Model of the Psyche." *American Ethnologist* 3:131–46.

Paulson, Rolland G.
1971 "Educational Stratification and Cultural Hegemony in Peru." *Journal of Developing Areas* 5:401–15.

Polgar, Sylvia K.
1976 "The Social Context of Games: Or When Is Play Not Enough?" *Sociology of Education* 49:265–71.

Powdermaker, Hortense
1970 "The Channeling of Negro Aggression by the Cultural Process." In *Education and Cultural Process: Papers Presented at a Symposium Commemorating the Seventy-Fifth Anniversary of the Founding of Fisk University, April 29–May 4, 1941*. Charles S. Johnson, ed. Pp. 122–30. New York: Negro Universities Press.

Rapoport, Amos
1970 "Symbolism and Environmental Design." *International Journal of Symbology* 13:1–10.
1976 "Sociocultural Aspects of Man-Environment Studies." In *The Mutual Interaction of People and Their Built Environment: A Cross-Cultural Perspective*. Amos Rapoport, ed. Pp. 7–35. The Hague: Mouton.

Richardson, Miles, ed.
1974 *The Human Mirror: Material and Spatial Images of Man*. Baton Rouge: Louisiana State University Press.

Roberts, Malcolm J., and Robert R. Bush
1959 "Games in Culture." *American Anthropologist* 61:597–605.

Rodgers, Daniel T.
1978 *The Work Ethic in Industrial America, 1850–1920*. Chicago: University of Chicago Press.

Rosenbaum, James E.
1975 "The Stratification of Socialization Processes." *American Sociological Review* 40:48–54.

Rosenfeld, Gerry
1971 *"Shut Those Thick Lips": A Study of Slum Failure*. New York: Holt, Rinehart and Winston.

Rosenthal, Robert, and Lenore F. Jacobson
1968 *Pygmalion in the Classroom: Self-Fulfilling Prophecies and Teacher Expectations*. New York: Holt, Rinehart and Winston.

Rozsak, Theodore
1969 *The Making of a Counterculture: Reflections on a Technocratic Society and Its Useful Opposition*. Garden

City, N.Y.: Doubleday.

Safa, Helen Icken
1971 "Education, Modernization, and the Process of National Integration." In *Anthropological Perspectives on Education*. Murray L. Wax, Stanley Diamond, and Fred O. Gearing, eds. Pp. 208–29. New York: Basic Books.

Schwartz, Audrey James
1975 *The Schools and Socialization*. New York: Harper & Row.

Scrupski, Adam
1975 "The Social System of the School." In *Social Forces and Schooling: An Anthropological and Sociological Perspective*. Nobou Kenneth Shimahara and Adam Scrupski, eds. Pp. 141–86. New York: David McKay.

Sexton, Patricia Cayo
1969 *The Feminized Male: Classroom, White Collars & the Decline of Manliness*. New York: Random House.

Shimahara, Nobou Kenneth
1975 "American Society, Culture, and Socialization." In *Social Forces and Schooling: An Anthropological and Sociological Perspective*. Nobou Kenneth Shimahara and Adam Scrupski, eds. Pp. 49–81. New York: David McKay.

Shimahara, Nobou Kenneth, and Adam Scrupski, eds.
1975 *Social Forces and Schooling: An Anthropological and Sociological Perspective*. New York: David McKay.

Sieber, R. Timothy
1979 "Classmates as Workmates: Informal Peer Activity in the Elementary School." *Anthropology and Education Quarterly* 10:207–35.

Siegel, Bernard S., ed.
1965 *Biennial Review of Anthropology*. Stanford: Stanford University Press.

Singleton, John
1967 *Nichū: A Japanese School*. New York: Holt, Rinehart and Winston.

Sitton, Thad

1980 "Inside School Spaces: Rethinking the Hidden Dimension." *Urban Education* 15:65–82.

Smith, Louis M., and William Geoffrey
1968 *Complexities of an Urban Classroom: An Analysis toward a General Theory of Teaching*. New York: Holt, Rinehart and Winston.

Sommer, Robert
1959 "Studies in Personal Space." *Sociometry* 22:247–60.
1965 "Further Studies in Small Group Ecology." *Sociometry* 28:337–48.
1969 *Personal Space: The Behavioral Basis of Design*. Englewood Cliffs, N.J.: Prentice-Hall.

Spindler, George D.
1955 "Education in a Transforming American Culture." *Harvard Educational Review* 25:145–56.
1974 "Schooling in Schönhausen: A Study in Cultural Transmission and Instrumental Adaptation in an Urbanizing German Village." In *Education and Cultural Process: Toward an Anthropology of Education*. George D. Spindler, ed. Pp. 230–71. New York: Holt, Rinehart and Winston.

Staples, Robert
1975 "To Be Young, Black, and Oppressed." *Black Scholar* 7:2–9.

Steward, Julian H.
1972 *Theory of Culture Change: The Methodology of Multilinear Evolution*. Urbana: University of Illinois Press.

Sutton-Smith, Brian
1977 "Towards an Anthropology of Play." In *Studies in the Anthropology of Play*. Phillips Stevens, Jr., ed. Pp. 222–32. West Point, N.Y.: Leisure Press.

Tuan, Yi-Fu
1977 *Space and Place: The Perspective of Experience*. Minneapolis: University of Minnesota Press.

Turner, Ralph H.
1961 "Modes of Social Ascent through Education: Sponsored and Contest

Mobility." In *Education, Economy, and Society: A Reader in the Sociology of Education*. A. H. Halsey, J. Floud, and C. Arnold Anderson, eds. Pp. 121–39. New York: Free Press.

Van Gennep, Arnold
1960 (1909) *The Rites of Passage Les Rites de Passage*. Translated by Monika B. Vizedom and Gabrielle L. Caffee. Chicago: University of Chicago Press (Paris: E. Nourry).

Vogt, Evon Z.
1965 "Structural and Conceptual Replication in Zincantan Culture." *American Anthropologist* 67: 342–53.

Warren, Richard L.
1967 *Education in Rebhausen: A German Village*. New York: Holt, Rinehart and Winston.

Washburn, Sherwood L.
1971 "On the Importance of the Study of Primate Behavior for Anthropologists." In *Anthropological Perspectives on Education*. Murray L. Wax, Stanley Diamond, and Fred O. Gearing, eds. Pp. 91–97. New York: Basic Books.

Watkins, Mark Hanna
1943 "The West African 'Bush' School." *American Journal of Sociology* 48:1666–75.

Wax, Murray L.
1971 "Comparative Research upon School and Education: An Anthropological Outline." In *Anthropological Perspectives on Education*. Murray L. Wax, Stanley Diamond, and Fred O. Gearing, eds. Pp. 293–99. New York: Basic Books.

Wax, Murray L., and Rosalie H. Wax
1965 "The Matter of Clothing." In *Dress, Adornment, and the Social Order*. Mary Ellen Roach and Joanne B. Eicher, eds. Pp. 257–64. New York: John Wiley.
1971 "Great Tradition, Little Tradition, and Formal Education." In *Anthro-*

pological Perspectives on Education. Murray L. Wax, Stanley Diamond, and Fred O. Gearing, eds. Pp. 3–18. New York: Basic Books.

Wax, Murray L., Rosalie H. Wax, and Robert V. Dumont, Jr.
1964 "Formal Education in an American Indian Community." *Social Problems* 11:1–126.

Wax, Rosalie H.
1967 "The Warrior Dropouts." *Transaction* 4:40–46.
1976 "Oglala Sioux Dropouts and Their Problems with Educators." In *Schooling in the Cultural Context: Anthropological Studies of Education*. Joan I. Roberts and Sherrie K. Akinsanya, eds. Pp. 216–26. New York: David McKay.

Whiting, John, and B. Ayres
1968 "Inferences from the Shape of Dwellings." In *Settlement Archaeology*. K. C. Chang, ed. Pp. 117–33. Palo Alto: National Press Books.

Whiting, John W. M., Richard Kluckhohn, and Albert Anthony
1958 "The Function of Male Initiation Ceremonies at Puberty." In *Readings in Social Psychology*. 3d ed. Eleanor E. Maccoby, ed. Pp. 359–70. New York: Holt, Rinehart and Winston.

Wilkinson, Rupert
1964 *Gentlemanly Power: British Leadership and the Public School Tradition, A Comparative Study in the Making of Rulers*. London: Oxford University Press.

Williams, Thomas R.
1972 *Introduction to Socialization: Human Culture Transmitted*. St. Louis: C. V. Mosby.

Wilson, Peter S.
1973 *Crab Antics: The Social Anthropology of English-Speaking Negro Societies of the Caribbean*. New Haven: Yale University Press.

Wittfogel, Karl A.

1963 *Oriental Despotism: A Comparative Study of Total Power.* New Haven: Yale University Press.
Wolcott, Harry F.
1974 *Looking at School Ethnography.* Boulder: Educational Resources Information Center for Social Studies and Social Science Education.
Wylie, Laurence
1976 "The School at Vaucluse: Educating the French Child." In *Schooling in the Cultural Context: Anthropo-*

logical Studies of Education. Joan I. Roberts and Sherrie K. Akinsanya, eds. Pp. 84–104. New York: David McKay.
Young, Frank W.
1962 "The Function of Male Initiation Ceremonies: A Cross-Cultural Test of an Alternate Hypothesis." *American Journal of Sociology* 67:379–91.
1965 *Initiation Ceremonies: A Cross-Cultural Study of Status Dramatization.* Indianapolis: Bobbs-Merrill.

Index

303